ma Samar was the conscience of democratic
ysician, human rights advocate, institution-
seeker. She embodied the ideals of her country's
but paid a heavy price. Her story is essential and
for all Americans, complicit as we are in a trag-
we must not turn away."—Steve Coll, author of

Sima Samar relates her lifelong struggles against
an Afghan girl, a medical doctor, a refugee in
built hospitals and schools, a government official,
n rights defender. Her story trenchantly illuminates
ust all learn from interventions in Afghanistan and
warning to the world at a time when women's rights
siege." —Emma Bonino, former EU commissioner and
reign minister of Italy

n is a *must read* for every woman—indeed for every person—
ports equality and human rights, especially for women and
r. Samar's life is an inspiration; she speaks truth to power
s repeatedly risked her life for doing so. Feminists worldwide
nd must learn from her experiences." —Eleanor Smeal, pres-
, Feminist Majority Foundation and publisher, *Ms. Magazine*

ghanistan's unsurpassably sad last half century ranks among
most dismal and disastrous episodes in all of human history.
ma Samar lived at the epicenter of this evil storm and has spent
er life working tirelessly to improve the lives of her fellow Afghans,
always holding on tenaciously to the hope for a better future.
Outspoken is a book that is sobering, necessary—and absolutely riv-
eting." Paul Kennedy, former host of CBC *Ideas*

"Afghanistan,
been described
men. This book p
I hesitate to say mo
the personal and t
and dreams, but who
and work stand in defi
promise for a better futu
world seems to have aban
UN High Commissioner for

"*Outspoken* is a book of mirac
book, an adventure story, a deep.
ing work that propels you from y
Samar gives bravery a face, from t
band taken away to be killed, to th
own life to save others. Illuminating t
recent history, *Outspoken* provides astoni
Honestly, I couldn't put it down." Lisa L
Human Rights

"*Outspoken* invites the reader into the heart of
its people's resilience and their strength. Despi
erous paths Afghans have traveled over more t
war, Sima Samar shows us the beauty of the Afg
wonder of Afghanistan. The very definition of coura
has fought tirelessly, through personal pain and tr
down successive repressive regimes—and even a few
West—in her quest for justice. She is a hero indeed." Kath
author of *I Is for Infidel*, former Associated Press news dire

"For two decades, S
Afghanistan—a ph
builder, and justice
revival after 2001
inspiring reading
edy from which
Ghost Wars

"In *Outspoken*,
patriarchy: a
Pakistan who
and a huma
what we m
serves as a
are under
former fo

"*Outspok
who su
girls. D
and h
can a
iden

OUTSPOKEN

*My Fight for Freedom and
Human Rights in Afghanistan*

SIMA SAMAR

with **SALLY ARMSTRONG**

RANDOM HOUSE CANADA

Unless otherwise indicated, interior photographs come from the author's
personal collection and appear courtesy of the author.

Library and Archives Canada Cataloguing in Publication

Title: Outspoken : my fight for freedom and human rights in Afghanistan /
Sima Samar with Sally Armstrong.
Names: Samar, Sima, author. | Armstrong, Sally, author.
Description: Includes index.
Identifiers: Canadiana (print) 20230486878 | Canadiana (ebook) 20230486967 |
ISBN 9781039007079 (hardcover) | ISBN 9781039007086 (EPUB)
Subjects: LCSH: Samar, Sima. | LCSH: Women—Afghanistan—Biography. |
LCSH: Women physicians— Afghanistan—Biography. | LCSH: Physicians—
Afghanistan—Biography. | LCSH: Women political activists—Afghanistan—
Biography. | LCSH: Political activists—Afghanistan—Biography. |
LCSH: Women—Afghanistan—Social conditions—21st century. | LCSH:
Women's rights—Afghanistan—History—21st century. | LCSH: Afghanistan—
Social conditions—21st century. | LCGFT: Autobiographies.
Classification: LCC HQ1735.6.Z75 S26 2024 | DDC 305.42/09581—dc23

Text design: Matthew Flute
Jacket design: Matthew Flute

Image credits: courtesy of the author; (sky) Guillaume Galtier / Unsplash

Printed in Canada

2 4 6 8 9 7 5 3 1

Penguin
Random House
RANDOM HOUSE CANADA

To the people who lost their lives and
whose graves remain unmarked as a result
of forty-five years of war in Afghanistan.

To the women of my country who live
under a regime of gender apartheid.

To all those who suffer from patriarchy
and gender-based violence worldwide.

CONTENTS

Map viii

Prologue by Sally Armstrong ix

One   EYEWITNESS 1

Two   GIRL CHILD 25

Three   STORM WARNINGS 59

Four   THE DOCTOR IS IN 77

Five   A FUNDAMENTAL THREAT 103

Six   ACCUSED 139

Seven   NO PEACE WITHOUT JUSTICE 173

Eight   THEY THOUGHT THEY COULD BURY US 205

Nine   TRUMP AND THE TALIBAN 235

Ten   THE IDES OF AUGUST 266

Eleven   GETTING TO NEXT 294

Acknowledgments 303

Index 307

AFGHANISTAN

PROLOGUE

by Sally Armstrong

IT BEGAN AS A QUEST and turned into an odyssey. The Taliban had taken over Afghanistan in late September 1996 and forbidden education for girls and working outside the home for women—basically putting women and girls under house arrest. During that time, I was the editor in chief of the Canadian magazine *Homemaker's*, and we covered many important issues of the day. I heard about a woman who was defying the Taliban edicts, keeping her schools for girls open and her medical clinics for women running. I wanted to interview her for a story I was writing about this incomprehensible return to the Dark Ages. But first I had to find her.

My quest included dozens of phone calls and scouring the news for the name of this woman. At last, I talked to human rights expert Farida Shaheed in Lahore, Pakistan, who said, "Come over here and we'll discuss this." Despite an editorial budget seriously strained by the cost of a flight, I left immediately.

I met Shaheed at her office, where women were being educated about the duplicity of their religious-political leaders. Shaheed was a fountain of information, teaching me the ABCs of militant fundamentalism. But then she told me, "I can't give you the name of the woman you seek—she's in danger of being killed." At about 5 p.m., when I was despairing my decision to fly across the world, Shaheed said, "There's a flight to Quetta tomorrow at 9 a.m. You should be on it. Someone will meet you in the arrivals lounge."

It was an easy flight to this city about 700 kilometers west of Lahore. By the time the plane landed my curiosity was thoroughly piqued. When I walked into the arrivals lounge a woman approached me, smiling. She extended her hand and said, "You must be Sally. I'm Sima Samar. I believe you've been looking for me."

And that's when the odyssey began. For the next week, I followed Sima around the hospitals and schools she was operating for women and girls. I discovered that she is the quintessential Afghan woman: she's strong, she adores her country, and she's had to fight for everything she's ever had. Sima Samar was only twelve years old when she learned the meaning of the words author Rohinton Mistry would later write that life was poised as "a fine balance between hope and despair." At that tender age she began to fight to alter the status of women and girls in her country. She fought the traditional rules for girls in her own family. She fought the Soviets, the mujahideen, the Taliban. She fought every step of the way to get an education and become a physician, to open her hospitals and schools for girls, and to raise her children according to her own values.

The article I wrote resulted in more than twelve thousand letters to the editor from women demanding action for the women and girls of Afghanistan. Some of the letter-writers started Canadian

Women for Women in Afghanistan, and similar associations sprang up around the world. They all asked Sima to come and speak. After 9/11 and the subsequent defeat of the Taliban, us president George W. Bush invited her to the State of the Union address in 2002 and introduced her as the face of the future of Afghanistan. At every podium in Europe, in Asia, in North America, she told her heart-wrenching story and was received with standing ovations, cheers and promises. She was a journalist's dream, sharing her stories with authenticity, passion and even humor. Little did I know that when my journalistic quest was finished the odyssey would continue for more than two decades.

As our friendship grew, I became her witness—when the Taliban threatened to kill her; when the government that formed after the Taliban was defeated in 2001 tried to sideline her; when she defied the naysayers and became the first-ever Minister of Women's Affairs; and when she started the Afghanistan Independent Human Rights Commission (AIHRC). I traveled to the central highlands with her to see her far-flung schools in action, and I was with her family when suicide bombers struck at the meeting she was attending at the Serena Hotel in Kabul.

When Sima visited Canada, she met my family and even swaddled my first grandchild. And when I visited her country, I sat on the floor cross-legged around the dastarkhan at dinner with her family and learned more about Afghanistan and Afghans than I ever could have imagined.

I watched her fight back, bristled at the threats she received and grinned at her audacity. When it comes to justice and equality, she simply does not take no for an answer. I remember one occasion when the Taliban demanded she close her schools for girls and said if she did not, they would kill her. She replied, "Go ahead and hang me in the public square and tell the people my crime: giving paper and pencils to girls."

I urged her to tell her own story when the Taliban, following on disgraceful backroom deals made with the United States, returned to power. While the world saw the twenty-year international intervention in Afghanistan as a failure, the truth is that during those twenty years, life expectancy in Afghanistan went from forty-seven years to sixty-three years, the boys and the girls went back to school, and nation-building began. That isn't a failure—it's a miracle. Sima was one of the leaders behind those remarkable changes, and I told her that the future of her country might depend on the honest telling of the chronicle of women, tradition, human rights and justice. What's more, she was in a position to know exactly why the government eventually collapsed. I saw her life of resistance and resilience as a cautionary tale to others who allow deception and misinformation about culture and religion and gender to overrule the history and ultimately the will of the people. This is her story.

One

EYEWITNESS

"I have three strikes against me. I'm a woman,
I speak for women and I'm Hazara—the most
persecuted ethnic group in Afghanistan."

IT BEGAN AS A SPARKLING MAY MORNING on an otherwise ordinary day. The weather was perfect, sunny and warm with a light breeze blowing springtime into Kabul. The blossoms had drifted off the trees, making way for leaves to burst onto the branches. It was approaching the end of Ramadan, the holy ritual that requires prayers and fasting for thirty days, so the anticipation of Eid, the celebration that marks the end of fasting, was on everyone's mind. Families and friends would gather to pray and give thanks and to savor traditional foods like steaming platters of Kabuli pulao, ashak, bolani, lamb kabobs, delicious sheer pira and, of course, each other's company. For a country that had experienced so much bloodshed and so many setbacks, this rebirth season of spring could have been seen as a sign of deliverance. But on that

1

day—May 8, 2021—at 4:27 p.m., when the first explosion tore into the Sayed Al-Shuhada school in Dasht-e-Barchi, a neighborhood in West Kabul where members of the Hazara ethnic minority live, my hopes for the future were dashed and my heart broke—again.

Although I could not have predicted it at the time, this was in fact the beginning of the end of the Afghanistan I had helped to rebuild. The events of May 8—the who, the why and the what—go a long way to describing the wrongs that need to be righted if my country is to see a new beginning.

The warning that day came by way of a beeping from my cell phone. I was in the midst of a meeting at Gawharshad University, where we were discussing a hopeful future, including a new research department and the enhancement of the program for women's empowerment. A horribly familiar chill crept up my spine when I saw the message that flashed on my screen—*explosion Dasht-e-Barchi*. In such a crowded part of the city I knew there would be bloodshed, but I hoped that the casualties would be few and the wounds minor. Still, it was impossible to forget the terrible attacks Dasht-e-Barchi had already experienced: at the education center, the sports club, the wedding hall, the maternity hospital, and several mosques. Casualties had been high.

The discussion at the table blurred as I kept checking my phone. The second text appeared minutes later with words that struck me like shrapnel: *girls, school, death*. By now everyone at the table was staring at their phones. Dasht-e-Barchi is the district where the Hazaras live, where men work menial jobs as laborers so they can scrape together the funds needed to bring their families from the central highlands of Afghanistan, which is the traditional home of the Hazaras, to the city and the promise of education for their children.

When the third text hit my screen, it felt as if the story was unraveling like Afghanistan itself. The first report was that it was a rocket attack on the Sayed Al-Shuhada school. Then a car bomb exploded at the scene as bystanders ran to help the injured. A third and fourth explosion followed, and casualties mounted.

Of course, I wanted to race to the scene—I'm a medical doctor, I'm a mother. But I knew the chaotic traffic and intense security checks in Kabul would hold up the rescue and I wouldn't be able to get there in time to help. I called a halt to the meeting and went home, where I turned on the television to try to comprehend the causes and consequences of this horrific act of violence on blameless schoolgirls.

The coverage was hard to watch. The street in front of the school was crowded with carnage—the bodies of little girls, their schoolbooks and backpacks and shoes strewn about. Limbs left at incomprehensible angles. People screaming, searching, panicking. Blood ran down the road like rainwater. Every means of transportation was being used to get the girls to medical facilities—cars, motorcycles, bicycles and rickshaws were pressed into action. The wounded were even being hoisted onto shoulders and carried away. Survivors were torn between running for their lives and staying to help classmates. Others called to onlookers to run to clinics to give blood. The injured were crying out for their mothers and begging for help while fires continued to burn all over the street. Journals of poetry and scrapbooks of artwork were consumed in flames. The notebooks held the dreams of becoming "a somebody," as the kids here like to say: a doctor, a police officer, an engineer or a teacher who could improve the life of the family and the future of the country.

I knew that poverty would prevent the wounded from being treated with the most advanced techniques. The father of a girl who suffered multiple fractures later said he had no money to buy the pins to rebuild his daughter's arm. As with everything else in their hardscrabble lives, they would have to put up with less. And for those who now had to deal with complicated injuries and disabilities, it meant more debt and hardship; for all of them, it would mark the beginning of an enduring trauma born from barbarity.

The school, which boys attend in the mornings and girls in the afternoons, stretches over a few city blocks backing onto a hill covered with small mudbrick houses where many of these families live. The girls, dressed in the ubiquitous black-dress-and-white-scarf uniform, had come to this place to learn. For the Hazaras who arrived here from the Waras district of Bamiyan in the central highlands, this neighborhood is stuffed with hopes. There's a mural on the wall at Sayed Al-Shuhada school with words that read: "Your dreams are limited only by your imagination."

They already know hardship. As is true for so many kids in this poor part of the city, their daily lives include a shift of carpet weaving to supplement the family income. The owners of the carpet companies have shrugged off the severe criticism for using child labor because they know it's the small fingers of a child that can weave the threads rapidly and follow the intricate patterns precisely. (While I have lobbied for a stop to child labor, I do not pass judgment on poor people who are trying to educate their children in a country that has no social security.) The children earn a meager amount, maybe ten to fifteen dollars a month, while they sit on benches just centimeters from the loom. Their fingernails are broken and split; the skin beside the nails is torn from threading the tough wool fibers through the apparatus. Because they are confined to a closed room, often working in tiers stacked on top of one another, they inhale the fluff from the wool and develop chronic lung disorders. They get few breaks, often falling asleep at the loom, and are forbidden to make conversation lest it distract them from the pattern. Silence at the loom is broken only by the sound of children coughing and the rhythmic tone of the shana, the comb used to pull the knots they make into the weaving.

Still, at school, these youngsters chased their dreams, even trying their hand at activism to fulfill them. Only a week before the attack a group of them went to the media to let the government know that the school didn't have enough books to go around. In their seriously overcrowded building, the children didn't mind sitting on the floor and out in the halls, but books were a priority they decided to fight for.

My thoughts were swirling around the events unfolding on the television screen when I glanced out the window and noticed a bird building a nest. I was immediately struck by how carefully the bird was weaving the tiny bits of twigs and dirt and string to build this nest where she would bring new life into this world, and how she was doing so without destroying any part of the environment. I watched that little bird working feverishly to prepare the nest and considered how easily a heavy rain or a fierce wind could destroy it. I remembered a woman from Kandahar coming to me and saying, "What have I done wrong in my life? Three times I built a nest and storms came and destroyed my nests, but the storms were man-made." So many in my country have suffered because somebody else wanted their land or their lives or to have power over them.

It had taken forty-five minutes for ambulances, fire trucks and police to get through the streets of Kabul to this west-end neighborhood at the height of afternoon traffic. The sounds of the sirens mixed with the shouting of parents and the pleas of the victims and the physical gore on the street to create a heart-stopping tableau of a people under attack—my people.

While no terrorist group took responsibility for this horrible strike, everyone here knows that trouble begins with the Taliban. If they didn't do it, they know who did.

Most of the world sees us as a people at war. And war has a way of coloring a country various shade of gray; the guns, tanks, dust, mud and rubble blur into a single hue. To most of the world Afghanistan has been presented in the recent past as nearly colorless, a sepia image of treeless mountains and endless deserts populated by beige-blanketed, bearded men with dashes of periwinkle blue provided by burka-covered women. The overall impression is of a place that is dreary, oppressive, backward and dangerous. But there is so much more to our country—from the legacy of the Persian cultural and linguistic sphere to the acclaimed lattice Jali woodwork and the celebrated Nuristani (chip-carving) techniques. Our Istalifi pottery and ceramics and calligraphy, even our beautiful carpets on display at the famous Turquoise Mountain in Kabul, are often missed by the masses of soldiers, politicians and diplomats who come here because of continued conflict. The best of us is overshadowed by the fabled stories of the British invasion in 1839 and the Russian occupation that began in 1979 and the 9/11 attacks in America that brought the world to our door.

In the wake of the terrorist attacks on September 11, 2001, the United States acted on the North Atlantic Treaty Organization's (NATO's) Article 5 on collective defense, which calls on all members to rally to the side of the one who has been attacked—in this case the United States—and prepare to make war on the aggressor, in this case the Taliban and Al Qaeda.

The invasion on October 7, 2001, named Operation Enduring Freedom, was welcomed by most Afghans. People were tired of conflict, of the violation of their rights, particularly women's rights; they were fed up with the lack of accountability and justice. But with rare exceptions, the story became a story of *their* soldiers and *our* poverty, of *their* sacrifices and *our* ethnic strife. There is so much more to this landlocked country on the ancient Silk Road: Both the spectacular Nuristan and Panjshir Valleys, with stunning landscapes of mountain peaks and a rushing river that by turns roars and gurgles through the provinces; the spiritual meadows of Bamiyan; the gentle Shomali Plain, our fertile breadbasket that contrasts with the deserts and stand-alone rock mountains and the endless dust of Kandahar and the brilliant colors of the historic mosques of Herat and Mazar-e-Sharif. As for the people—loyalty, friendship, protection and hospitality are in the DNA of Afghans. We are so much more than our quarrels.

There are four major ethnic groups in my country. While there are no clear boundaries and there is much overlap, each one is powerful in its own right. (A proper census has not been conducted since 1979, so population numbers and the precise ethnic makeup of the country are inexact.) Pashtuns, who make up about 40 percent of the population, are the largest ethnic group and the most influential in business and politics. Originating in southern Afghanistan and northwest Pakistan, they follow Pashtunwali, a traditional and cultural code based on honor, revenge and hospitality—and that is rooted in a strict patriarchy. Pashtuns were among the ranks of the mujahideen (guerrilla fighters) during the Soviet occupation. The recent presidents Hamid Karzai and Ashraf Ghani are Pashtun. So are the majority of the Taliban.

Tajiks, at about 25 percent of the population, form the second-largest ethnic group in Afghanistan and speak Dari as opposed to the Pashto language spoken by Pashtuns. Tajiks are one of the most ancient of the surviving Central Asian people. While they live in Herat, next to the border with Iran, and in Kabul, where they are successful merchants and craftsmen, they also have strongholds is northern Afghanistan and in the Panjshir Valley north of Kabul. Ahmad Shah Massoud, who was assassinated in 2001, was a native son of this valley. Ismail Khan, who ruled Herat for years, is also Tajik.

Hazaras are the third-largest ethnic group, at 20 percent of the population. We come from the central highlands and call our area, where we have lived for centuries, Hazarajat. We consider ourselves to be the originals—the native population of the country. We have always played a role in defending the country, including against the British and USSR invasions. After the withdrawal of the USSR and the collapse of the regime supported by them, the Hazara leader Abdul Ali Mazari called for equal rights for the people and inclusion of the Hazaras in government. But in the mid-1990s the Taliban declared war on the Hazaras, and the conflict has continued to this day.

The Uzbeks are the fourth-largest ethnic group, at about 10 percent of the population, and are often grouped with the Turkmen ethnic group. They live in the northern regions and developed a reputation as defenders of the country when, along with the Hazaras and Tajiks, they joined Ahmad Shah Massoud and the Northern Alliance and fought against the Taliban regime. When the Taliban was defeated, the Uzbeks took their place as some of the influential military and political leaders in Kabul.

A collection of about a dozen other ethnic groups make up the remaining 5 percent.

The Pashtuns, Tajiks and Uzbeks are all Sunni Muslims. We Hazaras, who make up one-fifth of the 38 to 40 million Afghans, are mostly Shi'ite Muslims, but some are also Sunni. (The Shi'ite religion was not officially recognized until the adoption of the nation's new constitution in 2004.)

The rich historical past of the Hazaras has contributed so much to Afghanistan. The capital of our region, Bamiyan, is a mystical place of shimmering poplar groves, babbling brooks and majestic copper-toned mountains where the ancient Buddha statues that were hewn out of the sandstone cliffs stood watch for more than fifteen hundred years. There were two statues: one was 38 meters tall and built around 570 CE; the other was 52 meters tall and built around 618 CE, when the Hephthalites ruled the region. There were many other smaller Buddhas in sitting positions located nearby, as well as in other valleys. In March 2001, the Taliban blew them all up in an act of cultural erasure. The act was perpetrated as theater to appease their hardline foreign supporters and distract from their inability to govern. It was also a convenient way to hide the mass graves that held the remains of those Hazaras who were executed by the Taliban during their takeover of Bamiyan.

During the five long years from 1996 to 2001 when the Taliban was in power, they failed to repair a single road or remove the heaps of rubble that had accumulated in the cities after the nine-year civil war that followed the collapse of the regime supported by the USSR. Nor did they implement any civic improvements such as garbage removal or clean water sources, or basic social services such as health care and education. However, there was one project to which they devoted incredible energy: destroying the ancient Buddha statues.

At first, they used army tanks to fire artillery shells at the icons, but that hardly caused a dent in these enormous structures. Then they planted explosives to bring them down, but that was also to no avail. Finally, the Taliban rounded up Hazara men who they considered to be infidels—and therefore disposable—and strapped bombs to their bodies. The men were forced to climb the Buddhas and plant the munitions in crevices; some of them were even hung from the top of the statues by their feet to make sure the bombs were strategically placed. The detonators from the bombs were wired and laid all the way to the mosque where the Taliban activated them, bringing more than fifteen hundred years of history to a thundering end while the onlookers shouted "Allahu Akbar." These were the actions of the men who were ruling my country while the world looked the other way.

Whenever I visit Bamiyan, the rhythm of life plays like the sound of a lute. When the sun sets, a quietude takes over that whispers of an enduring past. Frescoes discovered around the Buddha statues suggest Hazaras descended from the people who built them. The entire Bamiyan city was declared a United Nations Educational, Scientific, and Cultural Organization (UNESCO) World Heritage

Site in 2003. The declaration was to represent the artistic and religious developments from the first century to the thirteenth century and to mark the tragic destruction of the Buddha statues.

Bamiyan is located on the Silk Road, the network of ancient trade routes that linked China to western Asia. In fact, the route was so well-known for its role in carrying messages as well as goods that the United States Postal Service referenced it in their slogan. The Greek writer Herodotus, referring to the Silk Road noted:

There is nothing in the world
that travels faster than these Persian couriers.
Neither snow, nor rain, nor
heat, nor darkness of night
prevents these couriers
from completing their designated stages with utmost speed.

In recent years, the pride I've always felt in the heritage of my homeland has been stained by events that foretell a bleak future. To understand how we got here, we need to look at the root causes of Afghanistan's struggles. Chief among them may be the conflict between the two separate arms of Islam—Sunni and Shi'ite. The Sunnis make up the majority of the world's Muslims; the rest are Shi'ite. The differences between the two are like the differences between Catholics and Protestants, or even the differences within each group itself, such as the Roman Catholics and the Eastern Catholics or the Protestant Anglicans and Presbyterians. Or, for that matter, the various sects or branches of Buddhism, Judaism and Hinduism. It's all about minor interpretations of a religion that has a basic creed for everyone. We all worship the same god. We all believe in the doctrines of goodness, honesty, humility, generosity and service. How we express those beliefs is a personal and spiritual journey each of us takes or decides not to take. And yet religion is used as an excuse to discriminate, to punish and even to kill. Rather than bringing us together in service, one to the other, it drives us apart. Religion is used as a political tool to control people; this happens not just here in Afghanistan but in many parts of the world where strife is tearing civil society apart.

For example, the Taliban are adamant that their version of Islam is the real one, and all those who practice other versions, particularly the Shi'ite, are infidels and better dead. The Islamic State of Iraq and Syria (ISIS)—or the Islamic State of Khorasan Province (ISKP), as they're known here—believe in Wahhabism, a strict, puritanical form of Sunni Islam known for its harsh intolerance and ferocity and for its quick judgment of Hazaras as infidels. In fact, as in so many conflicts, various factions use religion to separate and divide people, to isolate and accuse others who choose to be different.

If you examine our history, you can see that our downfall began with the role assigned to women. By creating a culture that excluded women, politicians barred the way to sustainable peace. While the first girls' school was started by King Amanullah Khan in 1920, later, during King Mohammad Zahir Shah's reign, schools for girls were established in different parts of the country. And although numbers were small, there was a female presence on the police force and women were part of the government, even serving as cabinet ministers. I am a product of that time: I studied in a co-educational school in the country's southern province of Helmand, where I spent my childhood in the sixties and seventies.

In 1973, Mohammad Daoud Khan seized power from the longtime monarch and the country began to change. Although Daoud was ultimately tossed out in 1978 by the People's Democratic Party of Afghanistan (PDPA), a Marxist-Leninist group that paved the way to the Soviet invasion in 1979, the government had already started violating our human rights and restricting our freedom. For example, the pro-Soviet PDPA regime set a limit of just three hundred Afghanis (about ten dollars in US currency at that time, or about 11 percent of an average monthly salary in Afghanistan) for a woman's maher, an amount that is paid to the bride (the maher is not the same as the bride price, which is paid to the family). The maher, which had previously been as high as four thousand or even five thousand Afghanis, had provided some economic security for a woman getting married, since she didn't receive much from family wealth. The regime's new law exacerbated women's insecurity, and became a source of insult. I experienced it personally as a student at Kabul University's Faculty of Medicine; male peers would offer lewd jokes suggesting they could purchase each Afghan woman for about three hundred Afghanis. And some would say, "Look, I have six hundred Afghanis—I can buy two of you." The new law objectified women and further eroded their status. However, that was only the start.

It took a troika to entrap the women of my country: the mujahideen, the Americans and the Saudi Arabians. First, mujahideen factions, which were the main resistance to the communists, chose Islamism as their political ideology, probably because the Islamic ideals of the Muslim Brotherhood were spreading rapidly throughout the Middle East, and because Iran had already chosen a religious national leader. As well, in neighboring Pakistan,

President Mohammad Zia-ul-Haq had turned to Islamization.

Second, the Americans got involved. Zbigniew Brzezinski, the national security advisor to President Jimmy Carter, made use of Islam as a weapon of war in Afghanistan to create a counter force to defeat the occupying government of the USSR. He instructed the Central Intelligence Agency (CIA) to provide military supplies and humanitarian aid to the mujahideen, who were now branded as Afghan freedom fighters. In fact, although the West was taken up with the romantic notion of freedom fighters, the aid being sent was tailored toward militarizing the mujahideen to fight what would become a proxy war between the US and USSR. Ignoring Pakistani president Zia's dismal human rights record and his Islamization policy, the Americans entered a close political relationship with Zia. By January 1980, the month Ronald Reagan became the US president, lethal arms began arriving in Pakistan for use in Afghanistan. Financial and military support to the mujahideen increased dramatically.

Third, Saudi Arabia was brought into the picture because it was willing to match American funds for the mujahideen. For the Saudis, this was a unique opportunity to gain influence in the region and import Wahhabism, their anti-woman brand of ultra-conservative Islam.

The mujahideen, who received funds funneled through Pakistan from the United States, Saudi Arabia, the United Kingdom, China and several Arab countries, employed a politicized Islam as a means of fighting communism and selling their vision of Afghanistan to the broader population. How did they do this? Easily, by insisting they would ensure the safety of Afghan women. Under the guise of protecting women from foreign thugs, they wanted us cloistered behind purdah and walls that restricted our participation in society. This so-called protection of Afghan women is an argument that has been used by different regimes during forty-five years of war and continues to be used by the Taliban today.

After the Soviets ended their ten-year military occupation of the country in 1989, the international community assumed the Cold War was over and took off like a school of minnows. The result was a power vacuum contested by seven different factions of mujahideen, whose headquarters were in Pakistan—as well as the other groups in Iran. A fratricidal bloodbath erupted.

The mujahideen vowed they would return Afghanistan to its rich past by honoring Islam; they recalled how pro-Soviet occupiers had desecrated our culture by walking inside mosques with their shoes on or by beating a mullah and telling him to call on his God to come and save him. To gain public support, each faction one-upped the other when it came to how strictly the religion would be followed and how true to the ancient cultural traditions they would be. The result was that the status of women steadily declined as the mujahideen stripped their rights one by one, all the while claiming they were ridding the country of Soviet influence.

In fact, their goal wasn't to restore honor but rather to seek power in an internecine battle for control characterized by extraordinary brutality and lawlessness. It was a battle that brought the country to its knees and scorched the emotional earth of its citizens. For example, in 1993, not far from the neighborhood where the Hazara school girls were murdered at the Sayed Al-Shuhada school, the mujahideen were on a rampage. Warlords and their militia from different groups led raids on houses, looking for money and gold and kidnapping young men for ransom. The militia beat people to death, stole whatever they wanted, and even killed babies; they, too, demanded money, gold and jewelry. One woman was told to give them her gold wedding ring, and when she struggled to get the ring off her finger, even licking the skin around the ring to urge it away, the wretched brutes watching became peeved with the wait. They splayed her fingers apart and chopped one of her fingers off with a bayonet. When the ring tumbled to the ground, they scooped up their piece of gold and left. These atrocities were happening across the country, but the Hazaras got the worst of it. The fighting and the destruction, especially in the west part of Kabul, was brutal for all sides, and international laws of war were ignored.

Of the mujahideen groups vying for power, it was the extremist Taliban who came out on top. It began with their takeover of Kandahar in 1994 and continued with a march across the country; they defeated other factions along the way and arrived victorious in Kabul on September 27, 1996. These young men had been schooled in madrassas opened for Afghan refugee children in Pakistan—*Taliban* means "students"—but the curriculum was misinformation and hatred, and they were otherwise mostly illiterate. They promised peace, but in reality they hijacked Islam for political opportunism to deliver a toxic mix of misogyny and misery, all in the name of God.

Before the Taliban—and, in fact, before the civil war began—a tactic known as the night letter had begun to be employed. The original purpose of the letters had been to increase awareness, and to call on people to join protests. But the Taliban used night letters to intimidate and spread fear. Usually unsigned and distributed by hand in the dead of night, the letters would be nailed to a household door, a tree, a mosque, or simply tossed over a boundary wall. The letters invariably contained instructions or demands, with threats of dire consequences for failing to obey. News of the threat invariably traveled rapidly to the whole community—an efficient way of spreading terror and exerting control.

After their defeat in 2001, the Taliban continued their nocturnal postal activities, sending letters to anyone seen as supporting the government or the international community. In the face of such unwelcome threats, people rarely went to the police. In most cases, individuals assessed the seriousness of the threat themselves and took precautionary measures on their own, such as relocating.

These night letters are a microcosm of my country—a country in which hidden puppeteers hold the strings of the people and make them dance with fear: first this way, then that way, swaying in whatever direction the puppet master chooses. Some night letters, like the ones delivered during the pro-Soviet regime, succeeded in ridding the country of people who didn't respect our culture and religion. Others, like the ones from the Taliban, have prevented the elected government from taking our country into the twenty-first century. Plain as it is, just a scribble on a scrap of paper, the letter carries a mighty message. This underground networking is woven into the fabric of this land as a history of intimidation, a threat, and a way of reaching an entire village with one piece of paper nailed to a door. Violence is therefore predictable and recurs.

In fact, the same community where the attack on the school occurred in 2021 has also been the site of horrendous atrocities. Almost exactly a year before the attack, on May 12, 2020, a gang of assailants stormed into a maternity ward run by Médecins Sans Frontières/Doctors Without Borders (MSF) at the Dasht-e-Barchi Hospital and killed twenty-four people, deliberately targeting newborn babies, mothers, and women in labor. Among those killed were fifteen mothers and an MSF midwife, Maryam Noorzad. The attackers also killed two young children and six other individuals who happened to be in the hallway.

Because these terrorist attacks are not new to our people, many public buildings have created what we call safe rooms where people can hide. On that day, about one hundred people found shelter in the safe rooms of the hospital, including one woman who gave birth to a healthy baby in the midst of the terror attack. Others weren't so lucky. MSF sent out a press release that said, "Mothers, babies, and health staff were deliberately targeted. While the identities of the assailants remain unknown, this horrific crime appears to be part of a larger pattern of attacks targeting the ethnic Hazara community living in the area."

I wondered about the men who committed this crime and how they would celebrate their victory against women with their feet in stirrups on the delivery table and an army of newborn babies wrapped in blankets. To murder women while they deliver babies in a maternity ward and claim they are doing so to serve Allah is, for civilized people, an incomprehensible stretch.

Just a year later it was schoolgirls who were singled out for death. Several days would pass before the police and the media pieced together the awful events that resulted in the death of ninety-five schoolgirls, and the injury of more than two hundred. My heart ached for the mothers who were running from one hospital to another, checking every injured child, every dead body, one by one, hoping against hope to find their own girl alive. The hospitals and clinics were so overwhelmed that it was several days before they had lists of the wounded or the names of the dead.

Those bright-eyed little girls had made such an easy target because the school was so crowded, often having between fifty-two and sixty children in a class. And because security had been such a problem in the district, they dismissed the students in batches, the youngest first, then the middle grades and finally the seniors. The four explosions were carefully planned and executed to coincide with the hour the middle-grade girls—most aged twelve to seventeen— were dismissed.

I often ask myself what these men who target the poor, who seek to improve their lot in life at the expense of others—especially women and girls—are afraid of. Is it change? A man once said to me, "If I give women human rights, I have to give away my human rights." I tried to explain the concepts of equality and fairness and justice to him. I tried to help him understand that dozens of studies have shown that human rights are for all people and are a key to prosperity, to better outcomes for everyone. But he could process only the "giving away" part and stubbornly clung to his point of view. Eventually, I seemed to get through to him.

As day became night on May 8, the horrific scenes kept replaying in my mind. The same questions circled my brain like the whir of a wheel: When will this end? What can we do to tame the terrorists? When night came, I turned out the light hoping for relief, but those girls stayed with me; their faces played on the back of my eyelids and came to me in nightmares that left me weeping until the dawn.

Conflict in Afghanistan reveals a lot about governments and militaries around the world. Old concepts like the Geneva Conventions are no longer followed. What exactly is "the war on terror"? What do we actually mean when we speak of "endless war" and "perpetual war"? *Humanitarian law* and *war* are a contradiction in terms, and yet we pursue both.

And what happens to people during this period? We know conflict destroys buildings and bridges and that it kills mothers and fathers and children. But it also damages the way we act as citizens. Our behavior is shaped by the fear and anger and unpredictability that war brings. How can we imagine that forty-five years of war, and in particular the last eighteen years of suicide bombings and improvised explosive devices and attacks on our public institutions, will not contribute to emotional instability in Afghanistan?

The people are caught between the extreme left (communism) and the extreme right (Islamic fundamentalism). They're in the middle, with justice and peace up for grabs. I'm fascinated by how much we study war, analyze war, make movies about war and write about war, and yet never find the formula to stop it. That suggests to me that we've been looking for peace in the wrong places. Most wars today are civil wars. They are about insurgents and terrorists, usually rogue leaders and people who follow them blindly.

Historians say war has become easier to start and harder to stop. They also say Afghanistan will likely be the last international intervention that includes foreign boots on the ground. This is a possibility that all of us, not just Afghans, need to examine, because there are consequences for everyone. War is so destructive to human relationships; it makes even ordinary people resort to violence. In Afghanistan, and in every other war-torn country, poverty increases, and it is children, people with disabilities and women who get the worst of it. I remember seeing a child on the street during the first Taliban takeover; he was screaming his head off and all alone. The smoke from a bomb in his village was still rising. It was just one of many stark examples of how the suffering of children is part of the tapestry of conflict.

In war's aftermath the people are yoked to its consequences. Most suffer from the psychological trauma that comes with insecurity; others—the homeless ones, the orphans, the wounded, the malnourished—suffer no less grievously. All of them are paying the price for someone else's feud, and without help they grow up and keep the war kettle boiling, carrying the quarrel to the next generation.

And where does it end? It ends in places like the Hills of the Martyrs, a field with mudbrick houses scattered about that has become the resting place of the girls from Sayed Al-Shuhada school, the moms and babies from the Dasht-e-Barchi Hospital, and so many more from different attacks. I often ask myself why grandiose cast-iron statues of men on horseback with guns raised triumphantly are the monuments of war in the city centers of the world, while the blameless victims are buried together in cemeteries far away. Traditionally, when people died in the city their families took them back to the region they'd come from to bury them with their ancestors. But the increase in terrorist attacks in the west end of Kabul has moved people to claim the two rock-strewn dusty hills behind the school as a cemetery.

The cemetery came to be in July 2016, after an attack on people who were peacefully marching to demand a newly built electricity line to supply their neighborhood. Suddenly, the government had soldiers and barriers on the road that blocked the marchers' way to the city. Hundreds of men, women and even children were stopped and trapped in the middle of the road—a perfect target for the suicide bomber looking to strike. More than three hundred were injured, and eighty-six people died, most of them young boys and girls. It was decided to honor them as martyrs and to bury them on the hills not far from where they died. The government tried to stop this, but the voice of the people rang out louder than the grumbling of the politicians.

Suicide attacks had been rare in Afghanistan until 2006 but have since increased every year, influenced by jihadis outside of our country who began targeting mosques, sports clubs, wedding celebrations and election centers—wherever people gathered in large numbers. And the victims were mostly children dreaming to build a civilized, democratic Afghanistan. They found peace on those two little hills on the west side of Kabul.

While there had been other attacks, and children had been killed before, the May 2021 assault on girls leaving their school was like a rumbling coming from the core of the earth. It told all of us that inhumane terrorist killings were picking up speed. Even religion wasn't slowing the attackers down—the Taliban spokesman had warned: "Jihad during Ramadan is more valuable in the eyes of God the Almighty!" Although the Taliban claimed not to be responsible for the attack, the terrorist factions are interconnected: the Taliban, ISKP, and other bloodthirsty groups—all know what the other is up to.

The truly perplexing thing about all of them is that women and education are their Achilles' heel. Consider this: Between 1996 and 2001, women, who represent 50 percent of the population, were treated like slaves and like baby-making machines (and the more male babies, the better). Women could not speak out or talk back—they had no rights and lived obediently and submissively at home, suffering no end of violence. In 2001, when the Taliban was defeated, a lot of that changed; for the next twenty years, girls could go to school and become lawyers, journalists, governors, ministers, members of parliament, senators, teachers, doctors, entrepreneurs, artists and sportswomen. The universities were crammed with girls and boys who were reaching for the stars and imagining lives of fulfillment and success.

The young women had been joining the workforce as executives, and the government as ministers, and the judiciary as judges. In August 2021, they were even on the negotiating team that went to Doha, Qatar, for discussions with the Taliban to find a way to end the years of conflict. What's more, today 64 percent of Afghans are under the age of twenty-five. The Taliban may try to take their rights away, but they cannot erase the knowledge of the majority of its young citizens.

As summer began in 2021, many here were very afraid. So was I. We had stopped trusting the foundation on which the progress of the last two decades had been built. I kept reminding myself to look at what we'd accomplished: the institutions we built, the human rights record that's in progress, women taking their rightful place beside men in government and business, a flourishing media. After all that, after building and facilitating a democracy, imagine losing it all again. That is a loss not only for Afghans but for all people and countries who believe in human rights and democratic values.

I know the inside story of my country—the hijacking of the religion, the dishonesty, the collusion, the corruption, the self-serving leaders. I know the courageous women and men who have lifted the country to heights we had only imagined. And I know the blameless ones who simply want peace and a chance for their children's future. I have been an eyewitness to the US effort, to NATO's work, to the UN, the international community, and our own military. I know the players in this chess game called Afghanistan.

As a woman and physician, as a politician and activist, as a human being who has spent a lifetime witnessing one paroxysm of violence after another, I can say this: The hopes and dreams of the girls at Sayed Al-Shuhada school were the same as mine. Those girls perished simply because they were girls, because they dared to go to school to learn to think for themselves. They are my story. And I was their age—twelve—when I became aware that my country needed change.

Two

GIRL CHILD

THE SCENT OF FRESHLY BAKED BREAD wafting through a room has a way of tying each of us indelibly to a place. For me, that place is my home in the central highlands of Afghanistan, in a village called See Paya, in the district of Jaghori, in the province of Ghazni. Every nook and cranny is stored in my memory like a time capsule. We referred to dwellings like ours as muddy houses, as they are made from mud with straw, twigs and bits of small tree branches mixed in that is then packed around wooden poles. In the tunnels built under the floor and attached to the underside of the oven my mother used to bake what we call naan bread every single day. The smoke from the fire would spread, along with the scrumptious scent of the baking bread, through the tunnels that brought heat and a sense of sanctuary to the rest of the house.

An Afghan house is like an Afghan family—extended and sometimes complicated. Our house was attached by a corridor to my uncle Ali Asgher's house. It was a bigger house than his and more modern, with a few more windows and a second floor, which I presumed was because my father had worked outside the village and had seen other homes built this way before he built our house on the side of his brother's place. The flat roof was used during the summer months to dry apricots, mulberries, and almonds and to drain the yogurt and shape it into balls of qurut, used to thicken soups and other dishes. Most muddy houses had one small window to let the light into the main room and keep the winter cold and the summer heat out of the other rooms. Ours had three large windows facing south, which served both requirements—the heat of the sun poured into those rooms when it was cold, and we could read and do our stitching by its light all day long. The cooking room that my mother used in the winter months had a small alcove off to the side that we used as a private and warm place to bathe. In the summer, the cooking was done outdoors; whether inside or out, vegetables and meat were cooked over an open fire and milk was gathered from the livestock to be boiled into yogurt, butter and cheese. But no matter the season or the weather, the daily aroma of baking bread lingered—summer, winter, all day—and that memory stays with me and nourishes my soul.

The main room in the house where the family gathered was lined with mattresses and cushions and had no furniture. We sat on these pads on the floor around the dastarkhan—a large rectangular oil cloth—to eat our meals. The food was served on heaping platters and in bowls in the center of the dastarkhan, and everyone helped themselves to a meal that we ate with our hands. We also slept on the floor; there was not a lot of furniture in an Afghan house where I grew up. The mattresses, pillows and quilts were piled up in one corner of the house during the day in a stack called the *bars*. We each had our own bedding, but there were always extras for any guests.

Although we didn't have anything in the way of riches, I somehow knew we were a little better off than the others, partly because
most muddy houses were smaller than ours and didn't have large
windows, but also because the whole village used the services of one
shepherd to graze the goats and sheep, but our family had a shepherd of our own. Aside from the kitchen and sitting room that made
up the main part of the house, two stables were attached to the back:
one for the cows and donkeys and another for the sheep. Those
rooms, which brought welcome warmth to the house in the winter
months, led to the courtyard, and that's where the shepherd would
be every day at dawn to care for the animals. As soon as the weather
allowed, he would collect a lunch of yogurt and naan bread from my
mother and herd the animals into the hills for grazing. I loved watching them, especially during the first days of spring when they would
lift their heads high and make snorting noises in anticipation and
nearly run to the trodden paths, knowing that the sweet green grasses
had pushed through the earth and were waiting for them after a long
winter spent cooped up in the yard with only dried grains to eat.
The shepherd brought the animals back down to the courtyard in
time for the women to milk them before the evening meal. Day
in and day out, these were the rituals that marked my early years.

Our house had no running water or electricity. What's more, it
didn't have my father. That's the complicated part. My father,
Qadim Ali Yaqubi, lived in a modern house about 550 kilometers
away in Lashkar Gah in Helmand Province, with his second wife,
Halima, and their children. He had a job as an accountant at
Helmand Valley Development, which was a project funded by
the United States Agency for International Development (USAID)
to better manage the availability of water in the valley. Although

my father never had formal schooling and learned to read and write with the mullah in Jaghori, I always thought his success as a respected accountant spoke a lot about his intellect as well as his ability.

When I was very small, we'd all lived together in Jaghori: my sister, Aziza, nine years older than me; my brother, Abdul Wahid, six years older; and two children my father had with Halima at that time. They eventually had seven more for a total of nine children, which, when added to the three from my mother, made us a very large family. I was a toddler when my father moved away with Halima, so I don't remember the details. But it wasn't particularly unusual, as it was common for the male member of the family to be out of our district to find work. Aziza and Abdul Wahid left with them; Abdul Wahid would have more educational opportunities outside of Jaghori. One of the reasons my mother and I stayed behind was a matter of family business. My father and his brother owned the land, the livestock and the business they did in Jaghori together. My mother needed to manage and assert ownership of my father's side of the properties while he took a new job in Lashkar Gah.

Aziza and Abdul Wahid had treated me, the youngest, with so much love and attention that even as a three-year-old I felt the pangs of losing them to another province so far away. But my mother promised me we would see them again soon. For the next four years, while it was just my mother and me living beside my uncle and his family in Jaghori, my mother and uncle doted on me, giving me the best portions of food and all the attention I needed. I was naughtier than my uncle's kids and broke the rules a lot, but they let me get away with my shenanigans. I had a caramel-colored cat that went everywhere with me—to a friend's house, to my uncle and aunt's house, even to the mosque, where it waited patiently until it was time to walk back home. The rule was that it was never allowed to sit on my uncle's chapan (coat) because an animal's hair must never be present on clothing during prayer—but he never shooed my cat away.

It was a time for me to learn by way of observation: my mother managed on her own, and she made sure that my father's share was protected. She milked the cow herself and made delicious yogurt and butter for all of us—even sending some to the family in Lashkar Gah. She raised chickens too and exchanged the surplus eggs for colorful threads and fabrics for her embroidery. She was so patient with me and would sit down with pieces of white cloth and lovely threads to teach me how to stitch and make a design. It's something I do even today; the stitching brings me back to her and to those days when we were together. I was a willing student, and she had much to teach me about kindness, coping, self-sufficiency and tradition.

My father came to Jaghori to visit us during the summertime, occasionally bringing his second wife and my other siblings. They seemed like visitors to me, but my mother would tell me that they were my brothers and sisters, and that Halima was also my mother. I was too young to absorb these seemingly bizarre realities, but the look on my mother's face and the struggle in my own young mind kept signaling a misstep. Although I was a happy child living with my mother and beside an uncle who also had a second wife, it was during those early years that I began to question polygamy, and although I couldn't have put words to my feelings at the time, I was absorbing, as if by osmosis, some of the unfairness of being a woman.

My father also turned up in Jaghori on his own two or three times a year, because he also had a side business that sold natural ghee as well as a type of wood used for framing roofs, doors and windows to companies in cities like Kabul and Ghazni. Even though my mother welcomed him and encouraged me to do the same, and always emphasized that he'd gone away to a good job in Lashkar Gah, I began to wonder how their arrangement worked.

As a small girl I loved listening to my mother's stories and piecing together the tapestry that was her life. She told me that she'd gotten married when she was very young, which was the tradition then. I soon found out it was still the demand of some of the men and some of the mullahs who were part of the patriarchal system in our country and claimed that girls must be married before they menstruate. She had grown up in this town, the youngest of five children and the only girl. She often told me that she wished she had a sister. In fact, my uncle's daughter Ameena was the same age as my mother and was like a sister to her; they had played together as children, making dolls from wood and dressing them with bits of fabric they stitched into clothes. They became even closer when my mother married and moved into the compound as my father's first wife. My mother was so proud of that marriage certificate, which was issued in 1946 in our district of Jaghori, printed on parchment paper with beautifully ornate handwriting. It reads: *I Qadam Ali Yaqubi son of Yaqub Ali married Khursheed daughter of Ramazan Ali in the district of Jaghori on 1324* (the year in our calendar).

I've kept that certificate, and as I look at it now, it saddens me because today in Afghanistan this formality has been deleted from our tradition. I remember how much time and energy we spent in 2007 and 2009, when I was chair of the Afghanistan Independent

Human Rights Commission, working with all the related institutions and government ministries to finally agree on the written substance of a marriage certificate and to make it compulsory so that the wording would bring safety and respect to women in our country. We managed to make it law, but the implementation was complicated, and try as I might I could not revive it.

My sister Aziza was born soon after my mother had her first ovulation. Her second child, Abdul Wahid, was born three years later. I came along in 1957, 1335 in our calendar.

When I was six years old my mother took me to the mosque to study; there were about fifty boys in the class and only ten girls. Although my uncle had already started to teach me to read the Quran, my mother wanted more education for me, and the mosque was the place to learn to do math and to write as well as read. The mosque was close to our house, but I had never been there by myself and was very nervous about going inside without my mother. When she left me on my first day, I immediately burst into tears and ran after her, begging her to let me come home and telling her I was afraid of the mullah.

Of course, my mother took me back to the mosque, and in her gentle but persuasive way she convinced me to stay. Although today we hear mullahs who are more politicized ranting and raving about an endless list of sins (mostly committed by women), the mullahs in those days had authority in the village but were not to be feared. Every village had a mosque and a religious scholar who was chosen collectively by the villagers; he could read and write, while most people could not. From eight to four each day, the mullah taught whichever village children were able to attend, with a break only for lunch. He also performed marriage, funeral and religious ceremonies and tended to people in need. His job had nothing to do with politics; it was to solve village problems in good faith. In return, the mullah received his daily meals from the village families; the best meal in each house was always saved for him.

The mullah at our mosque was a young man who soon taught me the love of learning that would stay with me throughout my life: doing math was like playing games; books were like windows into another world; learning was a life-altering experience that thrilled me. I took to learning like a bee to flowers. I wanted to learn more and be better. Every Wednesday afternoon the mullah checked our lessons; if we hadn't done well, the punishment was to be beaten with a stick. But I was never beaten.

Thursday and Friday were our weekends. It was a time to be at home, to wander up into the hills near the village, to stir the pot of boiling milk until it was ready to be made into yogurt, to stitch a stitch that made my mother smile. We made dolls out of bits of fabric and played with balls we made from cow's hair. Those were the halcyon days of my early childhood. Learning a lot, rebelling a little and participating in ancient traditions. Weddings, for example, were big noisy celebrations that began when the groom and his relatives arrived with a horse covered in glittering fabrics. They came to pay the bride price, which had been agreed upon earlier, when the groom's family and their respected elders asked the family of the bride if their daughter would marry their son. This agreement—or refusal—was based on whether the bride's family wanted this boy for their daughter and whether the bride price was seen as acceptable. The bride price in my village would usually be about seven thousand to ten thousand Afghani, and the mehar (the amount of money paid by the groom to the bride) would be two thousand to five thousand Afghani, and a piece of land or a property, depending on the agreement made between the families. Once that was settled the bride's family also had to be compensated with clothes, jewelry, rugs, mattresses, quilts and household items that would go with the bride on the wedding day. Crowds of people from both families as well as village friends would gather to enjoy a delectable lunch and perform traditional dances. Then, at last, the bride would arrive dressed in the best clothing her family could afford. Wearing the traditional shawl over her head and a thin white veil on her face, she sat high on a horse that was led into the village by her groom with musicians and dancers leading the procession.

Afterward, when the bride arrived in the groom's home, a sheep, a goat or a chicken would be slaughtered right in front of her as a way of saying she was welcome and of acknowledging that she would bring food and happiness and prosperity to the family.

While everyone in the village loved these rituals, I have to admit I didn't understand them the first time I was old enough to take part, when my uncle's second daughter, Bakhtawar, was married. In fact, I sat on the steps of our house with a pocket full of stones, and one clutched in my hand, prepared to lambaste the people who were putting Bakhtawar on a horse and readying her for the day. I pelted them with my rocks while crying and begging them not to take her away from me. My poor mother, horrified by my actions, rushed to my side to stop me and convince me that my cousin would come back soon.

It was rare that outsiders came to the village, but when they did, they invariably attracted a lot of attention. For example, the few times we saw the police were when they came to round up the boys for military service. Every male had to serve at the age of twenty-one. If the boys were not educated in formal schools the commitment was two years in the army or police service; if they had graduated from high school, it was one year; and for university graduates it was six months of service—a wise enticement to promote education.

There was an anxiety attached to the police presence in the village. It's perhaps not surprising, then, that on a day when they came looking for someone who had broken the law, I managed to misinterpret what was happening and send my own fear running off in a completely inappropriate direction. At that time, the government was trying to formalize education and had started building schools. I was too young to understand the concept and somehow mixed up the police action of arresting someone with children being taken away from their parents to a jail called "school." When I saw the police, I ran as fast as I could and hid behind the stack of mattresses and quilts in the corner of the room and eventually fell asleep. Once the family realized I was missing they searched frantically for several hours—until I eventually woke up and wandered outside. I'd created quite a commotion. My father, who was visiting us at the time, put his arms around me and asked what had happened. I told him I was afraid the police were going to take me away. He replied, "No one will ever take my daughter." His words were reassuring, but I never did lose my distrust of the police.

My village was a place where people helped each other—whether bringing in the harvest or building a house, whether working in the fields or collecting firewood for their families or for the mosque—and the women and men worked together. There were families in other parts of the district, even the country and in our own village, who believed women and men should eat in separate rooms and boys and girls should play apart from each other. But it wasn't an issue that divided us; it was a preference, not a rule. No one was ostracized or mistreated, whether or not they mixed or separated the sexes. In our house, if there were no visitors we all ate together, but if we had male guests, we would serve the women and the men in separate rooms.

Mostly, during my early childhood, the rhythms of life in our village rocked gently with the passage of time. The crops were bountiful: almonds, apricots, mulberries and big juicy pomegranates, brought to the village by traders, that were as magnificent to look at as they were delicious to eat. Not to say farming was easy; the men, the women and even the children had to work hard to scratch a living out of that soil. There was never enough water, but we had a system called karez, an underground irrigation tunnel of vertical shafts that delivered large quantities of water to the surface by gravity and measured out the well water, monitoring the amount each family needed. Our lifestyle taught me not that we lacked resources but that being fair with each other meant no one went without. While the planting season of spring brought its own pleasures as seedlings flowered and flourished, the fall was a celebration of the harvest in which men and women together gathered the crops and stored the turnips, carrots and potatoes for the long cold months when the land would be buried in a meter of snow.

Harvest was always an exciting time for us because outsiders came to the village to buy our food; I was fascinated by these strangers: Who were they? Where did they come from? Did I dare speak to them? I remember one year we had surplus wheat and my uncle sold it to a man who was supposed to come with a truck to buy it. I had never seen a truck before and was very excited by this plan. But there were no roads to our village, so as it turned out, the truck couldn't come; donkeys carried the sheaves of wheat out to the edge of the village, where the truck waited. I scrambled up to the roof of our house to watch this noisy machine that wasn't being pulled by an animal. I hoped that someday I might get to ride on it.

Winter in Jaghori had its own charms. The mountains and meadows were blanketed in heavy snow that muffled the sounds of the village. We dressed in layers of scratchy woolen sweaters and coats and built forts and slid off the roofs of the sheds and hid behind snow drifts while throwing snowballs at each other. The women dried the fruits that had been harvested in the fall and sat at spinning wheels making wool from the shearlings collected in the late summer and all the while told stories and sang while refilling pots of black tea.

Now when I think about those days, I'm drawn to what a happy and peaceful time it was; the only guns we saw were for hunting wolf or gazelle or bighorn sheep for food, or in the winter months when the men would go to an open field with old British guns and shoot at a battered sign that was staked in the ground and used as a target. Teams of men from different villages competed against each other; the loser had to feed a meal to all the men on the winning team. It's hard to believe that today our villages are full of weapons and ammunition and a gnawing fear of each other.

Winter was also a time for the men to go to the mosque and listen to the mullah read the popular tales of Rostam, the mighty Persian holy warrior, and his beloved son Sohrab from the Persian book *Shahnameh*, written in the tenth century by the poet Ferdowsi.

The mullah had everyone's rapt attention while he recounted the story of Rostam's daring expeditions and the tragic fight with what he thought were enemies when in fact he killed his own son. Those evenings of storytelling were like the series we binge-watch on Netflix today. As a young girl I was allowed to join my uncle at the mosque, so I knew the stories as well. Once the mullah closed the book, a prolonged discussion followed. The mosque was a welcoming place, always warm, heated by firewood contributed by every family in the village. If anyone was traveling through our village they could find shelter from the cold in a mosque and stay the night there. In fact, there was invariably a hot meal, or at least hot tea and bread, provided to the stranger by a village family.

It was during those long winters that my mother taught me to sew and embroider and design patterns. Although she couldn't read or write, young girls and women from our village came to her for lessons. She would draw the design to show us what she wanted us to do, and we would follow her example. In return, one of my cousins came regularly to teach my mother, who was very devout, how to read the Quran. It took a long time, but she persevered. By the time I was six years old, my mother was reading the Arabic words from the Quran with ease. Her determination and effort made a lasting impression on me.

When I was seven my father came to Jaghori and showed us a book written for first-grade students. He asked me to read it and to do some simple math exercises. I believe it was at that time that he decided my mother and I should come to Lashkar Gah to live with the rest of the family so that I could be enrolled in a proper school.

As autumn began in 1964 my mother and I, along with my uncle Ali Asghar and his wife, Fatima, left on the three-day voyage to Lashkar Gah, the capital of Helmand Province. Our house and all of my father's belongings were left with my uncle's family. I couldn't understand why we were leaving, and I put up a strong argument to stay, but my mother kept assuring me that one day we would come back to Jaghori. For a girl who had never left the village, a girl who knew every lamppost and resident, this voyage was as wrenching as it was exhilarating. To prepare for the journey, my mother cooked khajoor—the delicious, deep-fried pastry we serve for special occasions—and packed it along with dried fruits and a stack of naan bread and the dried meat of two whole sheep. She put all our clothes and belongings in an iron box and several sacks and lined them up for the departure.

My anxiety about leaving was tempered by my excitement over riding in a truck—but first we had to get ourselves and all our boxes and sacks to the truck stop at another village. Led by my uncle, we trekked the few kilometers to the starting point beside donkeys ladened with our parcels. My uncle had made the hajj—the once-in-a-lifetime trip to Mecca that every Muslim who is able is expected to do. Ever afterward, those who have made the hajj are known by the title *hajji*. As we walked to the center of the small town, I heard people calling out "Hajji, Hajji!" I felt proud of my uncle and the honoring title he had earned. He carried a watch in his pocket that was pinned with a chain to a buttonhole on his jacket, which I thought made him look very important indeed.

It was mid-morning by the time we were loaded into the back of the truck and tucked in close to each other for the seven-hour journey to Muqur. We hadn't gone very far, maybe a few kilometers, when the thrill of riding in the back of a truck was replaced with nausea. Without any warning I started to vomit and was stuck in my own mess on a dusty, bumpy road with a day's drive stretching out in front of me. Thankfully I soon fell sound asleep and woke up in Muqur, where we stopped for the night in a local chai khana, a tea house divided into small rooms where people can eat and sleep if they want to stay overnight. After a dinner of the sweetened tea and bread we had with us, we slept until dawn and packed up again for our stopover in Kandahar. The road was long—it seemed never-ending to me—but at last, at noon on the third day, we arrived in Helmand Province. My uncle had to arrange for two horse carts to take us from the truck stop to my father's house.

While I thought arriving with two carts full of our belongings made us an impressive sight, I was in for a surprise when we reached my father's house. I'd never seen such a place. It was a cement house with running water and electricity. I wanted to turn on every tap and try every light fixture; to me it was like magic. And it didn't take long before I realized how much easier it was compared to lugging water and making fires and measuring the oil for lamps.

I was still taking in what seemed like a very large house—three rooms plus a kitchen and a bathroom with a toilet and a storeroom that led to a courtyard—when I saw my father riding a bicycle along a paved road and up the path to the house. He was a tall man, handsome, I thought; he had presence—he was one of those people who seemed to be in the center of the room even if he was standing in the doorway. He stayed at home only long enough for lunch that day and returned immediately to work while we were left to sort ourselves out in this new place with a second wife and, at that time, six more children.

My brother Abdul Wahid was away at a military prep school in Kabul, but my sister Aziza was there with wide-open arms to greet me—I had missed her immensely. She took me on a quick tour of my new surroundings. There were chickens in the yard, and vegetables much like we had in Jaghori. She told me our father also had another piece of land for milking cows and steers for plowing the land and that he had hired a man to help with the chores. It all seemed pretty grand to me. The house we lived in was provided by the Helmand Valley project for which my father worked. As in most company towns today, the size of the houses given to the employees was based on the position they held. We weren't rich by any means, but later my father had become the chief accountant for the project, so we had a house big enough for our growing family.

When my father came home at 4 p.m. that day after work, he carried a piece of black cloth with him and told Aziza to stitch it into a uniform for me so he could take me to school in the morning. I was perplexed—I had never been to a school and was a little frightened about what would happen. The next morning, without any explanation at all, my father picked me up, put me on the handlebars of his bicycle and pedaled a short distance to the school, where hundreds of children were lined up outside waiting to go in.

My father took me to the office of the headmistress, Mahbooba Safi, and told her that Marzia, which was the name I was called at the time, could read and write and do math at the grade-two level and that I should be tested for a higher grade than the other children my age were in. Accordingly, she took me to a teacher called Shafiqa who tested me for reading and writing and math. I did well. Then she began a test on religion.

The next thing I knew Shafiqa was marching me down the hall to Mahbooba Safi's office. Without saying anything about how I'd performed on the other tests, she reported to the headmistress that

I was "a stupid Hazara" who didn't know the religion. I had no idea what I had done wrong; her actions terrified me. I wanted to run, to hide, to get out of this strange new place as fast as I could, but I didn't know where to go. While listening to the diatribe, and struggling to understand the teacher's Kabuli dialect, I began to figure out the nature of my so-called sin.

Shafiqa, being Tajik, was a Sunni Muslim. She had begun the religion test with: "Who created you?"

"God," I answered.

"Who do you follow?"

"The Prophet Mohammad."

Then she asked, "Who do you love?" I answered, "Ali," because that's what the Shi'ite say. But the Sunni have a different reply to that question, which is "Char Yaar Ba Safa"—meaning "four honest friends" and referring to the four friends of the Prophet.

I didn't know that. I was horrified listening to her denunciation of me and started to cry. The headmistress told the teacher she would take care of it, and when Shafiqa left the office, she was gentle with me and asked me questions about the religion. When she got to the part that had made the teacher angry, I stopped, too afraid to say anything that would make the headmistress shout at me. She asked me to tell her what I had said, and when I did, she replied, "When you're at home you can say 'Ali,' but at school, you must say 'Char Yaar Ba Safa.'" I was only seven years old, but I understood that the words I had been taught represented a divide between my family and the teachers.

Mahbooba Safi told me to go back to the classroom. However, I decided not to go, as I was afraid of the teacher and now saw her as my enemy. But since I didn't know how to get home, I had to wait outside the building for my brothers to walk with me at the end of the school day. For two hours, I sat on the cold cement steps feeling the chill and trying to muffle my crying so no one would hear me. When I got home my weeping had turned into full-on wailing—I told my family I would never go back to those people who thought I wasn't as good as they were.

The next morning my father plunked me back on his bike, pedaled to the school, went directly to the headmistress and told her how he felt about the fact that they had insulted me. She apologized to my father and took me straight to the second-grade classroom. As far as my family was concerned, that was the end of the problem. I would better understand the politics that transpired during that brief discussion about being Shi'ite at home and Sunni at school when I was a lot older. But although I'd scored a victory of sorts in escaping the teacher who had insulted me, there was no escaping the hurtful truth that I had been singled out in front of the others because of my ethnic origins. It was my first lesson in discrimination based on my ethnicity; it wouldn't be the last.

In class I sat next to a girl called Qudsia, who quickly became my best friend and remains my friend to this day. She was Tajik and came from Kabul, but Qudsia taught me that being from a different place or even a different ethnic group didn't mean you couldn't be friends. We played together and studied together and visited each other's houses; as we got older, we wore each other's clothes. We would climb a tree that had a branch swooping out over the river, and that perch was where we told each other our secrets.

While I was getting used to school and my new life, there was another issue brewing in the family. I discovered that the real reason my mother and I had come to Lashkar Gah with my uncle and his wife was to arrange a marriage between their son and Aziza. While everyone seemed to be very happy about that plan, my beautiful sister was miserable, crying and begging my parents not to force her to marry this cousin. But as I found out, a deal had been struck when she was still a baby. My mother and father both had typhoid fever when Aziza was just old enough to crawl. Terrified that she would get sick too, they asked my uncle's wife if she would take care of Aziza until they were better. In return, they promised they would give my sister to their son in marriage. In our tradition there was no turning back on such a promise. When the engagement was announced, Aziza, who was eighteen, said she'd rather be killed than marry this man.

Weeks later, the marriage went ahead. I remember that day; she couldn't stop crying. I began to realize how intricate and potent family relationships are. This wedding was happening because my father was bound by our custom that says the older brother rules. The rights of my sister were not considered seriously; my father tried, but he could not persuade his older brother to change his mind.

When the newlyweds moved away to Jaghori, I was separated from Aziza once more. One year later, though, they returned to Lashkar Gah and rented a small muddy house near us. The place had no electricity or indoor plumbing, but at least my sister was close by.

Aziza was a good cook and a very talented stitcher. Her embroidery became known among neighbors in Lashkar Gah, and she and my mothers made crafts and other stitched goods that they sold all over the city, which I also did when I was older. But for all her talent and ability, it was my beloved sister's forced marriage that left the biggest impression on me regarding the blind adherence to culture and tradition over the rights of women.

I used to go to her house after school, and she would always tell me, "Study hard. Education is the only way to escape this way of living." She never did go to school because there had not been any schools for girls when she moved to Lashkar Gah. I believe my father did teach her to read and write.

Aziza's problems were compounded by the fact that she didn't get pregnant right away, and she had everyone hounding her to hurry up and produce a child. And then, once she did become pregnant, she and her husband and mother-in-law all got sick. She'd been so happy to be having a child and was busy knitting baby clothes when suddenly she became so ill that her skin turned yellow—the classic symptom of jaundice. A doctor tried to help, and we all thought she was getting better. In fact, when my father had about twenty guests coming to dinner, she did the cooking with the help of my mothers because she knew how to prepare delicious food and serve it in traditional Afghan style.

Then disaster struck. The day after the dinner party, Aziza went into labor and gave birth to a stillborn baby. When I got to the house that day, Aziza was in bed and the baby had been put in another room. My mother even lied and told her the baby was a girl—an effort to lessen the blow.

I crept into the room where the baby boy lay and was astonished to see how yellow this tiny infant's skin was. I would learn later in my professional career about jaundice, but on that day, I was struck by the abnormality that was being hidden from everyone. The next day, Aziza went into a coma, and the family rushed her to the hospital. It was there that my sweet and kind sister died.

Later, her husband, our father and family members, and the mullah took Aziza and her baby to the graveyard. With the family gathered around, they were buried in two plots, side by side. Aziza was only twenty.

In my professional life as a doctor, every jaundice and hepatic coma patient reminded me of Aziza's death. Losing her broke my mother's heart and left a pain in my own soul that has never gone away. What happened to her was one of the events that shaped my thinking about the conditions girls and women live with in my country.

My father, Qadim Ali, had two wives, which was a usual practice for many men. But it's a custom I've never approved of, and I could see how difficult it was to treat everyone with equality. I was the third child of the first wife, and once we were in Lashkar Gah with the second wife and her children, I realized that my mother, Khursheed, was being treated unfairly. The two wives lived together—in fact, when we'd all lived in Jaghori they slept in the same bedroom. I was close in age to the second-born of the second wife's nine children, so as babies we slept between the two women and were breastfed by both. But as I grew up, I saw the humiliation and the torment my mother had to endure.

By the time I was eight I had learned about power relationships and expectations. It was very clear that girls and boys had different roles: Girls could play with dolls; boys could play games outside. A man could ride a horse, but a woman could do so only if the horse was being led by a man. Girls should learn to do embroidery, cleaning and cooking. Boys could ride bicycles—although I used to take my brother's bike when no one was watching and ride it myself.

A girl could not be outside the house in the evening. A boy could stay out no matter how dark it was.

One of my father's sisters often came to us to ask for wheat. I found out it was because she was a sister in the family and the brothers did not give her the land from our grandfather that our religion says she was entitled to; instead, as the cultural tradition dictates, they took it for themselves. In Islam, women are supposed to get a share of their parents' property, even though it's not as much as the boys get. But in fact they usually get none at all, because it is assumed and accepted that women have lower status than men and are less valuable.

I sometimes think that despite the harsh realities of our lives, I managed to grab the brass ring. Because of the American agriculture project that was building a better water supply in our valley, the design of the city was modern. The high school I ended up attending was staffed by American Peace Corps volunteers, so the classes were coeducational, with male and female teachers and no boundary wall dividing boys and girls. And it certainly didn't follow the rules for girls that other schools did. I played basketball, volleyball and soccer on the school playing fields. I went to movies with my friends and ran along the riverbanks and climbed trees. We had labs for physics, chemistry and biology. I remember one day in the school lab getting to examine an amoeba—the one-celled parasite that can make you sick, even kill you. I began to understand the impact of science on health as I watched it under a microscope.

American families living in the city because of the USAID-funded project mixed with the local people. Every Saturday evening they had a program with music and dancing at what they called the

Staff House, and Afghans who worked with them were welcome. On Thursday nights, there was a movie—everything from Charlie Chaplin to a film about malaria, showing the health impact a single mosquito can have. Not only that, but the Americans were processing milk into ice cream and other dairy items such as yogurt, butter and milk, and they sold it to us. I thought the ice cream, which was different from the Afghan style of sheer yakh, was wonderful. Because of the American influence in Helmand, we not only had science labs and microscopes but also an English center that provided books at many different reading levels, and English classes. We equated the USAID logo with progress, change, learning and growing.

Many years later, in 2020, I saw that same logo in Kabul—the times were startlingly different, and the symbol now conjured up impressions of people merely surviving, feeling fearful and unsure. During a trip I made to Helmand in 2018 I could hardly believe the changes. There was a boundary wall around our house, and the students went to school for only three hours a day. The boys and girls were strictly separated. I didn't see any girls in the playing fields.

As a student, I was a voracious reader. Through books such as Maxim Gorky's *The Mother* and Victor Hugo's *Les Misérables*, I learned that other people didn't live by the same strict rules that the people in Afghanistan adhered to. By the time I was twelve, I knew I was a rebel, and that I could never accept my society's patriarchal traditions. I heard a mullah say that every menses was a crime because an ovum had been wasted. When I questioned him, he said girls should be married at the age of nine or ten, and he started shouting at me for daring to ask him such questions. I knew I had to find a way to change this thinking.

Those thoughts about altering the course of the status of women and girls were influenced by the significant differences in the way our school operated compared to other schools in the district. A female teacher called Mrs. Hitchcock taught us how to play games, and an Afghan man called Atrafi taught volleyball and football not just to the boys but also to any girls who wanted to learn. Later on, when civil war pushed all of us to different parts of the world, Atrafi and his family went to New Zealand as refugees. In 2007 I was invited by the New Zealand Human Rights Commission to attend an event in Christchurch. A dinner arranged by the Afghans was held in my honor because some soldiers from New Zealand had been part of the NATO-led International Security Assistance Force (ISAF) in Afghanistan after 9/11. To my great surprise, my sports teacher Atrafi was there with his family. We hugged each other and shed tears for what had happened in our country and reminded each other about how poor we had been but how happy we were with what we had. We talked about the days when he was a teacher and I was a student and girls in the school could play as freely as boys.

I did well in my classes and usually came first or second, which was a very good thing. Because I was skirting the family's rules almost all the time, I knew I had to stay on my father's approval list or he would yank me out of school. By then I was dreaming about becoming a construction engineer. It wasn't common for girls to go to high school—my sister Aqila and I were the first in the Hazara community in Helmand to attend one—much less talk out loud about becoming an engineer. Some of the conservative people in the city gossiped about us, but my father was committed to our education.

It was during my high school years that I became interested in joining the students seeking a better Afghanistan, with equal rights for all people. Although I had a lot to learn about human rights theory and practice, I certainly was aware of the discrimination against us Hazaras. The students who came from the other ethnic groups, including people from Kabul, used to say insulting things such as "a Hazara eating chocolate is like a frog sliding"—it doesn't translate very well from Dari to English, but we all knew it was to put us down. Such comments were flung at us all the time. Hazaras made up less than 4 to 5 percent of the student body, but most of us were the best in the class. I think it was our way of resisting discrimination.

Like student activists today, we began calling for changes in the country: better pay, fair employment opportunities for all, and better working conditions for laborers and farmers. I wanted equality for men and women, for rich and poor. I felt it was wrong that some people couldn't afford to eat.

Political activism had begun to flourish; the Cold War was well underway, and even in Lashkar Gah we heard the rumblings about Soviet politics and were becoming increasingly aware of the poverty and injustice in our own province. Various organizations formed to take sides: on the left were pro-Soviet and pro-China arguments; on the right was the Muslim Brotherhood.

We had a conference every two weeks on a Thursday afternoon, where we discussed current events. When we decided to elect a leader of the group, I had my first taste of true democracy. The competition for the leadership was open to the older and senior students; whoever won the most votes would chair the discussions on how to improve the economy and the development of the country. It was at these conferences that we first discussed forced marriage and child marriage and the selling of girls—problems that persist to this day.

We grew as activists and eventually began to call out injustices regarding the ethnicity of a student or favoritism a teacher was showing. At the same time, I noticed there were fewer girls than boys protesting, and I began to understand that equality begins at home; it's the bedrock upon which girls grow up to expect fairness and justice in society.

By the time I was in the eleventh grade, I had become a leader, and in that year and the year following, I spoke out against injustice and pro-USSR parties. The Pashtun students, who were the majority at the school, were with the Khalq party (a faction of the pro-Soviet PDPA), which wanted to overthrow the government immediately. But no matter how small, every political party in the country was represented at my school.

We organized lively debates on political issues both in Afghanistan and those that were playing out internationally, such as the USSR invasion of Czechoslovakia, the Vietnam War, the war in Bangladesh and freedom movements in North African countries. I saw it all as an encouraging sign of a developing democratic process and a brave new day in our country.

Then, in the summer of 1973, while King Zahir Shah was in Italy, there was a coup d'état led by Mohammad Daoud Khan, the king's cousin. He declared himself the first president of the country and established an autocratic one-party system with closer ties to the USSR and to Parcham, a faction of the PDPA comprising mainly Farsi-speaking Afghans. That event shifted the tone of our student discussions; rumblings about burgeoning democracy and power shifts had turned into rumblings about revolution, talk of which started in earnest among university students in Kabul and then spread to high school students and other educated people in the society. Daoud Khan angered some: the king's followers who felt a multiparty system would be a better successor to a monarchy; the ethnic minorities who mistrusted Daoud Khan's favoritism for the Pashtuns; and neighboring countries, particularly Pakistan, who anticipated unrest on their borders. (Later Daoud Khan would distance himself from Parcham and the USSR, which encouraged the PDPA to commit the military coup in 1978).

The quarrels affected all of us, of course; at my house it was the main topic of conversation with family and neighbors. However, there was a different development closer to home that took me by surprise. I was using my summer break to take typing and tailoring lessons at the women's association in the city when a marriage proposal arrived. My father reviewed the request and, to my enormous relief, abruptly said, "No." After Aziza died, my father had said he would never again force one of his daughters to marry. He told me that when I wanted to marry, I should tell him, and he would arrange it. So although he was reforming his view, he certainly wasn't relinquishing his power as the patriarch.

To be clear, in Afghanistan, the usual practice is for the family of the boy to approach the family of the girl with the proposal. Sometimes the marital arrangement is made as a way to settle a dispute, at which point it becomes a forced marriage rather than an arranged one.

It was during that summer that Abdul Ghafoor Sultani came into my life—first, as a visitor to our house. He was the nephew of my second mother, Halima. His grandfather, Halima's father, had died, and he had come to Lashkar Gah to pay his respects to his aunt. Ghafoor, as everyone called him, had spent six years studying physics on a scholarship in the USSR (several Afghan women were also given scholarships to study in the USSR) and was now a professor in the Faculty of Science at Kabul University. He was also a friend of my brother Abdul Kayum, who was studying engineering in Kabul. There was a lot of talk about physics and algebra as we relaxed at home after work and sat around the dastarkhan for meals. The subjects actually interested me a lot, so I joined the conversation with this man from far away.

He came for another visit during the winter break, this time bringing his two sisters and their husbands to see Lashkar Gah. It was not uncommon for relatives to come in the winter months because Helmand Province, unlike Jaghori, has a temperate climate with warm winters. But the next winter, he came back by himself.

By then it was 1974 and I was in my last year of high school. I was actively involved with radio stations such as the Voice of Germany (Deutsche Welle), because I wanted to learn how to speak the language, and All India Radio, so I could find out what people in other places were thinking. I was also preparing to write my final high school exams. That's when I received a letter from Ghafoor proposing marriage.

The proposal was both surprising and somewhat confusing. I didn't know what to do. I wasn't interested in getting married, but I was adamant about going to university. I brought the letter to my brother Abdul Kayum to get his advice. He liked Ghafoor and agreed that this was my chance to go to university; then he started talking about how well-educated Ghafoor was and what a good man he was. And Kayum reminded me that our father would not allow me to go to university and live in a city away from home. He had already stretched our tradition by allowing me and my sister to go to high school, which opened him up to gossip and criticism. My plan to study engineering seemed to be dependent on whether or not I was willing to get married.

Then one day in the late afternoon when I was sitting in the park with my friend Qudsia, one of my brothers came to find me. He told me we had a guest in the house and that I should come home immediately, which was code for something very important. Upon arriving, I found Ghafoor's father and cousin there. They had come to ask my father if his daughter could be married to their son. The whole family was happy with this proposal and so was I—because it meant I could go to university.

I was honest with Ghafoor, as I didn't want to enter this union with deceit—I'd already seen too much of that. I told him that I could not be an obedient wife, but I could be a good friend. And I also told him that one of the reasons I wanted to marry him was to continue my studies. He promised he would do everything he could to facilitate that. I knew he loved me, but somehow, I had grown up understanding more about loyalty than love. I had both fondness and respect for Ghafoor and, what's more, he offered me a rescue plan. And so, at the age of nineteen, I became officially engaged to Abdul Ghafoor Sultani, a twenty-six-year-old physics professor at Kabul University.

As soon as my high school exams were over, the engagement party—a simple tea for family and relatives—was held, and after that I dedicated myself full-time to preparing for the university entrance exams scheduled in January. Abdul Kayum came with me to Kandahar because tradition and the security situation at that time forbade me from traveling there on my own.

Just before I entered the exam room, my brother pulled me aside and said, "Select medicine as your first choice—it requires the highest marks. If you really decide you want to be an engineer, you'll be able to switch, but if you choose engineering now you won't be able to change to the medical faculty later." I took his advice, and it had a profound effect on my life.

Two months later, in the middle of March, the results were announced: I was accepted into the Faculty of Medicine. Then, as if to test my ability to navigate the rigid customs I had dodged for much of my life, an extraordinary opportunity came along: I was awarded a scholarship to study in Australia. But my father said a daughter who was unmarried could not go abroad to study, and he forbade me from accepting. Since I had already been accepted at Kabul University, I figured that would be my fallback plan, but again my father refused. When I suggested I could stay at a recently established home that was being used as a girls' dormitory, my father was horrified.

Now I had a new problem. The semester was starting on March 22. Although I was engaged, I was not married, so I was not permitted to go to Kabul. Ghafoor even came and asked my father to let me accept the scholarship. My father gave him a flat "No." Ghafoor didn't have the money to pay for the kind of wedding my father wanted, so that option wasn't available. Once again, I feared that my chance to make a life of my own was eluding me.

Finally, Ghafoor found a solution, borrowing some money from his uncle so that we could get married and move to Kabul. He was the sort of man who kept his word and fulfilled his promises; he was determined I would go to university. The wedding was held on a bright, sunny day in April 1975. The mullah came in the middle of the afternoon and asked us if we agreed to marry each other. Since it was required that my guardian speak for me, my father answered. Ghafoor answered for himself. The next day we went to the government office and signed the marriage contract. Then there was a dinner in the Hotel Bost, but as our tradition dictates, only the males in the family were invited to attend; the women stayed with me at the house, where we prepared our own meal.

Early the next morning my groom and his family, along with my second mother, boarded the bus for the ten-hour trip to Kabul. We arrived late on that Thursday night. Since Friday is the holy day, there was no work for Ghafoor or school for me, so we went to the Kabul Zoo. I had never been to a zoo before, and had only seen photos of elephants, tigers, lions, deer and exotic birds. It reminded me again that there was a wide world out there that I needed to know more about.

I had already missed a month of classes, so on Saturday morning I set out to begin this new phase of my life as a university student. Ghafoor accompanied me to the different departments to make sure the administrative work was done and that I would be allowed to join the classes. I worried about catching up with the other students, but I knew what lay before me was the opportunity of a lifetime, and I was ready for it.

There were 240 students in the class; only forty-five were women. Because I'd attended a coeducational school, I had an advantage in that I wasn't in the least intimidated by having classes and entering academic discussions with boys. Classes went from 8 a.m. to 5:30 p.m. Two boys from my high school class were also attending, so at first I walked with them to classes. But I wanted to get to know the Kabuli girls, who initially saw us as country bumpkins. Eventually I crossed that divide and acquired a host of new friends.

Ghafoor and I rented a house from one of his colleagues; it had two rooms, a small kitchen and a bathroom. There was electricity but no running water, and we had to scrounge to find furnishings. But starting our new life was fun. We walked together to university and came home together. Every Friday, on the holy day, we would do all the household work, receive guests and visit our relatives. Most Afghans live with their extended family, but we decided to live separately for the first three years of our marriage. After that, we shared a house with my brothers Abdul Kayum and Abdul Wahid, along with Abdul Rauf Naveed, a classmate of mine at school in Lashkar Gah and a nephew of my second mother.

Ghafoor and I had an arrangement that ours would be an equal opportunity household; the chores, the cooking, the laundry, the cleaning, even the banking would be shared 50/50. Everyone called us the "50 percent couple"; if I was out without him, or he was without me, they'd ask, "Where's the other 50 percent?" I went out to the cinema with his sisters or my fellow classmates whenever I wanted and without asking anyone's permission. Life was not easy, as we had very little money, but we were happy with what we had and Ghafoor started teaching math and physics in the evening to students doing university admission courses for some extra income.

Our lives were filled with working, studying and having friends over to discuss schoolwork and politics. As well, Afghanistan had become an attraction to young people known as hippies. We saw these men and women with long hair and disheveled clothing and backpacks walking freely about, traveling around the country and sampling hashish along the way. It was not part of my lifestyle, but once again the presence of people from away intrigued me and led me to ask more questions about sameness and difference.

I felt we were fortunate. But tradition played its role all the same. Our families kept asking us why there was no child, insisting that we fulfill our obligation to produce one. As much as we felt our decisions should be ours alone, we caved in to the pressure from our families after two years of marriage.

Fortunately, I had an easy pregnancy. Of course, there was much talk about the sex of the baby—at that time, having a boy was preferable to having a girl, but I was just delighted to be pregnant and didn't care either way. Ultrasound was not available then, and so no one knew the sex of the baby in advance. In the evenings I embroidered sleeping clothes and bedding and waited for this wonderful new person to arrive in our lives.

My mother had come two weeks before my due date to help me during the delivery of our child. I was attending school on my due date; the women in my class had planned to go to another classmate's home to visit her new baby. We all agreed to meet at the bus stop at three o'clock; I went home, wrapped up a present for my friend's infant and, all of a sudden, the birthing cramps began. I gave birth to our son, Ali, right there at our house. Since I could not go to my classmate's house, my friends came to me with the cookies and chocolate she had prepared and we all celebrated the arrival of little Ali. He brought such warmth and sweet sentiment into our lives that I soon could hardly imagine life without him.

My final exams had already started when Ali was born. After I'd finished my last one, we packed up and went to Lashkar Gah to stay through the holidays. But when the time came to return to Kabul I realized that studying while breastfeeding a colicky baby would be a balancing act—one I worried I wouldn't be able to manage. I think I was crying as much as the baby was. My mother took care of both of us, but eventually it was time for us to go.

Together, Ghafoor and I made a heartrending decision. I had to face that I could not take care of Ali and study at the same time. So, Ghafoor and I left Ali with my mother and traveled back to Kabul alone. I wept all the way on the bus, with Ghafoor trying to calm me and telling me that he loved Ali as much as I did, but now was the time to understand that Ali was in good hands and I should focus on my studies. He said, "When you are finished your dream to become a doctor, we will have Ali back with us, and in the meantime we'll go to Lashkar Gah every chance we get."

It was such a painful time, and we didn't have much money. Not being able to buy baby clothes for my son, I cut up my maternity clothes and stitched the fabric together to make outfits for him. I bought secondhand sweaters at the market and re-stitched them into little pants and tops. I felt guilty every single day we were apart. The plan was for it to be a temporary arrangement, and that we'd have him back with us before too long. What I didn't know was that our lives were about to be shattered by events much larger than us.

Three

STORM WARNINGS

THERE WERE SUBTLE BUT TELLING SIGNS that revolution was at hand. On an April day in 1978, classes were canceled and Radio Kabul, the only radio station in the country, suddenly switched from regular programming to pumped-up patriotic songs. My brother Abdul Kayum came home and said he'd seen security forces gathered around the radio station and heard there was fighting at the military base on the east side of the city.

As darkness fell over Kabul that night, the roar of low-flying fighter jets indicated that the rumors about a new coup d'état were probably correct. At 9 p.m., a radio announcement said everything was under control, which we interpreted as code telling us that the government had fallen to the revolutionaries. The next day the city was tense: most people stayed inside. The following night at 10 p.m. the news declared that President Daoud and his family were dead and the revolutionary forces of the PDPA had taken over the country. They named Nur Mohammad Taraki the head of the Khalq party, as president (the PDPA was a union of the two pro-USSR parties, the hardline Khalq and the Parcham faction, headed by Babrak Karmal). The next day all the offices were closed; people hid in their houses, afraid to venture outside. That spring would be the beginning of forty-five years of war, with all of the attendant killing, destruction, deception and corruption. It was called the Saur Revolution because it took place during the second month of the Solar Hijri calendar, Saur. Within a few weeks, the country was renamed The Democratic Republic of Afghanistan.

Almost immediately, people who didn't agree with the new regime were arrested, tortured, killed or disappeared; civil servants were replaced with unqualified people who belonged to the party. Anyone who didn't support the party was in danger. The resistance movement that I was already part of picked up speed, now turning against the pro-USSR government. We passed out pamphlets that told people what this new government would bring to the country. We wrote night letters to disclose the truth about the PDPA's connection to the Soviets. We focused on building awareness about the mismanagement of power. It was dangerous work. Suddenly, there were spies everywhere, even within families, and in my own medical school classes. No one dared to speak openly. Even making a joke about the new president could have you arrested or disappeared. Ghafoor was aware of the anti-Soviet work I was involved in and worried about my safety as an outspoken woman, but as far as I knew, he hadn't played a very active role in the resistance. Our home, however, became a center for debate and discussion. As the months went by and a new year, 1979, began, there was tension everywhere, as if a noose were tightening around our country.

Still, in our daily lives we sought normalcy while weathering the early part of the storm. On a cold March day, one of Ghafoor's sisters, Fatima, came over with her husband, Muhammad Akram; Fatima was five months pregnant and needed help making maternity clothes. She and I went off to the store to find fabric, and with the scarce Afghanis we had, found exactly what we needed. Fatima had been trying to get pregnant for several years, so the outing felt a bit like a celebration during those bleak political times. Akram had brought pine nuts and raisins to add a special touch to the dinner, and afterward, while Ghafoor, Akram and my brothers Abdul Kayum and Abdul Aziz were playing cards, Fatima and I stitched up the dresses. A stove that we filled with sawdust to heat the room kept us warm while we talked about politics. By the time we finished the two dresses it was midnight. Fatima was so pleased with my tailoring job that she planned to wear one of them the next day to her job at the Ministry of Mining. Because of the curfew imposed from 10 p.m. to 6 a.m., Muhammad Akram and Fatima stayed overnight with us.

The minute the curfew was lifted in the morning, the doorbell rang. Ghafoor rushed to open the door and found Akram's sister Husnia, wearing a burka and shaking with fear. He brought her into the house and listened in horror while she explained that during the night people from the intelligence service had come to their house and arrested a young man called Musa Khakash, whom they had been taking care of while he recovered from a car accident, as he still wasn't able to walk. What's more, she said, "They were asking for Muhammad Akram." We were worried; Ghafoor's eldest brother, an army officer, had already been arrested, and we didn't know what had become of him. It felt as though the bottom had dropped out of our lives. Did it mean all of us were now being hunted? Fatima left for work. We told Muhammad Akram not to return home, but he did anyway, insisting he had done nothing wrong and didn't want to be away from Fatima while she was pregnant.

A week later, on March 21—the Afghan New Year— Muhammad Akram was arrested. So were several of Ghafoor's cousins and his ninety-three-year-old uncle, a former senator with a serious heart problem. Fatima lobbied everyone she knew and went to every office she could to find out what had happened to Akram. Finally, after three months, she managed to get a meeting with the general secretary of the party, Hafizullah Amin, the most powerful person in the Khalq party. Ghafoor, who was devastated by these arrests, went to see Fatima when she returned, hoping for some good news; instead, there was an ominous message. Amin had told Fatima that she should have married someone in the Khalq party if she hadn't wanted her husband to be disappeared. He also said that Akram had joined the Ashrar—the government's term for the mujahideen who were fighting against the government and the USSR.

At that time, the mujahideen were truly fighting for Afghanistan; they had not yet been politicized and spoiled by the Americans, Saudis, Pakistanis and others. We saw them as heroes and assisted their work wherever we could. But when I heard these accusations about Muhammad Akram, I knew it could mean danger for us, and so I suggested to Ghafoor that we escape so neither of us would be arrested. He wouldn't consider it. "When we got married I promised you that I would do everything I could to facilitate your education," he said. "And now what I want more than anything is for you to get your medical degree. I'm not involved in any anti-government activities; they won't arrest me."

A week later my world fell apart.

It was June 23, 1979. I was in my fourth year of medical school at Kabul University; our son, Ali, who was sixteen months old, was still with my parents in Lashkar Gah. In Kabul, it was a bright and sunny Saturday. The rumor mill was busy, and we all anticipated danger. My sister, who was studying engineering at the university, even talked to me about what we should wear in case something were to happen. I decided on jeans, since I could run faster in them than in a skirt.

As usual for a Saturday morning, I had to go to the hospital to work. Our class had been divided up and sent to different hospitals—my group was at Wazir Akbar Khan Hospital that day. At noon, a bus went to each location to bring all the medical students back to the university in time for the start of classes at 1 p.m. We heard from the others on the bus that there'd been heavy fighting at the Chindawol police station; many had been killed when the government forces opened fire on people who'd attacked the station to get weapons.

Once we got to the campus, the administration announced a compulsory meeting for all the students and staff. Every time there was an attack on government forces or institutions, such as the one that had happened that morning, all students and public servants had to attend to denounce the attack and chant "Hoora"—something like the "hip hip hooray" cheer in English. I ducked out before the meeting began because I had a very uncomfortable feeling, and I told my friends that I was going home. The whole family was gathering, including my sister Aqila, my brother Abdul Kayum and Ghafoor's younger brother, Ataulha. Ghafoor was the last person to arrive because he'd attended the compulsory gathering at the university. Even though we were all together, I was worried. At about 6 p.m., Abdul Kayum said he would go out to buy some bread, and Ataulha said he'd go with him. Ghafoor told them to get extra bread since we were all anticipating trouble and didn't know what would happen next. Fifteen minutes later, Abdul Kayum returned alone. He said Ataulha had been taken by the intelligence services and that he'd also seen two of Ghafoor's cousins in the car: Dr. Mohammed Temor and his younger brother Nur Ahmad, who was only in the tenth grade. Dr. Temor would be released, but Nur Ahmad was never seen again.

I had started preparing dinner for the family, but when I heard this news, my heart was beating so fast I had to stop. I felt nearly paralyzed with fear. I began tearing the house apart, checking for books that were anti-government and gathering up the pamphlets I'd been distributing. I burned all that I could and flushed everything else down the toilet. I'd heard that when the secret police came to the house they even checked for evidence of burning papers, so I lit the firewood stove in the bathroom to burn the paper and then threw other items like wood and spices on the fire to cover the smell of the smoke. I worked furiously to protect everyone in my house.

I never got back to making dinner, but no one felt much like eating anyway. Since Ghafoor had to give a test to his students at the Kabul Polytechnic University the next morning, he busied himself preparing the questions for the exam.

Finally, we all went to bed. Ghafoor turned to me and said, "Poor Ataulha. I can't stop thinking about how hard it will be for him. I wonder if he will be tortured?" I told him my terrible fear that they would come to take him as well. I had no sooner uttered the words when there was a loud banging at the door. When we went to see who was there, twelve men were standing outside, and as soon as the door opened six of them barged into our home.

The leader of the group was one of Ghafoor's students. They said he had to go with them. I demanded to know where they were taking him. The student said, "Don't worry, we'll bring him back in a few hours." I told him I didn't trust him. He replied, "I swear to you I will."

I grabbed Ghafoor's coat and stuffed all the money I had, about twelve hundred Afghanis, into the pocket, hoping it might help him. "Wear your coat," I said. "It's a cold night." It all happened so fast—Ghafoor was still wearing his night clothes and plastic sandals on his feet when the men pushed him toward the staircase of the house and then stood between us. He glanced back at me with a look on his face that I knew well—it meant *take my words seriously*. "Don't go looking for me," he said. His eyes were pleading when he added, "It is too dangerous for you."

They were still on the stairs when that shameful student turned to me and had the nerve to say, "In case he's not back by tomorrow, bring the test papers to the Polytechnic." I told him it was his responsibility to bring Ghafoor safely home and shouted after him that it was his responsibility, not mine, to bring the exam to the students. He vowed again that he would bring Ghafoor back.

I never saw my husband again. Neither did his little boy.

None of us slept that night. In the morning I decided that to protect Ghafoor and myself, I would go to class as usual and that no one should know what had happened in our house the night before. All week I repeated my actions like a robot: go to school, come home, say nothing.

At the end of that first week, I received a telephone message from the chief of the physics department, Professor Husseini, asking that I bring in Ghafoor's notes and lesson plans for his classes. That meant everyone knew he had been arrested. I did as he asked. As I was leaving the office, I saw the student who had led the group that arrested Ghafoor. I stopped him and said, "You told me that you would bring him back in a few hours." He looked nervous. "Where is he?" I demanded. By now he was obviously scared. He replied, "Did he not come back?" I punched him in his chest as hard as I could and said, "You know very well that he didn't come back." He told me he would find out, but I never heard any more news from that scoundrel.

Since being silent hadn't worked, I began the agonizing task of going to every government department, to anyone who could have some information, begging for news of Ghafoor and his brothers. Whenever I heard of anyone being released, I would rush to their house asking for news. I hesitated only because it made the freed person nervous knowing the secret police were probably watching, but I had to try to find Ghafoor. And every Friday I went to the prison to ask for news, hoping someone would have something—anything at all—to tell me.

It was a painful ritual. It took three bus changes to get to the prison, followed by a long walk from the main street where the bus stopped. Pul-e-Charkhi was the biggest and newest prison built during Daoud Khan's presidency; it had six wings surrounded by high walls, and no one was allowed to enter except the people who worked in the building. Outside was a dusty area with no trees and no shade and no queue, but thousands of people: men and women, young and old, rich and poor, all looking for their loved ones. I would arrive with clean clothes for Ghafoor and a little money I had managed to save tucked into the pocket of a shirt.

The rule at the prison was that the guard outside would take the things we each brought for our relatives and go inside to deliver the fresh clothes (and hopefully not steal any hidden money); the guard would then come back thirty or forty-five minutes later with the unwashed clothes and news of the prisoner. I carefully wrote my husband's name on the bundle of clean clothes: *Professor Ghafoor Sultani*. Every single Friday I waited—in the sun, in rain, in the scorching heat of summer and the freezing cold of winter— hoping I would be one of the lucky ones who received a bundle of dirty clothes to wash, proof that my man was alive. I never did. Each time, the guard returned to me the neat stack of clothing I'd brought and said, "No one here by that name." I also routinely asked for his three brothers who had been arrested, but there was never any news of them either. By the end of each trip to the prison, in the late afternoon while I walked the distance back to the bus stop, I would be exhausted and crying and wondering how to carry on.

On one particularly hot and dusty summer Friday, as I waited with the crowds of people standing outside without water, shade or restrooms, a young woman who was pregnant and searching for her husband stood with us. When the crowd started shouting and throwing stones at the prison to express their frustration with the government, the young woman joined them. An officer opened fire and shot her; everyone ran from the area. Some were injured, but that woman and her unborn baby were shot to death. No one even took down her name. There was no report, no accountability.

As for the government, it felt as if the leadership was changing as quickly as the seasons. Hafizullah Amin had taken power in September, ordered Nur Mohammad Taraki killed, and released a list of the names of twelve thousand people who had been murdered while in custody. Of course, I rushed to the Interior Ministry to see the list, but the papers were smeared and torn, and I could not find Ghafoor's name on the few pages I was able to read. It was a horrible scene as some young women discovered the names of their loved ones; all of them were crying, and some even fainted. I watched the party members display a sickening schadenfreude at the heartbreaking human suffering on display.

It was a time of utter despair. I was a student with no income and no time or opportunity to work. The only thing I could do outside of my classes was tailoring and knitting and making clothes for women who could afford to pay me so I could stay in school. I began selling household items that no one would notice were missing because I didn't want any of my family members to know I needed help. Eventually I had to sell the embroidered bedcover that I'd made for our marriage. Then I sold the matching pillow covers. Then, one by one, the tablecloths, and eventually all of the embroidered things I'd made. All I knew in those days was fatigue and tears and defeat.

Then the rest of the world as I knew it blew up. It was December 24, 1979. I was preparing for final examinations; the subject was internal medicine. The whole week before had been filled with rumors and the constant roar of Soviet planes flying over Kabul. At 8 p.m., just after dinner, the firing of heavy artillery started in Darulaman, not far from where I was living. At about 10 p.m., while listening to the radio, we heard the voice of Babrak Karmal, the leader of Parcham, speaking from Tashkent, Uzbekistan. He announced that Hafizullah Amin had been assassinated and now he, Karmal, was the general secretary of the Central Committee of the People's Democratic Party of Afghanistan and chairman of the Revolutionary Council. The Soviets had arrived.

The next morning, during a heavy snowstorm, I walked to school for my exam and saw Soviet soldiers on the street guarding the city. A few days later, Karmal announced he would release the political prisoners. Once again people flocked to the prison in Pul-e-Charkhi and waited for their relatives to come out. I did not go; my brother Abdul Aziz and our friend Abdul Rauf Naveed went in my place because they were worried about crowds and trouble. Only some of the prisoners had been released, and the restless crowd pushed forward. My brother and Rauf got into the jail, but they couldn't find Ghafoor or his brothers, and they ended up being beaten by the guards.

The people who had been gathering as I did at the prisons every Friday speculated that our men had been taken to Siberia to work in camps and that most people in those camps didn't survive. The not-knowing crept over me day and night like a second skin. But as heartbreaking as it was, I knew I had to stay strong, and I vowed I would never give up. I had a toddler to care for and was more than halfway to a medical degree.

With Soviet soldiers on the street and a government spouting communist propaganda, the resistance movement was gathering strength. Rauf Naveed also worked in the resistance with me. Despite the frigid temperatures and huge snow drifts that winter in Kabul, crowds of people were shouting "Allahu Akbar" (God is great) every night for a whole week. People shouted from their windows and doorways from 8 p.m. to 10 p.m., chanting the words that would unite us and let the Soviets know they were not wanted here. In the daytime, between classes, I would distribute pamphlets asking people to join us at night.

But even as our numbers grew, it wasn't the Soviet military that used brute force to put down the demonstrations; it was the Afghans in the ruling regime who attacked and arrested the citizens on the street. Eventually the demonstrations stopped.

Classes at the medical faculty resumed amid all this turmoil. Since Ali was still with my mother in Helmand, I traveled there every time we had a break from the university. As if losing my husband was not enough, my little boy had been with my mother for so long by this time that he saw me as an auntie who had come to visit. I had to believe that eventually I could right this painful wrong.

By the time I was in my last year at medical school, we were assigned to the hospitals and doing a lot of practical work, for which we received a small stipend. Although I continued tailoring and knitting to make money, the added income made life easier for me. At last, in early 1982, our class graduated. Now I would be earning a salary, so my mother brought Ali back to me and decided to stay. My older brother Abdul Wahid had married; his wife, Nasreen, was also studying medicine and we were living together; my mother was there to help all of us.

We were told there would be no graduation ceremony, which we initially saw as merely mean-spirited. But to our astonishment, it was much more than that—the government had decided we would not be given diplomas. The reason was simple: the Soviets knew that most of the newly trained doctors would be across the border before the ink dried on the document. So instead, they gave each of us a certificate that allowed us to work in hospitals in Afghanistan but denied us the diploma that recognized us as medical doctors.

The aggravation continued like land erosion—every time we shored up our end, it resulted in more loss. For example, by the time we graduated there were eight women in a class of eighty-five medical students, and all of us wanted to work in the maternity hospital in Kabul. Since the education had been free, we were required to work in whatever government hospital they sent us to; doctors were not allowed to practice privately unless they had permission. The government sent seven of us to Wazir Akbar Khan Hospital, which was one of the best in Kabul. It had only two departments—surgery and internal medicine. It was known for its strict rules: visitors could come for only ninety minutes in the afternoon, and no food or drink could be brought to the patients by family or relatives. I wound up in the department of internal medicine, but during one of my first night shifts I nearly derailed my fledgling career.

It was late one night when three very drunk men were brought to the emergency room by the police. They were members of the ruling PDPA and, as such, had access to vodka. The men were vomiting, shouting and so out of control I was worried they would assault me. I asked the nurse in charge if we should call a senior doctor, but we decided not to. Instead, I gave each of the men a diuretic that would keep them busy running to the toilet through the night so they would leave us alone.

The next morning during the report to the doctors and head of the department, I explained my actions and quickly learned yet another aspect of Soviet rule. The senior doctor exploded when he heard what I had done, insisting I should have called him. I told him I didn't want to disturb him just to deal with drunk men. He explained that these drunks were powerful men in the government who could have had me arrested. It might have been a near miss, but in fact the three had fallen into a deep sleep after making several trips to the toilet and were only roused when someone came to get them in the early morning. Thankfully, I never heard another word about it. But I learned that part of surviving was being aware of when you were being watched.

It was hard for me to learn the lesson of keeping my mouth shut. On Wednesdays, the Russian advisor would accompany the doctors on patient rounds, listening as we described our patient's condition to the entire group. In one case, the advisor asked me which kind of viral hepatitis a patient had; I said I couldn't tell because we did not have the electronic microscope required to distinguish between the different types of viral hepatitis. He spoke with authority when he said, "It's hepatitis B." I said, "I am sorry, but this is not something you can decide without a microscope. It is a science issue."

The chair of the department was Dr. Toorpikai Saberi, a female doctor whose husband had also been arrested. She used to make a sign with her hand to stop me from arguing when a Russian doctor was present. After the incident with the patient with hepatitis, she spoke with me privately. When I insisted that I had been right, she cautioned me, explaining that I could be arrested for disagreeing with the Russian advisor and reminding me that I had a small child. It was all about trade-offs—and measuring how much silence you could manage.

But women like Dr. Toorpikai helped me enormously when it came to balancing my medical career and the crushing reality of Soviet rule. That year on Mother's Day, she called me into her office and said, "Your little son is too small to give you a present today, so I am giving you one for him." It was a bottle of perfume, a kindness I never forgot. She lives in Germany now; we're still in touch occasionally. Like mine, her husband never came back.

The medical work was never free of politics. One day when I was on duty, we had a patient who'd suffered an acute heart attack and needed to be in intensive care. The ICU had only three beds, but one patient seemed to be doing well, so the senior doctor moved her to the ward and made room for the new patient. The woman who was moved later died and her son, a party member, started threatening me and the other doctors. He demanded an official inquiry and got one. The head of the hospital, who was also a party member, came to our defense, but later he warned me to be very careful.

Life in Kabul was becoming increasingly challenging as party members seemed to watch every move we made. Freedom of expression was banned. The government controlled the media as much as they could. People were arrested for listening to the BBC. Village elders, mullahs and members of the Maoist groups and the Muslim Brotherhood were arrested and killed with no explanation; their bodies were not even returned to their families. Anyone who had opposed or even spoken out against the Khalq and

Parcham parties within the last decade was rounded up and disappeared. Even people who were pro–King Zahir Shah but wanted reform were detained.

I was distributing night letters everywhere I could—at the hospital after a late shift, in the neighborhood on the way home before daylight, every place I could do so without being noticed, considering there was a curfew between 10 p.m. and 6 a.m. But I knew I was tempting fate. My own family didn't approve of what I was doing. Eventually, I joined a group called the Revolutionary Association of the Women of Afghanistan (RAWA). Together we plotted the demise of the Soviets while I went to classes and later to work by day and attended secret meetings by night. The work we did was perilous, and some members disappeared, but we were undeterred. To rescue our country, we knew we had to get rid of the Soviets.

This routine of working shifts at the hospital, throwing my night letters and taking care of Ali went on until the summer of 1982. When the hospital decided to assign a man and a woman—both members of the intelligence services—to search each of us as we arrived at work every morning, it was the last straw for me. In late June, I decided to pack up a few of my belongings, take my child and go to Jaghori in the province of Ghazni—where I was born, and where Ghafoor's parents still lived—to start a medical practice on my own. My family members were not in favor of this move; they worried about my safety and whether my decision would put my brothers in danger. But I was adamant. I wanted to be a doctor and bring health care to people who badly needed it, and the area around Jaghori was not under the control of the government, as it had been freed by the local people two years before. When I submitted my request for twenty days' leave to the hospital administrator, he accused me of trying to run away. I didn't want him to know I was going to Ghazni so I said I was going to Helmand. He argued with me, saying, "It's too hot there. No one wants to go to Helmand at this time of the year." I said, "It's not hot for me. It is my home."

I went one last time to the Pul-e-Charkhi prison, carrying clean clothes for Ghafoor and handing them over to a guard. While waiting outside, I calculated the number of times I'd stood on that spot and figured I'd been there for more than a hundred Fridays since June 1979. And as had happened on each one of the other unhappy Fridays, the guard returned to me with the same bundle I'd brought and told me there was no one there by the name of Professor Ghafoor Sultani.

On the way home the awful reality sank in. I made the momentous decision that, upon my return to Jaghori, I would stop using my childhood name of Marzia. I feared the long arm of the regime could reach me, my son, and my brothers in Kabul and Lashkar Gah—and I felt I had to protect my husband wherever he might be.

An elderly man who was a distant relative of the family came to Kabul and agreed to accompany me and Ali on the bus journey to Jaghori. I packed all I could carry: a change of clothes for each of us, a blood pressure cuff, a stethoscope and a copy of the book *Current Medical Diagnosis and Treatment*. The only person sad to see me go was my mother, who worried about me going off on my own and of course about being separated from her grandson, who had slept in the same bed with her for four years and saw her as his mother. My father had come to Kabul on business, and he let me know he was adamantly opposed to my plan. It was my kind and honest mother who gave me the confidence to believe in myself. She stood in the doorway and stroked Ali's cheek and then mine. I can still see the tears on her face as she bade me farewell.

I wore a burka and held my son on my lap as we left Kabul. My medical equipment was hidden in a compartment of the bus as I knew there would be troublesome roadblocks along the way. My choice to leave was not an easy one to make. But I was happy and looking forward to an unknown future. Once the bus pulled away, I never looked back.

Four

THE DOCTOR IS IN

ALI AND I ARRIVED IN JAGHORI late in the afternoon and went directly to Sangi Masha, the village where Ghafoor's parents lived. They were shocked to see us, of course, but delighted to meet their grandson at last. We sat together drinking black tea and talking while I presented them with my plan. They worried that this action of mine could affect Ghafoor and their three other sons who were also missing. I explained that I was not safe in Kabul and that coming to Jaghori would protect all of us. I also told them that I would begin work as a doctor and contribute to the household finances. But even then, they worried. The mujahideen were active in the district and fundamentalism was spreading like a virus, so a woman-doctor-alone checked a lot of boxes for these meddling men.

What's more, Ali had never lived in a muddy house like this before, and at first, between missing my mother and feeling strange in this new environment, he didn't sleep. I took him out to the farmland full of fruit trees, hoping that by exploring these new surroundings he'd adapt to them, but leaving the house ended up creating other problems. For instance, wearing a scarf on my head hadn't been a requirement in Kabul, but here it was, and mine invariably slipped off my hair and landed on my shoulders or was left behind altogether. That wasn't the worst of my crimes. One day while we were out wandering, I spied a mulberry tree, and since I had a small bucket with me, I climbed the tree to get some berries for Ali. From my perch in the branches, I noticed my mother-in-law coming toward us and waving at me to get down. I thought I must have wandered onto someone else's property and was in effect stealing the mulberries, but that wasn't the case. "It's not that the tree doesn't belong to us, it does," she explained. "It's because women don't climb trees."

My actions bumped up against such cultural norms again and again. But what was harder to cope with was my little boy's sadness. One afternoon when we were sitting under an almond tree and I was breaking the shells for him, we saw a big truck driving along the road beside the Sultani land. Ali asked me if the truck had come from Kabul. I told him it had. Then he looked at me with that beguiling honesty children have and said, "Oh, it is so lucky! It saw my grandmother in Kabul." That innocent comment showed me just how acutely he was missing my mother.

It was time to launch my medical career, and I had the idea that Ghafoor's surviving brother, Muhammad Amin, who was living in Pakistan, should come home to Jaghori and help me. As a single woman, I could not travel to see patients unless I was accompanied by a man. I asked my father-in-law to write him a letter and also sent one of my own. Fortunately, he agreed to come.

We built the clinic from scratch out of a few empty rooms at the side of the house that had been bombed when the Soviets tried to take this district. We repaired the damage, cleaned the walls, and got a carpenter to build a desk, a chair and a bench for the patients. Someone donated an examining table. Médecins Sans Frontières/ Doctors Without Borders used to move through the area working in tents, and I asked them if they would help; they donated antiseptics, glass syringes and anything they could spare, as they knew the needs of the people and were happy that a female medical doctor was here to help them. As soon as I started seeing patients, word spread throughout the district and people flocked to the clinic: men and women, children and grannies, pregnant women, disabled people, truly sick patients. My dream of being a doctor was well and truly launched.

A few days later, I realized that my father-in-law was sitting by the clinic door and watching the lineup like a hawk. Later, he commented, "You are seeing male patients as well." I said, "Yes, but you must not worry. I promised Ghafoor I would never cheat on him and would be waiting for him. I do not see these people as men; I see them as my patients." He never sat there again and never asked me where I went or who I talked to or treated.

The people I was there to serve also began to trust me. The size of the task I'd set myself was startling; there was so much I could do to help the women, particularly with obstetrics and gynecology. No female doctor had been in the area before, and the women's needs were enormous. I relied on my medical book, reading about a disease at night and treating it the next day. The children suffered viral diseases like measles, chicken pox, whooping cough and diphtheria because there were no vaccinations—they'd all been stopped when the Soviets arrived. Every winter when these epidemics struck, almost every family lost one or two children.

There were no roads in the area so getting to my patients was often a challenge. Occasionally someone would take me by car, but a horse or donkey was the more usual mode of transport. Most often I went on foot. One time a woman had been in labor for three days when her family came to the clinic and begged me to come—I had to walk ten hours to get to her. On another occasion, I saddled up a horse and rode twelve hours over the steep, rock-strewn mountains to treat a child who was sick with measles and pneumonia.

My name was now a household word—everyone knew of Dr. Sima Samar. I helped them birth their babies and cared for their elderly, stitched up their wounds and soothed their pains. I taught them how to avoid illnesses and tried to convince the women to have fewer children. In the process, I learned as much as they did. My brother-in-law came with me on my district-wide medical rounds so no one could criticize me for breaking with tradition. Practicing medicine in a rural district demonstrated brutally that the lives of women were nearly unbearable and that lack of education and abject poverty were a direct result of the turmoil the country was in. I vowed that someday I would to do something about both conditions.

Interestingly, my medical practice brought Pashtuns and Hazaras together—after all, they suffered the same ills, and I was the common denominator. The work even created a bridge to the mujahideen, who were active in the district. In late October, Haji Khalilo, a mujahideen commander with Mahaz-e Milli, came to me and said there were a lot of sick people in Ajrestan—another district of Ghazni—who were not able to come to my clinic, but if I would agree, he would be happy to be my host and take me to them. I loaded up an old Russian jeep with supplies and made the trip, along with Ali, my brother-in-law Muhammad Amin, and Abdul Rauf Naveed, who had both been living in Jaghori with us.

We stayed in the house of Haji Khalilo and saw patients for a whole week. The situation was worse than in Jaghori. The patients were mostly suffering from malnutrition; the children were not being fed properly. It proved to me again that education was the way forward. These people didn't know what to feed their children to avoid sickness. One of my patients, a nephew of Haji Khalilo, had severe diarrhea due to malnutrition. Years later he turned up in my office in Kabul as a healthy thirty-eight-year-old man and recounted the story of me telling his mother that his hair was falling out due to poor nutrition and that he needed better food, including eggs. It was such a pleasure to see him again, but his story made me remember how his mother had told me she'd heard that eggs caused children to stop speaking.

The mujahideen were waging war against the Soviets, and occasionally their casualties landed on my doorstep. At nine o'clock one night, a young boy knocked on our door to say a car had been hit by a rocket. I grabbed a bag of basic medical supplies and went with him. Many were injured, but one seventeen-year-old boy had had his leg shattered so badly it was hanging on only by skin and splintered bone; his foot was already gangrenous. I knew I had to amputate the leg above the knee to stop the bleeding. I found a carpenter saw at the market site, poured boiling water over it, wiped it with alcohol and cut off the skin and the protruding bone fragments. I left them with antibiotics and clean bandages to stave off infection. I met the young man again when I was working in Pakistan and helped him to get fitted for a prosthesis—just one of thousands of civilians disabled in the war.

Whenever I left Jaghori to travel to Pakistan for medical supplies or to meet with other physicians, I witnessed the dangerous, difficult and sometimes enlightening circumstances in which we lived. I was always the only woman present and often ran into mujahideen on the road. One time, when I was coming back from Pakistan in the spring of 1983 with medicine for my clinic, I was carrying a letter from the mujahideen group called Harakat-e Inqilab-e Islami Afghanistan that said I should be allowed to pass. Suddenly, a group of young freedom fighters stopped the car. I told them I had a letter granting me safe passage. The boys said they couldn't read, so I suggested I read the letter for them. They were so shocked to see a woman read that they grabbed my hand and kissed it. Then they asked me to pray for them because they were about to attack a government military post nearby. I told them they should not be sharing their battle plans with strangers or they might wind up being killed themselves.

In Jaghori, the MSF doctors came by our house sometimes on Fridays for a cup of tea or lunch. Since we had fruit trees, I always sent them home with a bag of fresh produce. We built relationships, referring patients to each other. I was finding my way with others in a world I was getting to know.

There was a German leprosy specialist by the name of Dr. Ruth Pfau who came every spring and fall to take patients with her for treatment in Karachi. She always stopped at my clinic, and I was inspired by her treatment of vulnerable people who were often ignored by their own families and sent to live in caves because of the taboo around leprosy and the lack of knowledge about it. My medical practice felt like an ongoing learning experience, and it energized me to bring help to these people.

During the winter of 1984, when we'd had more than a meter of snow, a French doctor from MSF came to me to ask if I could help with a woman called Fatima who had been in labor for six days. It had taken twelve hours for ten men from her family to carry her to the MSF hospital. The MSF doctor told me in English (so the relatives would not understand) that she might already be dead by the time we got to her, but her family had asked them to get me. It took us an hour to get to the hospital. The family members had already put her face toward Mecca, which is what we do in the final minutes of a person's life. A few men were reading the Quran, which is supposed to ease the last breaths the person takes. I checked the woman's pulse; it was very weak. I suggested a shot of adrenaline to accelerate her heart rate. The MSF doctor refused so I did it myself, as I saw no other way to save her. I was able to pull out the stillborn baby—it smelled so terrible that I figured it must have been dead for several days—and then the placenta, which was also foul-smelling. I cleaned up the patient, started antibiotics and hoped for the best. Half an hour later, when I was still there drinking tea with the doctors, she opened her eyes and started asking questions. It had been a very close call. She'd lost her baby, and I discovered she also had a vesicovaginal fistula (an abnormal opening between the bladder and the vagina) that needed treatment, but for that night all ended well. I saw her again in Pakistan a few years later and repaired the fistula.

Traveling around the district was also eye-opening. People were on the run from conflict between the competing factions of mujahideen trying to take territory. Thousands of families were forced to leave their homes for safety in Iran and Pakistan. They would leave the fireplace full of wet wood so the smoke would drift up the chimney for days, making it look like they were still at home while they ran away.

My situation was further complicated by the fact that the mujahideen in the area felt that schools were only a place to teach people to be communists, and therefore were forbidden. When it was time for Ali to begin his formal education, I knew I had to part with him again. I was utterly heartbroken when my mother came and took him with her to Kabul. Ali was my solace, my reminder of Ghafoor and the life we were supposed to share together as professionals in Kabul. My boy was all the world to me. When he left, my life became completely consumed with my work.

In the midst of all of this—the clinic work, the journeys into the highlands to treat patients, the increasingly fractious warring between mujahideen factions and government forces—a man called Haji Qamber turned up at my clinic and spoke five words that stopped me in my tracks: *I have news of Ghafoor.* I was instantly caught between renewing a dream and reliving a nightmare. He explained that his son, who was with the PDPA, had sent a message to say that if I would work with the government, Ghafoor would be released. In the meantime, there were rumors that the government was sending troops to capture Jaghori from the mujahideen. I didn't believe they had news from Ghafoor but dared not deny their request outright.

A week later, two more men came in a Russian jeep and told me the daughter-in-law of Haji was in labor and needed my help.

It was after dark; I said I wouldn't go at night and suggested they bring her to me; otherwise, I would go in the morning. They parked the jeep behind our house and stayed there all night. In the morning, they asked again. I didn't believe there was a patient waiting for me, and by now I'd heard that troops were advancing, so I told them I would give them medicine to take to the woman. They left without the meds. Later, Haji came back and said again that if I cooperated, they would release Ghafoor. I replied, "If you can bring me a letter from Ghafoor—just two words in his own handwriting—I will work with the government." That was the last I heard from Haji.

Near the end of 1984, I developed whooping cough. Despite the fact that the local population thought I could cure any ailment, I couldn't kick the persistent cough and I kept losing weight. I decided to travel to Pakistan to seek treatment and sent a message to my mother to bring Ali, now six years old, so I could take him with me. But I knew it was not possible for me as a young woman to travel on my own. Three of my brothers were in Iran to avoid military service in the PDPA. I sent a letter to one of them, Abdul Samad, asking him to come to Jaghori and accompany us to Pakistan.

The voyage was formidable. The roads were controlled alternately by mujahideen and government forces, both of which made the travel difficult. We hid by day and traversed the mountains by night in the dark. It took two days and two nights to get to the city of Quetta, situated across Afghanistan's border to the southwest.

Once there, I discovered a burgeoning Afghan diaspora. It felt like the next best thing to home; maybe it was time to build another nest. I decided to stay in Quetta and find a job. The dusty, rock-strewn landscape that unfolds from the huge mountains here at the west end of the massive Hindu Kush range is similar to the land the Afghan refugees had left. The miniature yellow wildflowers that push defiantly out of the scrubby soil grow like symbols of their struggle.

Within days of arriving my cough improved, thanks to the warmer weather; in fact, in a few weeks it had disappeared altogether and there was no need to see a doctor. Now I needed to find a house to live in, a job to earn a living and a school for Ali.

I applied for a job at a one-hundred-year-old British-built facility called Mission Hospital. There I met a retired British Pakistani police officer called Frederick Ines who was now the director of the nongovernmental organization (NGO) Inter Church Aid—a consortium of churches providing funds for Afghan refugee relief programs.

I told Mr. Ines I was a medical doctor and that a classmate of mine was already working at the hospital. He asked if I had a medical diploma. I said, "Yes and no." I told him the pro-Soviet regime had deprived the graduates of a certificate so they could not practice outside the country. Then I explained that I'd gone to Peshawar, a city on the other side of Pakistan where diplomas of all sorts were sold for three hundred rupees (US$10 at the time), and had bought a medical diploma. He laughed out loud at my audacity. I said I'd be happy to take a test and suggested he get in touch with Dr. Pfau from the leprosy clinic or the MSF staff, all of whom would attest to my work.

We went to see Dr. Lutter, who was the medical director of the hospital as well as a surgeon and eye specialist. Dr. Lutter asked me a couple of questions about the diseases I was treating and then said, "Dr. Pfau has spoken to us about you. If you want the job, you can start tomorrow." I told him I wanted to learn to do surgery; he agreed to teach me. The next day I went to work, for a salary of five thousand rupees a month (about US$450).

Afghan women didn't have many more rights in Pakistan than they did in Afghanistan. The refugee quarter in the hospital was funded by Inter Church Aid and was open only from 8 a.m. to 1 p.m., and those were also the hours for the health clinic and the maternity department. They were not open for emergency cases after hours, and a doctor was on call only for patients who had already been admitted. I tried to explain that women in labor don't follow the clock, and that they needed someone to keep the clinic open because babies had a way of deciding themselves when they'd arrive. But no one wanted to make changes for women.

I soon became aware that the Hazara people in Quetta who had moved from Afghanistan to escape persecution decades earlier were not being treated fairly by the Pakistani government. As a result, Hazaras protested and clashed with government forces. Eventually, following these protests, the Hazara refugees were pushed into a camp called Mohammad Khail two hours away from the city, along with some Pashtuns, Balochs and Tajiks from northern Afghanistan. Inter Church Aid opened a medical clinic at this newly established camp, and I immediately volunteered to treat the women there two days a week. Their already difficult lives were made worse by being banished from the city.

Not that the Afghans still living in Quetta were treated well either. In fact, one of my colleagues at the hospital was forever complaining about how dirty the Afghans were. One day I responded to her judgmental remarks by reminding her what they were dealing with. "They don't have access to water for a bath," I said. "They live in tents in the dust of the desert, with a limited amount of water to drink. They are not rich. They did not come here to picnic; they were pushed from their villages and homes. They were traumatized, separated; and witnessed the killing of their loved ones and the destruction of their properties and animals. They have dignity and pride just like you." I repeated this speech many times, but it didn't change her behavior, so finally I went to Mr. Ines and said I could no longer work in this place that allowed innocent people to be insulted every day. He spoke to Dr. Lutter, and the woman was fired.

I began taking fabric and sewing kits to the women at the camp because I knew they could embroider tablecloths, napkins and pillow covers to earn a little income. When a Swiss woman called Vreni Frauenfelder saw the embroidered work in Quetta, she bought some to sell in Switzerland. It was the beginning of a collaboration that carries on to this day. (Vreni had visited Afghanistan during the hippie days in the early seventies and had wonderful memories of the people she met. When the Soviets invaded in 1979, she and her friends decided to do something to support Afghan people. Her Help Committee Schaffhausen has been a lifeline to all of us, and her friendship to me everlasting.)

While I did learn surgical technique from Dr. Lutter, I was also learning that the policies around fighting the Cold War with the Soviets were hurting the very people they were trying to save. Formal education was denied to the refugees, while big madrassa religious schools funded by the United States, the United Kingdom, Saudi Arabia and several Arab countries were built by fundamentalists in order to brainwash boys. The students came from families who were poor and had too many children; they were promised the boys would be provided with food, clothes and an education. But rather than studying science and math, they were taught hatred and revenge, particularly against women and modernity. The goal of the West was to support these conservative groups in order to defeat the communists. Pakistan was steeped in Islamization, and so was neighboring Iran. I could see that Afghanistan was being squeezed by these influences, all in the name of fighting to protect our religion and our land, but in reality it was a Cold War game. The people were victims of the shortsighted policies of the superpowers.

With Ali enrolled in a proper school and me working full-time at the Mission Hospital, my life took on a semblance of normalcy. But I couldn't ignore the thousands of Afghan refugees living in appalling conditions around me. I couldn't dismiss the women whose efforts to cope with and care for their children were hampered by some of the mujahideen factions and patriarchal traditions that forbade them to visit male doctors and harassed those who ventured from their homes to work or attend school. It made me see even more clearly that the role of women in society is diminished under the guise of protection. Conflict and war always create insecurity for women and children, disabled people, and unaccompanied minors, particularly girls. In these times, people were separated from their families, and girls were sold to smugglers along the roads to Pakistan and Iran or traded to rescue a male family member who had been taken. In the refugee camps opportunistic men took advantage of people who couldn't read and write and declared themselves elders, using that status to enrich themselves. Women's needs were never a priority, even in relief programs. For example, no hygiene products or contraception was included in the relief distributed in the camps. Women's access to reproductive health and rights was not even discussed, let alone facilitated. The refugees in the camps became increasingly poor, with no job prospects and no income. And they were producing more children—the raw material to turn into militants who would fuel the conflict and violence.

A tragic incident at the hospital convinced me of the need to change our direction. It was early morning, before the hospital opened, when a young, pregnant Afghan woman developed eclampsia. Her condition deteriorated rapidly as her high blood pressure increased and was followed by convulsions and loss of consciousness. I ran everywhere to help her. The pharmacy was closed; the delivery room was closed and would open only at 8 a.m. I had to refer her to a maternity hospital, but she got there too late, and she died.

Afterward, I was so upset that I went to Mr. Ines. "I want to start a hospital for Afghan women and children that will be open twenty-four hours a day," I said. He was sympathetic, but he told me there was a major obstacle: fear that the fundamentalists would attack their office for funding a hospital for women. I promised him I would not tell anyone who was supporting the hospital. Our discussion underscored the issue I felt was the root of the problem—policies were made by men for men with guns, and not for refugee women and children.

A week later Mr. Ines came back to me and said he had met with the Inter Church Aid board members; they had agreed to fund my hospital. I started to look for a building immediately and began translating nursing books from English to Persian. I hired Afghan doctors and nurses and prepared a training program for female nurses and midwives. We found a building in the middle of the town and named our new hospital Malalai, after an Afghan woman who famously fought off the British at the Battle of Maiwand on July 27, 1880, during the Second Anglo-Afghan War. It took six weeks to staff and stock the hospital, and on the day we opened we saw more than one hundred patients. Malalai Hospital was a source of hope for Afghan families, and the number of patients increased every day.

An old adage warns us to be careful what we wish for. While my new hospital became almost instantly famous, and I was thrilled to be part of helping so many in need, the increased attention caused my own security to plummet. By now the fundamentalists had started employing their anti-woman policies under the guise of protecting women. They saw me as their enemy because I was promoting the rights of women every chance I got. The special branch of the Pakistani police force was after me as they were receiving reports that I was working for the pro-Soviet regime to secure the release of my husband. The fundamentalists even threatened to kidnap my son if I didn't stop my work for the refugee women.

To me, it was clear that strong steps were being taken to destroy our nation. First, degrade half of the population by controlling the lives of women and making them the property of the males in the society, particularly the politicians. Second, destroy the education system and use it as a political tool to deny science and promote political and financial interests. Third, deny human rights values and principles. In this way you promote supremacy: men are superior to women; one ethnic group is superior to the other; this color and religion has more value than that one. The end result? More conflict, more poverty, more discrimination, and much less human dignity, as well as continued conflict. That is precisely what happened to Afghanistan during the 1980s, and we have never fully recovered.

In May 1988, the Norwegian foreign minister, Thorvald Stoltenberg, came to visit the area and was so impressed with the work I was doing that he asked how he could help. I decided to take a chance and ask if he would fund a hospital in Jaghori, where people were dying from communicable diseases due to lack of treatment and from pregnancy complications that could be dealt with in five minutes. To my amazement, he asked if I could have a proposal ready before he left for home the next day. I'd never even heard the word *proposal* before, but I said yes and asked an engineer I knew to draw a design for the hospital and calculate the cost, and to have it to me before he left for work at eight the next morning.

A week later I received the first check for the hospital. I bought a Toyota four-wheel-drive, and Inter Church Aid gave me an ambulance to start a mobile clinic during construction. We acquired medicine, hired a male medical doctor and a female nurse, bought cement and building supplies, and left for Jaghori to start the construction on a piece of land that belonged to Ghafoor. Two months later, one of the local mujahideen groups attacked the hospital and stole the Toyota, the ambulance, the medicines and even the cement. Undeterred, we kept up our efforts, but the thefts persisted and were continued in Sangi Masha by one of the Hazara mujahideen groups. And they weren't the only ones stealing our goods—other mujahideen groups outside of Jaghori were helping themselves too. Then, one day, I came face-to-face with one of their leaders.

We had sent a shipment from Quetta—a few metric tons of rebar for reinforcing cement as well as BP-5 high-protein biscuits to treat malnutrition in children—but it was stolen by one of the Hezb-e Islami people who were located near Jaghori. A few days later the commander of that group happened to bring his mother to me at the clinic for treatment. I knew right away that she had pneumonia and needed an antibiotic. But I admitted her to my fledgling hospital and told him to come back the next day. When the commander returned, I sat him down and said, "The biscuits and the iron your friends took belong to the hospital in Jaghori. If you want me to treat your mother, give them back." He went himself to collect the remaining items and return them to me. Mind you, half of the biscuits and some of the rebar had already been sold.

Because of all the interference from the mujahideen, it took four years to complete the construction of the hospital. But it was a beginning. We trained nurses, started a midwifery program, and began a mass vaccination drive against tetanus and the viral diseases that had been making the children sick. We taught hygiene to people who were simply unaware of the importance of washing hands or sterilizing instruments for birthing babies. We trained thousands and gave them the basic equipment to deal with deliveries—they'd been cutting umbilical cords with kitchen knives, sometimes even with stones.

Afterward, we sent the newly trained staff out to the towns and villages that had never had medical help before. The maternal mortality rate for mothers and infants, which had been one of the highest in the world, began to drop in the villages that our trained midwives were in. We trained teams—a sister and a brother or a husband and a wife—so they could travel to distant villages together without being stopped by the conservative people who forbade women to travel alone. In fact, some of these newly trained nurses and birth attendants went on to be elected to provincial councils; some became members of parliament. I'm immensely proud of the work we did.

While I was consumed with medical clinics and schools, the conversations around the dastarkhan made it clear the detested Soviet government was not sustainable. At last, that conclusion was reached by the players holding the cards for our future. On April 14, 1988, with the United States and the USSR as guarantors, Pakistan and Afghanistan signed the Geneva Accords, a collection of agreements that included Soviet withdrawal by February 1989. Notably, not a single woman had been part of the long negotiation for that accord.

The accord was full of promises made among the four players: Pakistan, which represented the mujahideen in Afghanistan; the United States and the USSR, who were the guarantors; and, in Afghanistan, the government of Najibullah (also known as Dr. Najib), who was president during the Soviet occupation. In fact, they all failed to meet those promises. Although the Soviets left, as agreed, Najibullah stayed in power for three more years. He failed to win support nationally or internationally and, in 1992, his government collapsed because his own tribal militia turned against him, and he was overrun by the mujahideen.

As for Pakistan, the Inter-Services Intelligence (ISI) continued writing the playbook for a proxy war with Afghanistan. They had held talks with the mujahideen that cemented policies that continue to hurt the country to this day: although we petitioned and marched and begged to be included, women and ethnic groups other than the Pashtun and Tajiks were denied seats at the table. Even the UN, which claimed to be seeking a nonviolent transition of power, turned its back on women. While the Taliban can be accused of gender apartheid, they were following in the footsteps of this earlier anti-woman policy.

When the Soviets withdrew their troops in 1989, the international community, including the NGOs, closed up their offices and left the country. We were no longer of interest to them—the Cold War was over, so they quickly left us on our own. It was a move I knew would have enormous consequences. Couldn't they see that the vacuum they left would be filled by fundamentalists? What did they think would happen? Several different factions within the mujahideen were vying for power, so after the long, loathsome Soviet occupation was finally, truly over, an internecine battle for control of the government erupted. It raged from 1992 to 1996, bringing the country to its knees.

At the same time, my schools and clinics were crammed with women, men and children who needed everything from bread and medicine to schoolbooks and the milk of human kindness. Despite the lack of funds and materials, we struggled to serve the blameless people.

We were dealing with a host of medical problems for women and children in Quetta—everything from simple skin diseases to surgeries such as cesarean sections, appendectomies, hysterectomies and tonsillectomies. And there were fibroids and cysts and gallbladder attacks and kidney stones on a regular basis. I worked with outpatients and in surgery and the delivery room, and even did the emergency cases at night because my house was close to the clinic. I had learned how to do surgery while I was at the Mission Hospital, but now I was also able to hire an Afghan surgeon who'd been living in Iran and had come to Quetta, as well as a few other Afghan doctors. We started every day at eight o'clock in the morning and operated until 1 p.m. While surgeries were usually scheduled, except for emergencies, the delivery cases had to be dealt with too. In the afternoons, we took time to teach nursing and midwifery courses.

In March 1989, I was invited to Norway, Sweden and the Netherlands to discuss funding for my programs. Not surprisingly, the voyage began with a blip at the office of the Afghan Commissioner, where I needed to get a travel document. I was told a woman had never been in this office before and asked to come back the next day with permission from my father or husband to travel. One man even asked if I'd made a mistake just entering the office (I wondered if he was aware that women had been astronauts since 1963). In the end, I got an official piece of paper with my name on it.

The trip was a watershed for me. In Norway I met again with Foreign Minister Stoltenberg, who agreed to fund the schools I wanted to start. When he asked me the cost, I told him that I could run a school with 200 to 250 students for US$1,000 a year. He agreed to fund ten schools per year. In Sweden, the Swedish Church was my host, and a Mr. Gerhard arranged to send two huge containers of medical equipment for my hospitals. In the Netherlands, Karel Rose from the Inter-Church Organisation for Development Cooperation (ICCO) arranged several meetings with the leadership of the NGO as well as with the European Union (EU) in Brussels. He also took me to see the beauty of the tulips the country is so famous for. On the train to the EU meeting, I noticed a group of men with pink earrings, and when I asked the man from ICCO who they were, he said they were homosexuals; that was a first for me. All of it took me back to the intense curiosity I'd had as a child in Jaghori when I saw strangers and wondered if I could talk to them and what I might learn from them. While there, I did radio and newspaper interviews, which was helpful for raising funds for my work. And I also learned there were people out there in the wide world with human rights aspirations similar to mine.

Later in the year, along with five men from different mujahideen groups, I traveled to the United States for three weeks to learn about American laws and governance; I have to say it was not an easy trip. We were taken to different towns, including a stop in Atlanta to visit the Martin Luther King Jr. Memorial Library, which inspired me greatly. By the time I returned to Afghanistan I was full of ideas for change. The first thing I did was to face the fact that Malalai Hospital, which I had founded along with the Revolutionary Association of the Women of Afghanistan, wasn't fulfilling its mandate; it had become too political, and my work with RAWA was not helping me meet my goals. So I withdrew from both the hospital and the association. The doctors, nurses and most of the staff left with me.

I went back to Mr. Ines and told him I wished to start another clinic and asked if he would help. After he discussed my idea with others, he agreed to fund a hospital for women and children. That's when I realized I could combine all my dreams into one. In August 1989, I opened a health clinic called Shuhada (meaning "martyr"), a name I chose as a tribute to Ghafoor and others who had lost their lives for freedom. Now was the time to achieve the first of my lifelong goals: to get the women and girls of Afghanistan educated and into a health care program.

Shuhada started with medical clinics and hospitals because that seemed to me to be the most acute need. Within a year we opened schools for boys and girls. We built one hospital in Quetta and, with support from Oxfam, created a school in Quetta for Afghan refugees there as well; we named it the Aryana Girls' School. The teachers were university-educated Afghan women refugees. We opened the doors to 250 girls.

Shuhada was successful right from the start. Hundreds of eager students flocked to the schools, and the lineup at the clinics stretched out into the street. I started sewing and quilting projects so the women could earn money, and trained people as health care workers and midwives. I tapped every international aid organization I could find for the funds to operate. But nothing was ever easy. For example, I wrote a book for a literacy course for teenagers who had missed out on education but could not sit in a class with seven-year-olds. The book included health education, such as the feeding of babies, vaccination, personal hygiene, and family planning. I asked UNESCO to print the book for my students, but they refused because the material also included information on family planning. Even the UN refused. I taught the girls anyway, but I was astonished that these international NGOs and UN agencies didn't understand that for the female half of the population of Afghanistan, family planning was of vital importance. So many of the organizations at that time were focused on male domination and a patriarchal system in Afghanistan. Still, despite the challenges and the trouble all around me caused by increasingly extreme fundamentalists, I felt like a changemaker who'd been given the chance of a lifetime.

With the USSR out of the way, the UN started promoting the creation of Afghan NGOs, but they only registered and paid the core
budget of male-operated ones. When I tried to register Shuhada
I had no success. As well, the UN claimed their funding was for
emergency situations, and my health and education projects were
classified as development issues and therefore didn't qualify. In
fact, my programs were very much needed by these people caught
in a humanitarian emergency.

A UN meeting about the future of Afghanistan, held in Peshawar
in 1993 and chaired by a man called Mahmoud Mestiri, was the
first occasion for women to be invited to participate in such a
forum. But what surprised me was the vehemence of some of the
women in attendance. A group who were fully covered in black,
calling themselves Khwaharan Musalman (Sisters of Muslims),
attacked women like me. They said we were not Muslims because
we were not wearing proper hijab, and that people like us did not
have the right to talk or to have space in Afghanistan. When it was
my turn to speak, I said that no program would be successful if we
ignored the participation of half the people in the country and all
the minorities. I realized my work was cut out for me, but I was
certain I would win.

As the mujahideen continued their rampage, violence against
women, kidnappings, child marriage and forced marriage sky-
rocketed. And refugees were arriving in the thousands to Quetta
again. I hired doctors, nurses and teachers to open more clinics and
schools; I equipped them with supplies and paid them with a UN
food-for-work program. I continued to approach international aid
organizations for funding, all the while hoping that this would be
a temporary solution and that soon we'd be able to go home.

In 1990, I decided it was time to expand Shuhada's work into Afghanistan. Once again, I went to Inter Church Aid to ask for support to construct a school for girls in the village of Sangi Masha in the center of the Jaghori district. The construction was almost complete when a man from the Norwegian Refugee Council came to see the projects in Quetta and together we decided to travel the long road to Jaghori to inaugurate the Shuhada Girls High School.

I must admit that although the road was long, bumpy and dusty, I was very excited to show off the work we were doing and, in particular, our new principal. To reduce the expected opposition to educating girls, we had hired a mullah as principal. He was highly respected among the people in the village and, thankfully, had taken the very bold step of registering two of his daughters as students in the school. We started with grades one to three and found a woman who had studied teacher training in Helmand to be the headmistress. The rest of the teachers had only gone as far as the sixth grade, but soon enough we started a teacher training program for them. While the building process had been interrupted by looters on more than one occasion, the Norwegian Refugee Council was sufficiently impressed with our progress to provide the support we needed.

The trip back to Quetta began with some drama when we were warned that a mujahideen group had plans to capture me along the way. I wasn't worried; I just told the driver to take a different route. But the episode was eye-opening nonetheless. I was starting to realize that although I had developed a reputation in certain circles as a changemaker, to others I had become a holy threat.

Fundamentalism was spreading rapidly and menacingly. The mujahideen who were roving the countryside in Afghanistan had bases in Northern Pakistan. They were still being funded by the countries that had lined up to fight the Cold War alongside the Americans, and they understood that the way to an Afghan heart was to promise a return to spiritual roots. But factions had developed among the mujahideen. To gain popular support, each group used religion and culture to prove they were more anti-Soviet than the others, and to persuade people to come to their side. Consequently, the lives of the refugees in Quetta took on a suffocating and threatening aspect similar to what our compatriots were experiencing in Afghanistan.

In the midst of all this, Ali and I had a new and heartwarming addition to our family. My friend Abdul Rauf Naveed had married in 1989. The next year, he and his wife had a child, a little girl called Tamanna. Unfortunately, his wife left him when she was pregnant, and after the delivery she had to give the child to the father, as tradition and religion required. Since Rauf was already living with my family, he brought his little daughter to us. I felt she would do well with us and suggested he give the girl to me to raise. Rauf was delighted with the plan, and together we made it happen.

The arrangement worked out well. Rauf, who is an organizational wizard, was helping to run Shuhada. He had always been part of our family. When I was a medical student he had lived with Ghafoor and me, along with some of my other brothers who were sharing the house. He even lived with us when he was married. So it wasn't unusual that when he was in Quetta he would stay at our place. He was back and forth between Pakistan and Afghanistan, taking care of the logistics and administration of the Shuhada projects. Although the situation in Afghanistan was chaotic, he would always manage to distribute the relief we provided—such as quilts and medical supplies—to internally displaced persons (IDP) in Bamiyan, Mazar-e-Sharif, Pul-e-Khumri and Kandahar. Rauf and I understood each other and worked hard to make Shuhada the best NGO in the region. Together, we made a great team at work, and with our new family connection, we became closer still. Eventually, in 1998, Rauf and I married.

By 1992, the puppet government left behind by the Soviets had collapsed entirely, and Afghanistan fell into civil war. My brother Abdul Wahid saw his house destroyed by the fighting in Kabul and, realizing he and his family were not safe, came with them and my mother to Quetta. Then my father arrived from Lashkar Gah with his second wife, Halima, and their family. The province of Balochistan, where all of us were now living, straddled the border between Pakistan and Afghanistan and reached toward Kandahar, the Afghan city that had become home to a new group of mujahideen called the Taliban.

I knew the mujahideen posed a big threat to women and girls, and the Taliban seemed more menacing than all the others. Soon we were confronted by the oblique threats of this newly powerful faction as they strutted through the refugee camp proselytizing. When they emerged victorious in Kandahar in 1994, poised to take over in Afghanistan, the tension in the diaspora in Quetta ratcheted up again. Whisper campaigns began, and gossip took on the nature of hard currency, turning the lives of women like me into a high-wire act between life and death.

Five

A FUNDAMENTAL THREAT

A COLLECTION OF MOSTLY ILLITERATE, twentysomething men calling themselves the Taliban emerged in Kandahar in 1994. Mainly from the Pashtun area of eastern and southern Afghanistan, the Talibs had been educated in madrassas in Pakistan. Strutting about menacingly in their signature black turbans in Kandahar as well as in Quetta, where they were supported by the Pakistan government, they promised an end to the internecine war the mujahideen were waging—but they also pronounced the end of the emancipation of women.

A new wave of refugees crowded into Quetta. I plucked the teachers and principals, the lab technicians and doctors, the logisticians and nurses from the arrivals and put them to work. Meanwhile, I tried to raise the alarm about this hyper fundamentalism, but with both the UN and my international connections failing to respond swiftly, I knew I couldn't wait. I decided I had to defy the extremists and protect my students and patients in Quetta as well as in the schools and medical clinics across the border in Afghanistan.

People were becoming frustrated with the ongoing conflict, and many were beginning to look favorably on the Taliban's promises to collect the weapons from the mujahideen and bring back the rule of law. They were even saying the former king, Zahir Shah, would be brought back to the country. In a galvanizing incident in 1994, the Taliban leader Mullah Mohammed Omar gathered his Talibs together to provide security for goods being moved from Pakistan to Turkmenistan. When the mujahideen attempted to muscle their way into the delivery, the Taliban attacked, stopping the looting and providing safe passage for the transport. It created the impression that they were able to enforce the rule of law.

But the dark side of these Talibs became clear as soon as they took over Kandahar. They shuttered the girls' schools and told women to stop gathering in public. The public baths, which most people used because they didn't have hot water at home, were closed to women. Then the Taliban started a relentless march across the country. In September 1995, they took Herat from Governor Ismail Khan, who was certainly no friend of women's rights but was not as severe as the Taliban. Then they went on to capture most of the provinces in southern Afghanistan.

As much as we were all focused on what was clearly a dangerous force taking one town after another, I'd also been busy lobbying the UN to expand their offices in Afghanistan, particularly to the central highlands, the remote part of the country where the Hazaras live. The organization had already opened offices in Kandahar, Mazar-e-Sharif, Jalalabad, Kabul, Kunduz, Gardez and Herat. They'd also set up shop in Bamiyan, although they were doing very little there. To be fair, the UN had visited Bamiyan before, but most of their time was spent at the ancient Buddha statues and Band-e-Amir, a remarkable site like the US Grand Canyon. Located in the magnificent Hindu Kush mountains at an altitude of about nine hundred meters, it is an exceptionally beautiful place featuring six deep, blue lakes separated by natural dams. In 2009, it became Afghanistan's first national park.

As much as I appreciated the UN's interest in our national treasures, I was more concerned about the poverty in the area. Many people, including Hazaras, had been killed in Kabul as various mujahideen groups fought each other. As a result, thousands of Hazaras had been displaced to Mazar-e-Sharif and other parts of the country. (The city was seen as safe, as it was divided between the different political parties, who seemed to keep to themselves.) What I wanted the UN to understand was that Afghans, and in particular Hazaras, were on the run and that their fates were in the hands of these splinter groups; a UN office in the midst of the region would be useful for starting small development projects such as building schools and clinics, repairing roads and creating job opportunities.

To give you an idea of what things were like then, let me share a story about a trip I took to Kabul in 1993 to bring medicines, food and clothing to those affected by this fighting. I was wearing a burka and traveling with my bodyguard, Safar. We arrived in Kabul in the late afternoon and hired a taxi to take us to the Shuhada clinic in Karte Seh, but the driver refused to take us there; the Hazaras would kill me, he said. I didn't argue with him and suggested a hotel instead, as it was getting late. He told us to stay in the car while he asked if there was room at the hotel. When he came back, he said there was a room with five beds and we'd have to pay a thousand Afghanis for each bed. Otherwise, if more guests came, they would be sent to the empty beds in my room. There was no power, no water and no food; for another three thousand Afghanis we got a candle, a bucket of water and two cups of tea. I heard gunfire all night long as the different factions in the city fought each other.

The next morning, we finally made it to Karte Seh, where I could deliver the goods the people needed. While there, I wanted to go to my brother's house to see if I could find any of the personal belongings I'd left behind when I moved to Jaghori in 1982. I found only a few old photos, but I was invited to stay for dinner with the family and just happened to be part of a joyous event. Their son, who had been taken hostage five months before by one of the mujahideen in the Paghman area, had just been released, so I got to witness the reunion.

The week I spent in Kabul was shocking: everything was destroyed; the people were terrified; there were armed thugs all over the city. It was like a bad movie. When it was time to go back to Pakistan, Safar and I boarded a minibus and were waiting to depart, Suddenly, Safar was yanked out of the vehicle and told he could not leave the country because they claimed he was Uzbek and had to stay to fight. It took twenty minutes to talk our way out of that situation. Once on the road we were stopped three more times by three different groups, all demanding money, threatening to kill us (in particular Safar, who was wanted as a Hazara man), and holding us back. By the time we crossed the border I had a visceral understanding of the anarchism and wholesale fury of the mujahideen. For example, even the Kabul museum was fully destroyed. All that was left were a few Buddhas that were too heavy to transport. I wondered what it would take to save my country.

At last, in June 1995, we persuaded the UN to meet in Bamiyan. I saw it as an important step forward; it turned out to be another lesson in the confounding conditions we were dealing with. The commander of Hezb-e Wahdat-e Islami stole the World Food Programme's vehicle and the one from the United Nations International Children's Emergency Fund (UNICEF); as a result, the UN said the meeting could not proceed. I refused to give up on the opportunity and decided to go with my group by road from Mazar-e-Sharif to Bamiyan to get the vehicles back. I convinced some of the NGOs to come with me so the UN could not use the excuse that they did not have partners on the ground.

It took three days and two nights of traveling and provided yet another lesson in rural living. We stopped for the night in a small village called Zard Sang, where one person living there was able to read and write. Most of the young men were away working in Iran and sending money back home for their families to survive. One of the community members had a tape recorder and went house to house so that family members could record messages for their loved ones. (Since there was no functioning post, whenever people were coming or going to Iran they relayed messages this way.) Since the people in the village wouldn't take money from us for allowing us to sleep at their houses, we left them cash to buy batteries for the tape recorder instead. We traveled eight hours again the next day only to discover that the local mujahideen commander had taken the UN cars to another province—and so the UN canceled their journey to meet with us.

As we were still in Bamiyan, we went to see Shahr-e Gholghola, a historic archaeological site also known as the City of Woe. In 1221, the entire population here was massacred, and the city destroyed by Genghis Khan. Watching out for land mines, we climbed the hill, but once at the summit we heard heavy artillery and decided we had better beat a hasty retreat. It took eight hours of driving to get to a safe district. By the next day, the Hazaras in Bamiyan had been defeated by the government forces of Burhanuddin Rabbani. It would be another few months before we could persuade the UN to come back to visit the area and start their work again. We never did get the UN vehicles back from the commander.

While the political future was becoming increasingly unclear, my work was starting to attract attention. The awards that came my way allowed me to bring my concerns to the world and the world back to me. It began with two women from the Philippines who came to visit Shuhada in 1994. They were doing research on my schools and clinics because I had been nominated for the prestigious Ramon Magsaysay Award. Later, I found out that I was the recipient, along with a gentleman from China, in the community leadership category. I was told I could bring one member of my family with me for the events surrounding the presentation of the award in Manila; I brought Ali. The ceremony was very moving; we all wore our national dress, and the president of the Philippines presented our award and asked each of us to speak. I spoke about the truly worrisome facts facing Afghans: violence against women, forced marriage, child brides, the total absence of human rights and the lack of security for all of us. As honored as I was to receive this award, I found myself choking back tears on the way to the podium. Every other recipient—whether from China, India,

Argentina, Thailand or Malaysia—had their country's ambassador in the audience. No officials from Afghanistan attended. During the reception, a couple of Afghans who worked for the Asian Development Bank introduced themselves to me, which was a nice surprise.

In 1995 I received the Global Leader for Tomorrow Award from the World Economic Forum (WEF) in Davos, Switzerland. My old friend Vreni Frauenfelder met my plane and showed me around Zurich before I took the train to Davos. Each recipient was given a certificate from the chair of the WEF and invited to speak in front of the gathering of world leaders; afterward, I met with the chief of staff for the WEF about how he could help. Bill Gates was there too and had given out machines for the conference that did something called email. I had never seen such a thing before; nor had most of the others.

I wanted to meet Madam Sadako Ogata from Japan, the United Nations High Commissioner for Refugees (UNHCR), to talk to her about the perilous situation of the people who were returning to Afghanistan from Iran and Pakistan, particularly through central Afghanistan. With some assistance, I wrote my very first email to her. I was thrilled when she agreed to meet, as she turned out to be extremely well-informed and willing to help. She later became Japan's Special Representative for Afghanistan, and we would see each other often in Kabul.

I was invited back to Davos a few more times, and in 1999 I had the privilege of listening to Nelson Mandela speak about apartheid and the Truth and Reconciliation program in South Africa. As I took part in these opportunities that allowed me to listen to leaders speak and to seek advice from others, it felt as if I were weaving a tapestry that was showing me piece by piece what needed to change and how I might help. And in what became an annual tradition, Vreni and I sold Afghan crafts and dried fruits and honey at community functions where I would speak about the oppressive status of women in Afghanistan and my projects to raise money for my work back home.

In September 1995, along with other NGO members, we managed to reschedule the UN visit to the central highlands, where we were able to push the UN agencies to start their activities in Bamiyan. That trip started in a dramatic fashion. We arrived late in Yakawlang, at about 7:30 p.m., and stayed at the staff house of Yakawlang Hospital, which was being run by the Iranian Red Crescent Society. Dr. Shakiba Habibula who was working for Oxfam, came to me and asked if I could see a woman who had been in labor for three or four days. Of course I agreed.

The patient was weak, pale and very dehydrated, so I started an IV and asked if they had anesthesia equipment; the woman was at serious risk of dying and needed a cesarean section. Since they didn't have the equipment, I had to use ether to sedate her. The uterus had ruptured, and the baby probably had been dead for several days, so the tissue was fragile. I removed the fetus, performed a hysterectomy and, frankly, hoped for the best. It was well past midnight when I checked on her and told her husband to give blood at the very basic hospital lab so she could have a transfusion. The next morning, I went to the hospital to see if she had survived. To my great surprise she was sitting on the bed; her husband was lying down. When I asked him if he had given blood the night before, he replied, "No, because she had a C-section last year while we were refugees in Iran and I gave blood then." I was so angry that without thinking I slapped that man and told him that we women bleed every month and we don't die. He was shocked, but he promptly rolled up his sleeve and donated blood to his wife. She survived.

The situation in Afghanistan was deteriorating rapidly. It's fair to say that the Taliban owed its success to the actions of the mujahideen, whose lawlessness and constant violation of people's rights led to a loss of support among the public. Furthermore, the various groups were not able to come together and establish the united front required in order to act as a government. In fact, as the mujahideen were pushed from their strongholds, they started taking revenge on each other. For example, Jamiat-e Islami supported the Taliban to get rid of other mujahideen groups such as Hezb-e Islami and Hezb-e Wahdat Islami. The fratricidal bloodbath was tearing the country apart.

The Taliban continued to take other parts of the country, mostly without much resistance. On September 27, 1996, they took Kabul easily, thanks to the extraordinarily shortsighted thinking of President Burhanuddin Rabbani and Ahmad Shah Massoud, the mujahideen leader in the north—both of whom somehow thought the Taliban would leave them alone.

In an act that would foretell the future Taliban brutality, former president Najibullah, who had been under UN protection in the UN compound, was murdered along with his brother. Their bodies were hanged from streetlights in a public square, their cash and cigarettes stuffed into their pockets and stuck on their bloating fingers.

Then the situation got even worse.

The Taliban's shocking edicts were announced to a stunned population. Females were put under house arrest: Girls were not to go to school; women were not to go to work. Women and girls were not allowed to leave the house unless they were in the company of a father, husband, brother or son and also had a permit to be outside. It was mandatory for females to wear a tent-like burka, which, for most women, resulted in a debilitating loss of personal freedom. Women in the cities complained that they couldn't see through the mesh strip over their eyes and feared falling as a result of a view they described as similar to wearing horse blinders. Their own breath dampened the cloth in front of their mouths, and that moisture attracted the dust from the war-wrecked roads, which made them feel as if they were suffocating in stale, dirty air. The psychological damage was intense. One woman described it by saying, "No one can see me. No one knows if I am smiling or crying. I can't see where I'm going. There are holes in the roads, it's easy to step into one and fall down. There's no one to help you up. No one in the world wants to help us."

In the space of twenty-four hours, Afghan women disappeared: from their jobs, the streets and public life. In contrast, the war with the USSR—during which the puppet regime forced all young men to join the national security forces—had had the indirect effect of making women more visible. When young men either joined the army or fled the country to avoid fighting and death, their departure created space for women and girls in the university and led to job opportunities as teachers, journalists, civil servants and more. While it hadn't been the intention of the regime to promote women's rights, a side effect of their actions was that women had been able to take advantage of the situation, at least in the big cities.

The edicts got crazier as each day went by, as though the Taliban was using its newfound power to make up punishments. Windows had to be painted over so no one could see women inside their homes. Makeup and nail polish were taboo. The Taliban didn't like the *tap-tap-tap* sound made by a woman's high heels, so women had to wear wedge shoes. White socks were forbidden because white was the color of the Taliban flag. Photographs, even those taken at wedding ceremonies, were banned. So were sports for girls. Radio and television and music were also banned, as were children's toys. Little girls were told to throw their dollies into a bonfire. Flying kites, a national pastime, was forbidden.

The shops were closed to women. The bearded Talibs patrolled the streets, whipping anyone who disobeyed. They called themselves the Department for the Propagation of Virtues and Prevention of Vice. Their leader, Mullah Mohammed Omar, said flatly, "A woman's face corrupts men." Female patients had to leave the hospitals since the staff included male doctors. In a stupefying rationale, Mullah Omar explained that the Taliban's actions against women were being taken because "[o]therwise they'll be like Lady Diana."

The Taliban announced their rules in a series of numbered edicts that had everything to do with appearances and nothing to do with the health, safety or well-being of the people. Here are a few examples:

- There is to be no exit [from homes] or traveling of sisters [females] without the escort of legal close relatives.
- The person in charge of collecting fares for sisters in buses, minibuses and jeeps should be under ten years old.

- To prevent sedition and uncovered females, no drivers are allowed to pick up females who are using Iranian hijab [which allows the face to show]. In the case of violation, the driver will be imprisoned. If such kinds of female are observed in the street, their houses will be found and their husbands punished. If women use stimulating and attractive clothes and there is no close male relative with them the driver should not pick them up.

- If any music cassette is found in a shop the shopkeeper should be imprisoned and the shop locked.

- If anyone is observed who has shaved and/or cut his beard he should be arrested and imprisoned until his beard gets bushy. [This rule had a grace period of one and half months before going into effect.]

- To prevent British and American hairstyles, people with long hair should be arrested and taken to the police department to shave their hair. The criminal must pay the barber.

- To prevent keeping pigeons and playing with birds: within ten days this matter should be monitored and the pigeons and any other playing birds should be killed.

- To prevent washing clothes by young ladies along the water streams in the city: it should be announced in all mosques and the matter should be monitored; violator ladies should be picked up with respectful Islamic manner and taken to their houses, and their husbands severely punished.

I wanted to say to the Taliban: "If a woman wears clothes that don't fully cover her body and a man cannot control himself, whose fault is that?" It's not our fault, because we are women. If men don't have enough self-control to hear the tapping sound of a woman's footstep or see her hair showing or her fashionable clothes, it's their problem, not ours.

But those transgressions were nothing compared to the actions of a woman who had wronged the religious police. To disobey was to die. A woman seen in the company of a man who was not her relative was accused of zina (any sexual relationship with a man who is not your husband) and carted off to the soccer stadium, where the Taliban would toss her to the ground, form a circle around her and throw rocks at her head until she was dead. It was stipulated that the rocks must not be so big as to kill her quickly.

There is nothing in the Quran to support the actions of the Taliban. But the world was looking the other way.

The tension in the diaspora ratcheted up again. The lineup at my clinic in Quetta grew ever longer. My schools for girls had to operate in shifts because I didn't have the money to rent more space. The women mounting resistance to the Taliban's barbaric rules—who had as much power here in this refugee district of Pakistan as they did in Afghanistan—became discouraged in the face of the silence from the world community. And some international agencies began justifying the abuses by saying, "At least there's peace under the Taliban." Except, for women, living in prison isn't peace. The silence in the graveyard isn't peace. The threat of being stoned to death isn't peace. Painting your windows over so you can't be seen isn't peace. Being without music isn't peace. We women were being asked to wait a long time for peace— or so it seemed.

By this time I had founded four hospitals, twelve health clinics and forty-six schools in Afghanistan, and two clinics, a hospital and four schools in Quetta. We were delivering more than a hundred babies a month, conducting multiple surgeries daily, and seeing between six and eight dozen patients a day. The rule for paying was this: if you were destitute, it was free; if you were able to pay, it was twenty rupees (thirty-four cents). This was when I decided to collect all our work under a single name; I called it Shuhada Organization.

While the struggles with the Taliban swirled around the streets outside my clinic in Quetta, I was busy trying to find funds for my hospitals and schools. By now I knew there were people who were sympathetic to my projects and goals. I met these people in Norway and Sweden and Holland and the United States. What's more, I had known since the early 1990s that the concept of gender equality was being discussed by NGOs and the UN. I'd been to a meeting with Oxfam in Mazar-e-Sharif for what they called a "gender training program" for their staff in the northern regions. This kind of talk was becoming more common even though the Taliban and other mujahideen around us were beating a different drum.

I watched the Taliban strutting around the streets and even barging into my clinic demanding medical treatment for themselves and their wives and wondered how they had arrived at such erroneous conclusions about gender. I wanted to explain that together men and women are the two wings of a bird. Both wings have to be healthy and whole—not wounded or broken—to enable the bird to fly.

In Quetta as well as in Afghanistan, religion was being misused politically and damaging one of the wings. I felt it was a question of education. If you don't know what's in the Quran, or you don't understand the meaning of the words, you are liable to misinterpret religion and use it to trample women's rights. Most of the edicts promulgated by mullahs are misguided because the language of the Quran is Arabic. In Afghanistan people speak Dari and Pashtu. Not only that, but 85 percent of Afghan women and about 75 percent of Afghan men were illiterate at that time and couldn't read the Arabic text. In fact, a common expression in Afghanistan equates illiteracy to blindness. If you ask a woman if she can read, she'll say, "No, I'm blind." If you ask her what that means, she'll tell you, "I can't read, so I can't see what's going on."

I attended a program in Uruzgan Province and listened to elders complaining that their people didn't have female teachers and doctors. As the last speaker, I addressed the issue plainly: "Change needs to come from you. Who is going to be the lady doctor to deal with your wife and daughters if you refuse to send your daughters to school? Who will be the teacher to teach your girls? Your daughter's brain is not smaller than mine. I am able to do the work. Your daughters can too."

Afghanistan became known as a country where being a woman was to be a target for religious extremists, an object of so-called cultural practices. It became a place where the girl child was fed last and least, and denied an education. She was sold as chattel, given away in forced marriage as a child bride and used in any manner that benefited a father or brother.

The atrocities committed against women and girls throughout the country were shockingly brutal. An eighteen-year-old girl was in labor for four days because a female doctor was not available. Her family tried to help her with hot compresses that burned her abdomen and endless concoctions that made her increasingly sick. When they finally brought her to the hospital, I did a cesarean section to save the girl's life and removed the fetus, which had been dead for days. And losing the baby wasn't the worst thing that happened to that girl. I had to do a hysterectomy because all her reproductive organs were gangrened—the result of waiting so long to get help. Now she'd be considered useless and dismissed as a servant because she couldn't bear children and was therefore unworthy to marry.

Although people had begun to leave Afghanistan as early as 1979, when the Soviets arrived, the biggest exodus by far occurred after the Taliban took over the capital city, Kabul, in 1996. In a matter of months, Afghanistan became a pariah state to most of the world: a major narcotics exporter producing 70 percent of the world's heroin, and a haven for terrorists as well as arms dealers and smugglers who were like GoFundMe units for the Taliban. The United Nations tried to interrupt the increasingly disturbing outcomes by slapping sanctions on the country that was harboring Osama bin Laden, who had been accused of bombing American embassies in East Africa. The aim was to restrict the Taliban's movements and cut off their financial support from other countries; they also hoped it would flush out bin Laden.

The oppression and human rights violations and the discrimination against the Hazaras went on unabated. Somehow, Osama bin Laden flew under the radar, keeping impressive estates in five major cities, his gardens lush with green grass and blooming flowers during the worst drought the country had known in decades, and welcoming jihadis from all over the world to train for their future violent actions. Through it all, women remained behind their painted windows.

In 1996 I took my friend and benefactor Vreni Frauenfelder to Jaghori to see the programs she was funding. She applied for a visa, but since the Taliban was running the Afghan consulate in Quetta, and she was not accompanied by a male, she was refused. I told her that we would hire a car, cover ourselves with burkas, and I would say she was my mother and couldn't speak. The Taliban hassled us, mostly because they were looking for forbidden audio cassettes.

Halfway from Kandahar to Qalat, we saw some Kochi (nomad) children playing with a metallic object. I had just enough time to realize it was an unexploded mine before it exploded.

We stopped the car. The blast had instantly killed two children and injured a girl who was about nine or ten years old—she needed hospital care. I was worried that if her back or neck were moved, her injuries could be made worse. The male member of the family tied her onto two wooden sticks wrapped with a blanket. There was no room for the makeshift stretcher in our car so we fastened her to the top with her uncle crouched beside her. We drove her to Shajoy, a district of Qalat, where there was a small clinic.

By now it was too late to travel farther. We spent the night in a room with no toilet or electricity or windows or even a door, and we slept on the ground, which was crawling with cockroaches. I have never forgotten that night: I was with my people in my country, but Vreni was a Swiss woman over the age of seventy. I saw proof of her personal dedication to the people of Afghanistan.

My rage at the near silence from the world community continued to grow. The UN held meetings in Peshawar and Quetta in early 1997 for all the various factions to discuss Afghanistan. No women were invited. I was later invited to attend a meeting in Washington to discuss the situation in Afghanistan. Each delegate was allowed six minutes to speak. As the only woman, I told the other attendees that I represented more than half the people in Afghanistan. I asked, "How come I only get the same six minutes as all these men?" The chairperson replied, "You can speak as long as you like."

Death threats toward me—sometimes by night letter and other times as shouted warnings—became as common as the viruses I was treating in the clinic. I stood my ground and told the fundamentalists, "You know where I am. I won't stop what I'm doing." Then they instructed me to shut down my schools for girls. I tried to avoid their attention by stating that the schools taught girls only up to the sixth grade, even though they actually went all the way through high school. Eventually the Taliban got tougher with me. I remember them saying that if I didn't close my schools, they would punish me. I answered them just us directly: "Go ahead and hang me in the public square and tell the people my crime: giving paper and pencil to girls."

I developed a strategy for getting around both the increasingly paralyzing rules of the extremists as well as the age-old customs of people who'd never been to school and believed fervently in the teachings of mullahs (who hadn't been to school either).

Much of the suffering of women and girls comes from often-incorrect religious interpretations adopted in places like Pakistan and Afghanistan that put the onus on girls to protect the honor of the family. One day a sixteen-year-old girl came with her parents to my clinic. A quick physical examination and ultrasound told me what I suspected. She was six months pregnant—and terrified. She confided in me that she had been raped. The law according to Sharia is that a woman who is raped must have four male witnesses to prove that it was rape rather than consensual sex.

Naturally, no such witnesses are ever available. Without this proof it is the family honor that must be protected.

This girl had kept her terrible secret until she could hide it no longer. If I didn't do something for her she would be killed. So I quickly hatched a plan.

Since most people I treated didn't have a lot of information about biology, I could explain things without going into too much detail. I told the parents their daughter had a tumor and needed surgery. I said she was too sick and anemic to have the operation right away and she would have to stay at the clinic.

I kept that girl for three months. When the baby was due, I performed a cesarean section. The family waited outside the operating room because it was the custom to show the family what was found in the surgery. I put the placenta in the surgical basin, showed the so-called tumor to them and told them their daughter would be fine. Then I gave the baby to a woman who was in a different sort of trouble: being married and infertile.

The people who came to my clinic suffered all the ills common in refugee camps: malnutrition, anemia, typhoid fever, malaria. In the lineups at the door they whispered news of the Taliban's latest atrocities and decrees. Women were being severely punished for being seen with a man who was not a relative. And yet these same men would travel several days to get treatment for their wives at my clinic. One Talib told me his wife bled from her nose whenever she worked hard in the fields. I told him, "She's full-term pregnant; she shouldn't be working so hard." He replied, "She has to work. Fix her nose."

Another young patient I had to protect had been bleeding for eleven months. Her blood pressure was dangerously low. She was as weak as a sparrow. Except for the dark circles under her eyes, her face was the color of bread dough. At first, I thought she might only need a simple D&C (dilation and curettage), but culture interfered—she was a virgin. The simple operation would destroy her hymen, and consequently the proof of her virginity, which in turn would destroy her life. So abdominal surgery was scheduled. I asked for a blood donor for the surgery and told her parents, "Go get me blood from your family, and don't bring me anyone who's been fooling around sexually or taking opium." The family scurried away to find the donor.

The next morning after a cousin had been procured and the blood drawn and bagged for the surgery, another doctor and I, along with one assistant and three nurses, scrubbed and began our work in the operating room. A tumor the size of a large baked potato was removed. I didn't think it was malignant but sent it to the laboratory to be sure. It would take several days to get the lab results. But as custom required, I had to send the nurse out to show the family what was found and have them decide whether the girl should have a hysterectomy or not. After much discussion, they decided on the hysterectomy. I said to the nurse, "Go back out there and talk to them. She is unmarried. No one will marry her if she has a hysterectomy. Ask the family to give her a chance. We can maybe save this uterus." Eventually I went outside myself with the fibroid tumor in a jar. There was high drama as the father, mother, sisters and aunts questioned me. At last I won the debate. I returned to the operating room and sewed the girl up.

As the war against women continued, a new and menacing problem started to turn up at the clinic. Many women developed osteomalacia. Confined to the indoors or cloaked beneath burkas, they were no longer exposed to sunshine, and their bones were softening due to a lack of vitamin D. As well, they were surviving on a diet of tea and naan bread because they couldn't afford enough nutritious food. On top of that, depression was endemic because the future was so dark; people were living in constant fear. But at the same time, the little girls in my schools were still dreaming of being doctors and scientists and artists and even politicians.

By this point in my life I had a lot of experience in fighting the suffocating rules girls like me were raised with. I fought every step of the way—to get an education and become a physician, to open hospitals and schools for girls in Quetta and various cities in Afghanistan, to raise my children the way I thought they should be raised. I fought the Soviets and the mujahideen. And now I had to do battle with these Taliban, these illiterate boys who thought they could teach us a lesson. I was the one doing the teaching— of the girls in the schools and the nurses and doctors in the clinics. Thousands of girls learned to build self-confidence and self-respect and reach for the stars at our schools, and thousands of women regained their health at our clinics. The refugees and the Afghan people we were serving saw us as heroes, but the Taliban considered me the enemy.

Our rights were continually eroded, in part due to the monetary aid flowing in from Arab states such as Saudi Arabia and Sudan, which called for the segregation of men and women and the active implementation of their militant brand of Wahhabism. Women were simply forbidden to go to a hospital, and no male doctor could see female patients. So I saw them—at their homes or in my clinics.

Families, particularly women and children, were living in a perpetual state of fear as the Taliban perpetuated extraordinary violence against anyone deemed to have disobeyed. For example, under the Taliban rule, playfields became sites for public executions instead of soccer games; women and girls were seen as a threat to holiness and were whipped or beaten simply for showing a hand while paying for food or making a sound while on the street.

This throwback to a medieval era created a strange wall of silence. The UN wrung its hands, and government leaders the world over looked the other way. There were women who saw this cataclysm coming a decade before the Taliban took power and raised the alarm, but only a few internationally recognized voices joined their protest. One was Carol Bellamy, the executive director of UNICEF in New York, who, in March 1997, predicted a social and economic catastrophe for Afghanistan because of the treatment of its women. Other Afghan American women—in collaboration with the Feminist Majority Foundation, Amnesty International USA, Refugee Women in Development, the Women's Alliance for Peace and Human Rights in Afghanistan, and Canadian Women for Women in Afghanistan—started a campaign to raise awareness of the plight of Afghan women.

In November 1997 Canada's minister of foreign affairs, Lloyd Axworthy, invited me to come to Canada to assist him in discussing a strategy for dealing with the Taliban and for taking further action on women's rights in Afghanistan. I told him that one of the problems for us was that some people talked about this terrible oppression as though women accepted it, which simply wasn't true. I also urged Canada to put pressure on the Taliban to change its policies—to allow girls to go back to school and women to return to work. I said that Canada had the ability to be effective by making alliances with countries such as the United States to put pressure on countries that supported the Taliban, such as Pakistan, Saudi Arabia and the United Arab Emirates (UAE). After that meeting, I spoke out to the women of Canada and said we needed solidarity and sisterhood—that we wanted them to speak for us because we didn't have a voice in our country at that time.

Later, Foreign Minister Axworthy took twelve thousand letters from Canadians—written in response to a *Homemaker's* magazine article by Sally Armstrong about Afghan women's human rights—to the UN General Assembly. After that, the UN spoke out, but not with tangible results. In fact, they sent a delegation to Afghanistan led by Angela King, the Special Adviser on Gender Issues and Advancement of Women. Upon returning she released a statement saying that the situation of women was not so bad after all, and that the Taliban had brought security to Afghanistan whereas the previous groups fought among themselves and killed a lot of people. While that last part was true, I was apoplectic. Several women joined me in replying to this statement from the international body that is the guardian of the Universal Declaration of Human Rights and all other conventions—and therefore responsible for the rights of *all* people. Our message: liberty can never be the price of security. Security is more than silencing the guns.

In 1998 I was invited to the United States, along with a Talib who was head of the Red Crescent in Herat. Fortunately, there were some empty seats on the plane, so as soon as we took off from Karachi I removed my scarf, pulled up the arm rest in the middle seat and curled up to get some rest. He was on my case immediately, asking how I could possibly be seen without my scarf. I dismissed him, saying, "I don't want to argue with you. I want to sleep."

We arrived in New York and took another flight to Washington before noon and agreed to rest for a while and go out for some food later in the afternoon. I knocked on the Talib's door at 4 p.m.; we went outside to a 7-Eleven store to buy sandwiches. He'd never been outside Afghanistan and Pakistan and was worried about whether the food was halal (allowed in Islam). We bought some cookies and fruits and then, instead of seeing him continue to worry, I went to my relatives in nearby Virginia and brought back some Afghan food for him and assured him that it was halal.

One of the first stops we made was at a clinic for illegal immigrants. The doctor talked about how some of the women there were victims of domestic violence. Then she mentioned that she was from Mexico and said that in her culture if a girl got pregnant outside of marriage she would be kicked out of the house. I said, "Your culture is much better than ours, where we kill the girls who get pregnant without being married." The doctor was shocked. She jumped to her feet and said, "You're killing the girls?" I said yes. Then she asked, "What happens to the man?" I told her that the man runs away. The Talib started to talk to me in our own language, saying he'd deal with me when we get out of there. When we left, he started accusing me of speaking against Islam, which I strongly denied. But I asked him, how often is a man killed because a woman is pregnant even after she was raped? He had no response.

At every meeting, my Talib colleague kept trying to control the narrative and talk about the bravery of Taliban fighters, whereas I continued to raise the rights of women and the importance of equality.

Our next meeting was at the University of Maryland, a short ride on the Metro. It was summer, and a young woman wearing shorts sat near us. My travel companion was trying not to look at her but could not avoid stealing glances. When we arrived at the university, I suggested we go to the cafeteria for Kentucky Fried Chicken before going to our meeting. He said, "No, that's not halal." I told him it was a lot more halal than the way he was looking at the young girl on the Metro.

We ate the fried chicken; he said it was tasty.

Toward the end of our trip, the Talib kissed my hand and said, "You are my older sister." His example illustrates my belief that, deep down, the Taliban are more ignorant than cruel. They have been brainwashed and have never been exposed to another life. They were brought up in madrassas without the love of a mother and being taught hateful messages about women from an early age. And so they too were victims of the Cold War and the political Islamization of the region.

On the Talib's last night in the United States we were in Atlanta at the home of a Dr. Nasiri and his daughter Humaira Nasiri, who worked at the World Bank. When it was time to leave, the doctor offered me his medical books. I was very pleased to have them and asked the Talib if he could take the books to Quetta for me because I was staying in the United States for another two weeks. The daughter filled a suitcase with the books, and I told the Talib my husband would meet his plane in Quetta. Rauf picked him up at the airport and took him to our house for lunch. He also gave him a prayer mat as it was soon time to pray. The Talib then said he'd been told that Hazaras are not Muslims, but, he said to Rauf, "I see you are Muslim."

Poor guy—he was subsequently removed from his position because he had committed the double sin of first, traveling with a woman, and second, one who was Hazara. Since he belonged to a powerful family in Kandahar, he became the head of a military hospital in Kabul, where he took a first aid course and called himself a doctor. One of his duties was to transport injured Taliban soldiers to the Aga Khan University Hospital in Karachi. He used to call me at night on the phone—at a late hour, as he didn't want the Taliban to know he was in touch with me—and ask lots of questions about religion and our culture. When the United States defeated the Taliban in 2001, he escaped capture by speeding off in an ambulance to Spin Boldak on the border with Pakistan. He sent a note to me saying I should send someone to get the ambulance and take it back to Kabul. We stayed in touch for a brief time but eventually lost contact. He remains proof to me that when people get to know each other and share their views, they can begin to look outward and find their shared humanity.

There were so many issues cropping up because of the Taliban that I could hardly keep track of all of them. Before the fighting began, family planning was available. But then most of the budget was used for war rather than social services. I was concerned for this young generation, most of whom had four or five children by the age of twenty. Many girls became pregnant while still breastfeeding the last born. As a result, they suffered from anemia and osteomalacia; it was also why the mother and child mortality and morbidity rate in Afghanistan was second-highest in the world after Sierra Leone.

The Taliban were (and still are) so obsessed with their version of purity of women and girls that they were simply incapable of running a government. The collapse of systems of governance was obvious when a 6.1 magnitude earthquake struck northern Afghanistan on February 4, 1998. Communications were so poor it took two days for the news to reach Kabul. Reports claimed that hundreds of people died, and thousands more were left homeless. The Taliban had to rely totally on the international community to direct the rescue.

I could not seem to convince the people with the power to interfere, to take action. I vividly recall meeting with Tom Hushek, the us desk officer for Afghanistan in Washington, DC. My intention was to engage in a meaningful dialogue, advocate for educational aid and voice the dire human rights needs of the Afghan people. I highlighted three key realities: First, the Taliban had turned Afghanistan into a training camp for terrorists, which was dangerous not only for Afghanistan but for the rest of the world. Second, there was the drug trade, particularly the opium harvesting and exporting that was thriving in Afghanistan and destabilizing regional security, and how it would ultimately destroy the lives of young people everywhere. And third, Afghanistan had become a prison for women and girls.

Hushek's responses sank my heart. He said that their information did not show that Afghanistan had become a training ground for terrorists. He said even if Afghanistan were to become the largest producer of opium, the supplies would not reach the United States, which was more concerned with drugs coming from Colombia. As for women's issues, the United States must respect the "Afghan religion and culture" toward women and therefore should not take any action in this regard.

Of course I countered every one of his arguments and stated unequivocally that putting women under house arrest was not our "culture." Moreover, I told him it was the responsibility of his country to support human rights in my country. It was the United States that had given support to the conservative groups in order to fight the USSR. While I wasn't in favor of military intervention, I did want to put pressure on the countries that supported the Taliban and their mentalities. When I walked out of the State Department I was crying.

The conversations I'd had not only isolated the women I came to talk about but also foreshadowed the conflict to come. But while the Afghan desk in the United States failed us, I have to say that American women spoke out strongly for us. On December 10, 1998, First Lady Hillary Rodham Clinton marked the fiftieth anniversary of the Universal Declaration of Human Rights with a speech about the women of Afghanistan. She said, "Perhaps the most egregious and systematic trampling of fundamental human rights of any person is taking place in Afghanistan today against women. . . . We cannot allow these terrible crimes against women and girls—and truly, against all of humanity—to continue with impunity. We must all make it unmistakably clear that this terrible suffering inflicted on the women and girls of Afghanistan is not cultural, it is criminal. And we must do everything we can in our power to stop it."

The Feminist Majority Foundation in the United States mobilized more than 225 women's rights and human rights groups to join their campaign to stop the American government from recognizing the Taliban and to stop gender apartheid. Some of the female members of the US House of Representatives and Senate also supported the campaign. Their voices were welcome, particularly since their own government was actually contemplating support for the Taliban.

It was also astonishing that the US government would under-estimate the growing threat of the terrorist group Al Qaeda. In 1998 Al Qaeda had claimed responsibility for suicide attacks on the American embassies in Kenya and Tanzania, and later, in 2000, for another attack on the USS *Cole*, a guided missile destroyer that was refueling in Yemen's Aden harbor. Seventeen US sailors were killed and thirty-seven were injured. To retaliate, the Americans fired missiles into what they thought were Al Qaeda's training camps. But the irony was that Pakistan, on which the Americans were probably relying for intelligence, was playing both sides: they gave Osama bin Laden warning to leave the camps before telling the Americans to fire on them. In the end, the only casualties were a few young Al Qaeda members; their leaders escaped.

In 1998, I was asked to speak at a UN conference on Afghanistan in Ashgabat, Turkmenistan. Invited were all the donor countries and international NGOs and some Afghan NGOs to discuss what had clearly become an international crisis. The United States wanted to place sanctions on Afghanistan because the Taliban refused to hand over bin Laden for his crimes in Kenya, Tanzania and Yemen, but a Spanish diplomat, Francesc Vendrell, as Special Representative of the UN Secretary-General, claimed sanctions would destroy the meetings he'd planned to hold between the Taliban and the Northern Alliance. When it was my turn to talk, I asked if there was a space for women at the peace table discussions between the Taliban and those who opposed them. No one answered my question because no one had considered the participation of women in this conservative, male-dominated Afghan society. In fact, under the Taliban, we did not even exist. I explained to this gathering of mostly men that denying women a place at the table during peace talks was unconscionable. They might think that since men make war, men should make the peace, but women, being the victims of war, should be at the center of every program related to building the peace.

Now that the Taliban had stopped stealing the UN's cars and food and kidnapping their staff, the organization's representatives began showing sympathy for them. While most Western countries were employing the platitude of "respect for the culture and religion" as an excuse to avoid interfering, the Americans were still dabbling with formally recognizing the Taliban, mostly because they wanted to secure the contract for a major oil and gas project.

Again, it would be American women who picked up the torch. The Feminist Majority Foundation campaign dramatically increased visibility for Afghan women and kept up the pressure on the United States and the UN to deny the Taliban official government status. Feminist Majority Foundation president Eleanor Smeal and campaign chair Mavis Leno appeared on all the major news shows, and after a letter from Leno appeared in the syndicated "Dear Abby" newspaper column, more than fifteen thousand people joined the protest.

In a bold put-your-money-where-your-mouth-is initiative chaired by Mavis Leno, the Feminist Majority Foundation challenged one of the Taliban's potential funders. For several years, Unocal Corporation—a US energy company based in California—was the leader of a consortium to build an oil and gas pipeline from Turkmenistan through Afghanistan to Pakistan. The Feminist Majority Foundation protested the project in campaigns across the country, during Unocal's annual stockholders' meeting, and in demonstrations outside its corporate headquarters. Brilliantly dramatic posters depicting a woman in a burka with a gas nozzle held to her head were created for the campaign. Unocal canceled the project and lost an expected $100 million.

Some people asked Mavis Leno, the wife of television host Jay Leno, why she got involved. She told a story about her father being buried in a mining accident. She said, "He was dug out and he was fine, but he told me that while he was buried the hardest thing was that he had no way of being sure that anybody was looking for him. They could think that maybe he hadn't gone to work that day, or that he was someplace else, not buried. Or maybe they would think, yes, he was buried, but he was dead. Maybe they wouldn't look for him. That's what came to my mind when I heard about the situation with the women in Afghanistan. They don't even know if anybody knows what has happened to them. They don't even know if people are trying to save them. And that seemed so terrible to me that I felt I had to be one of the people that was looking for them."

Emma Bonino, the commissioner for humanitarian affairs for the European Union, also took up the cause. When she came to Kabul at the end of February 1998, the Taliban arrested her for taking photographs at the hospital for women. The UN intervened and she was released after a few hours, but she had been an eyewitness to the facts of life under the Taliban. When she returned to Brussels, she held a press conference on March 8, International Women's Day; since I was in Germany at the time attending another meeting, she invited me to join her. I attended the press conference but wore a burka to mask my identity and asked them not to use my name but rather to just introduce me as an Afghan doctor. I was known for being outspoken, and since I was on my way back to Pakistan, I decided for the sake of safety to be anonymous.

Emma Bonino told the media what she had seen in Kabul and how shocked she was by the appalling status and condition of women in Afghanistan. Grateful for her solidarity, I explained that the human rights for women as well as minority groups were being violated with impunity. Emma then launched the "A Flower for the Women of Kabul" campaign and called upon member governments of the United Nations, all international organizations, and in particular the EU countries, to wear a flower as an expression of support and to do whatever was in their power to help restore the basic human rights of women in Afghanistan. She said, "These women have no help right now other than us." It was at this press conference that I first met Eleanor Smeal of the Feminist Majority in person, an encounter that began a long-lasting collaboration and cooperation to support women's rights in Afghanistan.

Another voice of support came from London, England, where Fatima Gailani, who holds a master's degree in Islamic jurisprudence, had fled with her family. (She is the daughter of Pir Sayed Ahmed Gailani, the spiritual leader of the Sunni Muslims, who was also living in exile in London). Outraged by the Taliban's interpretation of Islam, Gailani said, "I can prove that any action of the prophet, his wives—and the Quran—has nothing to do with this; it goes against the Quran in fact. For example, a woman with a covered head is not more honorable than a woman without a covered head. The Taliban are against Afghan tradition, against Islam, they only continue because presently there is no alternative."

I had also been working directly with a network of women from different Muslim countries called Women Living Under Muslim Laws (WLUML). Their goal was to stop the isolation of women and to provide linkages and support to all women whose lives were being affected negatively by patriarchal laws. The network was a response to punitive interpretations of Muslim law that were harming women during the mid-1980s. Women were being arrested and jailed without trial for discussing issues such as the family code of honor. Women had been stoned to death for alleged sexual impropriety. They were being refused divorces even when the law permitted them. And some women who managed to get a divorce were refused custody of their children.

The WLUML network highlighted what they saw as two equally important issues: First, Muslim laws sometimes vary radically from one cultural context to the other. Second, there are several different legal codes that coexist in each cultural, social and political context. At the very least, each society has a codified legal system and a parallel system of customary laws and practices. Further complicating the matter were subdivisions of the laws into two formal codes in some countries, one religious, the other civil. And within that context the customary laws were diverse and often interpreted at the whims of the local mullah or religious leader. All of these laws were almost always detrimental to women.

Until 1991 WLUML stepped softly, holding workshops on Quranic interpretations by women and organizing cross-cultural exchange programs. But with militant fundamentalism on the rise, they became more vocal and more forceful, and, as a result, exposed themselves to more danger. By 1996, when the Taliban took power, the network was the leading voice for women living under Muslim laws.

Farida Shaheed, the Asian coordinator of WLUML in Lahore, Pakistan, won't even use the word *fundamentalist*. "It suggests a return to cherished fundamentals of Islam, which it certainly is not," she said. "They aren't religious at all. This is political opportunism. Their strength is in disrupting the political process and using that to blackmail those in political power."

I was in the United States in 2000 and had a meeting with Secretary of State Madeleine Albright. Joined by Eleanor Smeal, Mavis Leno and Jennifer Jackman of the Feminist Majority Foundation, I spoke with Secretary Albright about the Taliban regime and the harsh treatment of women in Afghanistan. When she asked what her government could do, I said, "You can pressure the countries who have recognized the Taliban regime: Pakistan, Saudi Arabia and the United Arab Emirates." Albright responded that they could not put pressure on Saudi Arabia because the price of oil would go as high as twenty-five dollars per barrel, and the "road map to peace between Israel and Palestine will fail." They couldn't put pressure on Pakistan because Pakistan had an atomic bomb and the moderate civilian government could fall to the hands of the fundamentalists, which would be very dangerous. And she also said that the United States did not have much leverage with the Emirates.

Well, fast-forward: We have seen the price of oil soar, and we saw the Twin Towers fall. The short-term policy for Afghanistan led to the terrible crimes of 9/11. That cycle is repeating itself today and my people are the victims of the proxy war being fought in Afghanistan. As we say in our language, the people are firewood for the political ambitions of the superpowers.

As time went on, Shuhada's work was complicated by the Taliban's relentless sanctions against the Hazaras. We could not even supply our hospitals and schools. Pashtun colleagues from other NGOs carried supplies for us to Ghazni, and we did plenty of smuggling of the goods we needed, but many Hazaras lost their lives trying to help others. Even our polio vaccine campaign was thwarted by the Taliban. The rule of law was lost in the country; the more violent the group, the more powerful they became.

And yet goodness prevailed among many. One time in June 1998 when I was checking on projects in Ghor, we saw a very poor man standing on the road with his hand raised to us. We stopped the car and heard him ask, "Is Sima Samar there?" I said yes. He told me his story. "I have only one child, a girl, ten years old. Please take her and educate her." I was emotionally shaken by his action and his words. A person who had never seen me before trusted me to give his only child an education. I knew I could not take her with me because I was flying on a UN plane to Pakistan, so I told the Shuhada staff who were with me to bring her to Quetta by road when they came later. Sadly, Bamiyan and Ghor were taken by the Taliban, and we couldn't locate that man; his hope for his daughter was lost, and my promise never became a reality.

In September 1998, they took Bamiyan, but the fight continued in other districts. In January 2001 the Taliban was responsible for a massacre of Hazara civilians in Yakawlang. Three of the Shuhada hospital staff there were killed, the building was bombed, and the equipment was looted. In exceptionally frigid winter weather, families fled into the snow-packed mountains. Some were so exhausted from carrying the very young and elderly that they wrapped them in shawls and blankets and tried sliding them down the mountains, hoping they could catch up with them at the bottom. Many died. The survivors had no choice but to leave their family members under the snow, knowing they'd be eaten by wolves. By the time

they staggered into Quetta they had lost their homes, their liveli-
hoods and, in so many cases, their loved ones.

The brutality had been unrelenting for five long and agonizing
years. And then, on a bright and sunlit morning, four planes took
off from American airports. It was September 11, 2001.

In grade 10 at Lashkar Gah High School (front row, fifth from left), 1973

At Kabul University Medical School
(on the right), 1978

The ruins of the Kabul Museum,
destroyed during the Civil War, 1993

Scrubbing for
surgery at the
Shuhada Clinic
in Quetta, 1997

Showing the results
of the surgery to the
patient's family, as
required culturally

Writing a prescription
for the mother of a
newborn baby (© 2001
Courtesy of Olivia
Heussler, Zürich)

In the office of US Secretary of State Madeleine Albright. From left to right: Jennifer Jackman, Mavis Leno, Secretary Albright, Eleanor Smeal, me; 2000

With General Fahim Qasimi, President Hamid Karzai and Mohammad Mohaqiq during the inauguration of the Afghan Interim Administration in 2001

Meeting with Senator Joe Biden, chair of the US Senate Foreign Relations Committee during the time I was Minister of Women's Affairs, 2002 (Photo by Paula Bronstein/ Getty Images)

At the emergency loya jirga when I was deputy chair, 2002

Proud of my students at a computer course in Kabul in 2002—they were paving the way to the future

With my students in Dikundi in 2003; their enthusiasm filled me with hope

The inauguration of the AIHRC office in Herat with the UN's Special Representative Lakhdar Brahimi, 2003

The presentation of the *Call for Justice* report with UN Special Representative Jean Arnault, me, UN High Commissioner for Human Rights Louise Arbour and President Karzai; 2004

At the White House prior to the State of the Union speech. From left to right: President Karzai, President George Bush, me, First Lady Laura Bush, Foreign Minister Abdullah Abdullah; 2002 (Photo by Eric Draper, courtesy of the George W. Bush Presidential Library)

Receiving an honorary
Doctor of Law Degree at
Brown University, 2005

Meeting with civil
society leaders in
South Sudan, 2008

Cutting a ribbon
at the opening of
the Shuhada Clinic
in Bamiyan with
Vreni Frauenfelder,
2009

Receiving the Ramon Magsaysay
Award, from H. E. Fidel V. Ramos,
President of the Philippines, 1994
(Photo from the Ramon Magsaysay
Award Foundation archives)

Receiving the Profile in Courage
Award from Caroline Kennedy and
Senator Ted Kennedy, 2004 (Photo
by John Wilcox, courtesy of the
John F. Kennedy Library Foundation)

Receiving the Geuzen Medal,
accompanied by Rauf Naveed,
and being congratulated by
Prince Willem-Alexander of
the Netherlands, 2011

Receiving the Right Livelihood
Award—also known as the Alternative
Nobel—from Monika Griefan and
Jakob von Uexkull, 2012 (Photo
by Wolfgang Schmidt, courtesy of
Right Livelihood)

Meeting with members of the provincial council in Uruzgan, 2012

One of the joys in my life was addressing the shining young students at the schools.

With Australian Foreign Minister Julie Bishop in Brisbane, Australia, at a conference on international law, 2017

Accompanied by Ahmad Ali Yaqubi at the internally displaced persons camp in Herat, 2020

Six

ACCUSED

ON THE AFTERNOON OF SEPTEMBER 9, 2001, two journalists went to the city of Taloqan to interview Ahmad Shah Massoud, the mujahideen leader of the Northern Alliance that held 5 to 10 percent of the country. The pair activated a bomb hidden in their camera, killing Massoud—it was the first suicide bombing in Afghanistan. Some analysts believe Massoud's death, ordered by Osama bin Laden himself, set the stage for what would follow.

It was just before suppertime in Quetta on September 11 when we learned what was happening in the United States. Four planes had been hijacked by terrorists: two had flown into the famous Twin Towers in New York, another hit the Pentagon, and the fourth plane crashed into a field in Pennsylvania when the courageous passengers overtook the hijackers. Nineteen hijackers had committed murder-suicide, killing 2,996 people and injuring more than 6,000.

Like others the world over, my family and I followed the aftermath with immense sorrow and also disbelief that this could have happened, especially on US soil. Soon after, the truth came out and the president of the United States, George W. Bush, demanded that the Taliban hand over Osama bin Laden, who was said to be the mastermind of the attack. Of course the Taliban refused. We all waited for the reaction: What would President Bush do, and how would it affect us?

Every day we waited for the American response. We listened to the news 24/7 and worried about ordinary Afghans who had already suffered so much under the Taliban; we wondered how we would keep them safe now.

Just twenty-six days later, on October 7, we were watching the 8 p.m. news when we saw footage of the first bombs landing in provinces that were known to be Taliban strongholds, places where Al Qaeda had its training camps. The destruction was extraordinary, and the fear created in ordinary people—the women, the children, the elderly, the innocents who had already been deprived, beaten and threatened by the ruling Taliban—was heartbreaking.

I was still living as a refugee in Quetta at the time, but that didn't keep me out of the fray. As soon as the US bombings started in Afghanistan, the security forces in Pakistan went into high gear—restricting movement, putting up checkpoints and trying to keep the journalists already in the city blocked from leaving the Serena Hotel, where they were staying. It felt like the entire city was under siege.

The aftermath of 9/11 in Afghanistan was startling. The Taliban were scuttling across the border into Pakistan, shaving off their long, scraggly beards; some were even hiding themselves under the burkas they had forced women to wear. Because the United States had acted on NATO's Article 5 when they launched the military intervention—when one of the allied nations is attacked, it is considered an attack on all—the world arrived on our doorstep in the form of soldiers. First there were the airstrikes from the United States and the United Kingdom; then Australia, Canada, France, Germany, Norway and others joined in an operation called Enduring Freedom. Although the US military had been on the ground since a few days after 9/11, soldiers from a total of forty-nine nations eventually took part in the International Security Assistance Force, which came under the command of NATO in 2003.

The Taliban was no match for the onslaught. As soon as they surrendered on December 9, 2001, diplomats and policy professionals and humanitarians in their thousands poured into the country with plans and equipment and funds to help rebuild everything from education and health care systems to infrastructure and governance.

In those early weeks I did dozens of interviews with journalists flooding into Quetta. For a while it felt like a game of cat and mouse we were all playing with the Pakistani police. They wouldn't let the journalists out of the hotel, but I wanted the true story to get out to the world. So when Tristana Moore from the BBC's Channel 4 and Elaine Lafferty from the *Irish Times* called me on the first evening of airstrikes and asked if I could assist them, I told them I would meet them in the lobby of the Serena Hotel. We decided that one of them would come with me in the car and the other one would jump from the wall behind the hotel and we would pick her up from the other side. I brought them to my house so they could file reports on the situation in Quetta, where there were violent demonstrations against the United States by Pakistani religious leaders and madrassa students as well as some Afghans who were supporting the Taliban.

I had been invited to speak at a conference in Germany and decided to go. By now I was receiving speaking requests from cities around the world in support of the women in my country. I turned down a request from the UN asking me to come to New York since I was eager to be back in Quetta.

Suddenly, American attention was lasered on Afghanistan. While women's rights had previously been overlooked out of supposed respect for the Afghan culture and religion, now those same rights were a crucial tool that the US government could use to garner national support for an intervention to oust the Taliban from power. The periwinkle-blue burka became a flashpoint in the Western media; those images depicted the brutality of the Taliban and created a groundswell of support around the world.

The White House came on board, with President Bush claiming in speeches that the "people of Afghanistan have suffered under one of the most brutal regimes . . . in modern history; a regime allied with terrorists and a regime at war with women," and that American "responsibilities to the people of Afghanistan have not ended. We work for a new era of human rights and human dignity in that country."

His wife, Laura Bush, addressed the issue of women's rights within Afghanistan on November 17, 2001. In describing the oppression of Afghan women, she said, "Civilized people throughout the world are speaking out in horror, not only because our hearts break for the women and children in Afghanistan but also because, in Afghanistan, we see the world the terrorists would like to impose on the rest of us." Following her speech, the UK prime minister's wife, attorney Cherie Blair, along with members of parliament and cabinet ministers, made a similar plea on behalf of

Afghan women, claiming, "The women in Afghanistan are entitled, as the women in every country are, to have the same hopes
and aspirations as ourselves and our daughters."

I'd been hoping for this kind of worldwide response ever since
the mujahideen had started to restrict the rights and freedom of
women, first as a means to fight the USSR and then as a way to har-
ness their own power. Now the brutal treatment that Afghan
women had endured was being revealed on television reports
and in publications around the world. A video of a woman being
killed with a bullet to the head surfaced; years later *Time* magazine
featured more chilling proof of what we all knew about brutality:
a photo of a young woman whose ears and nose had been cut off.

Once the international community arrived, Chicken Street in
Kabul became a tourist attraction. Restaurants flourished, as did
businesses. New institutions, governance styles and banks were
booming. Those were life-altering days for a country that had been
under Soviet occupation and the wrath of the mujahideen and
the punishment of the merciless Taliban for twenty-three years.
Change was in the wind, and it looked like the sky was the limit.

At the end of November, the World Bank organized a three-day
conference on the reconstruction of Afghanistan at the Marriott
Hotel in Islamabad. They invited most of the Western countries
and the UN agencies as well as national and international NGOs to
discuss a plan for rebuilding the country. I felt that *reconstruction* was
not the right word; Afghanistan had never been well constructed,
and whatever basic infrastructure we had had been destroyed by
many years of war.

There was also a major conference in Bonn, Germany, around
the same time, to work on a roadmap for the new Afghanistan, to

select a leader of the interim government and to establish the International Security Assistance Force. I had been invited but was unable to go, having flown to Canada to receive the John Humphrey Freedom Award, named for the Canadian lawyer who wrote the first draft of the Universal Declaration of Human Rights.

I kept abreast of the Bonn conference details and the events at home while traveling to cities across Canada to speak about the situation and particularly about the women of Afghanistan. I was also on the receiving end of a media blitz, since the invasion of the country was headline news everywhere: the Taliban was considered defeated; Osama bin Laden had escaped and was presumed to be hiding in the mountainous region of Tora Bora in the east of the country. Afghan militias from nearby Jalalabad and the American Special Forces conducted a lengthy operation to find him. Later, the world learned that he was in Pakistan.

In Canada, a bright young woman called Isabelle Solon Helal from Rights & Democracy, the NGO that presented the award, accompanied me across the country. We were in British Columbia on December 5 and had an early morning flight to Edmonton, Alberta, for another event, so when my phone rang at 4:30 a.m., I presumed it was a wakeup call. Instead, it was my son, Ali, who by then was a student in Texas. I had that heart-stopping moment when a family member phones you so early in the morning and immediately thought he must be calling with bad news about my elderly mother in Quetta. I asked him what was wrong. He laughed and said, "Not to worry. I'm calling because I just heard on the BBC and also on CNN that you are in the cabinet of the new government: You are the vice president for President Hamid Karzai and minister for women's affairs."

I could hardly believe my ears, so I turned on the TV for news, and there it was: the leaders in Bonn had agreed on an interim government and distributed positions to different ethnic groups and political parties, including to many mujahideen commanders. And I saw my own name come up again and again.

I took a hot shower to wake myself up, and then called Rauf in Quetta to see if the news was really true. He said that the UN had already contacted him to see where I was. There were crowds of people outside our house showing their support for me.

When I got to the hotel lobby, I filled Isabelle in. She made the observation that it wouldn't be an easy job. We had been hearing that some of the participants at the Bonn meeting had argued that war criminals and those accused of crimes against humanity and gross violations of human rights should be excluded from the transitional government. But that recommendation had never made it to the final document that was signed on December 5, and it worried me. The mujahideen leaders and other tribal leaders were not interested in justice or accountability. Their main goal was to divvy up the spoils of war for themselves.

I was weighing these issues and considering my next steps on my way to the airport. By the time the flight took off I knew I would accept; otherwise, my opponents would accuse me of shouting about the rights of women without taking responsibility for them. By the time the plane landed in Edmonton, the gravity of all of it hit home; as we taxied up to the gate I heard an announcement: "Dr. Sima Samar, please identify yourself to the crew." Isabelle and I were taken to the front of the plane, where protocol officers from the Canadian government were waiting to assist me as a member of the government of Afghanistan. As we walked with them they asked for our luggage tags, fetched our bags and took us to an official car headed to the hotel.

We had several meetings all over the city that day, so I didn't get back to the hotel until late that night. As if the VIP treatment at the airport hadn't been unusual enough, the clerk at the reception told me that my room had been changed to a suite. When I got there, two men in black suits were standing on either side of the door. I stopped in my tracks, automatically thinking something was wrong. Then one of them said, "We're here for your security. We won't bother you and no one else will either." It was the Royal Canadian Mounted Police, and they would be at my side for the rest of the tour. I knew what it was like to have people harassing me when I spoke. Now I had officers protecting me. The change in circumstances was so enormous I could hardly contemplate it all. Sleep evaded me that night as I pondered all that had happened and what was coming at me.

The Canadian tour continued and I began to understand how celebrities feel: every event was packed with people, standing room only, and my speeches made the front page of the newspapers and sometimes led the evening news. At one event at the University of Toronto, someone asked, "What would you do if the mujahideen tried to implement the Sharia law?" I replied that I did not believe in the Taliban interpretation of Sharia law. I did not think much of it at the time, but this remark would come back to haunt me.

Those were heady days in Canada. I met Prime Minister Jean Chrétien and was introduced to the members of Parliament in the House of Commons. I was moved to my core when those men and women stood up to pay respect to me and the women in my country.

The next stop on my trip was the United States and a meeting with Secretary of State Colin Powell and his undersecretary, Paula Dobriansky. I told Powell that the cabinet that had been put together in Bonn was a collection of powerful commanders, each with its own militia. I also said, "I am a woman, a member of a minority ethnic group, and I'm on my own when it comes to protection. Who is going to guarantee my security?"

He said that as the first Black secretary of state in the United States, he could understand my situation. Then he explained there would be international forces in Kabul before the government was even installed. I also shared with him my view that the United States had supported the most conservative groups in Afghanistan during their Cold War fight against the USSR, and that the Taliban was the product of that support. Then I told him four things we needed from his government:

1. That Afghanistan not be abandoned as it was after the fall of the pro-USSR government in 1992.
2. That the same amount of money be spent on reconstruction and job creation as had been spent on bombing the country.
3. That women's empowerment programs be supported seriously, and focus put on education as a strong tool to change the mentality in our society.
4. That more females be assigned to the US embassy and that female soldiers be sent to the country so our people could see women capably handling those roles.

His response to my requests was straightforward: the United States would not abandon Afghanistan; the same mistakes would not be repeated. He said he would try his best to send more women to Afghanistan and mentioned that the Afghan foreign minister had said in an interview that Afghanistan did not need soldiers from Western countries. I told him that Afghans had experienced disrespect and hardship from foreign soldiers in the past and we needed assurance that our people, especially our women, would be respected this time. I believed he was sincere and I was hopeful that the Americans would not repeat past mistakes.

The women I had been collaborating with began to worry about my security. Ariane Brunet from the NGO Urgent Action Fund said her organization would buy me a satellite phone, which was very new at the time and also very expensive to use—US$3 per minute. The Feminist Majority Foundation said they'd pick up the phone fee.

My original plan had been to spend the rest of December with my son, four brothers and one sister who were all in Dallas. But that would no longer be possible, so Ali came to see me in Washington, DC. He offered to come home with me to help in this gargantuan task I'd been given, but I said no; it was more important for him to complete his university studies. On December 17, I went back to Quetta, where literally thousands of Afghans turned up at the airport to greet me. There was a sense of overwhelming hope for the future of our country, and seeing the people's happiness filled me with the courage needed to get ready for another adventure.

Two days later, a UN plane took me to Kabul. My brother Ahmad Ali Yaqubi and General Muslim Hamed, plus a bodyguard and driver, went ahead of me. As we were landing, I looked out over the hills surrounding Kabul, the muddy houses on the out-skirts and the city close to the airport. I thought of all the refugees who had been displaced in twenty-three years of war, all those who had been lost, I thought about Ghafoor. By the time we landed and I walked down the steps to the tarmac, my eyes were brimming with tears—even though my heart was full of promise.

We rented a house in Wazir Akbar Khan and had to furnish it with everything from saltshakers and spoons to mattresses and quilts. Kabul was cold; heating equipment was scarce. Everyone was searching for what they needed to survive during those early days. Two days after we arrived, Elaine Lafferty, the American journalist I had helped in Quetta, came to my house and asked if I had seen anyone from the government. All the other cabinet ministers were housed at the Hotel Intercontinental. I'd been contacted about staying there but felt I'd be better off in my own house. When I told her I had not only not seen anyone but also didn't even know the new president, Hamid Karzai, she gave me his satellite phone number. When I called the president he picked up the phone himself. I said, "I am Sima Samar, one of your ministers." He asked me to come to the palace at 8 a.m. the next day; we would go together to the inauguration.

The task in front of me was enormous: I would need to navigate ancient customs, brutal tribal disputes and militant politicized mullahs clinging stubbornly to their record of human rights abuses. There was no working infrastructure, not even enough electricity in the capital. People were starving; there was a measles epidemic and wild polio virus was out of control. The girls' schools had been closed for five years and the few health clinics and hospitals still operating were damaged. We had been given a six-month interim term in the Bonn Agreement. It felt like we were trying to turn around the *Titanic*.

The next morning, when I went to the palace, I was greeted by the president's brother Qayum Karzai at the gate—we'd actually met before, at his restaurant in Maryland in 2000. On this crisp morning I suggested that he ask his brother not to wear the traditional Afghan dress because shalwar kameez was a Pakistani style and the Afghan men and women were wearing suits at the office. He grinned at my suggestion and said, "He is wearing chapan [an Afghan coat]—you can tell him yourself."

Once inside, I saw that President Karzai was reading his speech for the transfer of power from Burhanuddin Rabbani, who had been the president in exile in Tajikistan after the Taliban took over Kabul in 1996. After we'd exchanged a few customary pleasantries, I brought up the matter that was on my mind and asked him to please wear a business suit to the swearing-in ceremony. He replied, politely but firmly, "I will not." While we were talking, President Rabbani came into the room, so I stopped arguing with Karzai about his wardrobe.

What a day. The swearing-in was held in an auditorium at the Ministry of Interior. It was very encouraging to see the auditorium full of representatives from countries around the world and all the UN agencies. If hope and optimism could be measured in facial expressions, the smiles and sparkling eyes in the room that day would have guaranteed our success—although I was disappointed to see how few women were represented. Sitting with me in the front row were some people who thought they owned the country and the lives of Afghans; I did wonder if I was a suitable choice for this team. I knew I would need to prove to them that a woman could do the job as well as they could.

I turned my thoughts to the new foundation for Afghanistan in the aftermath of war and to healing the wounds of the people. The suffering was over; the killing and bloodshed had stopped. Mind you, the poverty—even there, in the richest neighborhood of Kabul—was shocking: the children barefoot, their wounds and scars evidence of deprivation and the brutal past. But while their faces showed their malnourishment, their eyes glimmered with hope for a better future.

As Minister of Women's Affairs, I started with nothing: no office or budget or staff. In fact, when I finally got an office, I brought in some of the women we had trained in computers and English at Shuhada Organization in Pakistan. Delegations were arriving from all over the world to meet the deputy to the chair of the interim government in a country where women had been invisible for so many years. I needed people who were computer literate and could speak to our guests in their own language.

When Colin Powell came to Afghanistan in January 2002 and President Karzai introduced us, Powell grinned and said, "I already know her. She gave me a hard time in Washington." The Russian foreign minister, Sergey Lavrov, came as well, and invited us to make an official visit to Moscow. I was also receiving a great many Afghans from different sectors of society, showing their support and high hopes for a better future.

I had to take most of these early meetings at the Presidential Palace, as I couldn't even offer these dignitaries a cup of tea, as is our custom—not only did I not have an office, but I also didn't have any cups. One memorable visit was with Madam Sadako Ogata from Japan, who was by then Japan's Special Representative for Afghanistan. When she arrived, it was so cold in the room that we found a locally made diesel heater to ward off the chill—but the room filled with smoke. Once I'd managed to air it out, I asked Madam Ogata to have a seat. As soon as she sat down on the couch, which had been left by the former owner, it broke underneath her. I was so ashamed and kept apologizing, although she was very gracious and understanding of the circumstances. I found a chair for her, pulled myself together and sputtered out the plans I had for the ministry and for the women in my country. She promised her country's support, and Japan did contribute a lot; however, the level of support for women ended up being below my expectations.

The other issue that confounded me were the policies of the countries coming to help us rebuild; their approach was not based on the needs of people and did not fully take into account the complexity of our situation. As such, the policies were superficial and easily broken; each country conducted its own program rather than establishing cooperation and coordination with the other donor countries. The issues the government and the world community faced were enormous: no money in the banks (the Taliban had taken it with them when they ran away) and no functional systems and infrastructures in the cities (they'd been demolished). The people in charge were the ones who arrived first, not the ones qualified to do the jobs.

One evening I was called by Karzai's office to go to the palace and join the delegation traveling to Bagram Airport north of Kabul to meet UK prime minister Tony Blair's plane, which was arriving at midnight. It was bitterly cold and snowing when we set out. The huge military plane arrived just after midnight, and the president's entourage met with Mr. Blair in one tent while I was sent to meet with his wife, Cherie, in another tent. I pressed my case for women, asking for help with education at all levels, access to health care and, in particular, access to reproductive health, including access to contraception. I also asked her to help us with job opportunities that would lead to economic independence from the male members of the family. She promised me that her husband's government would deliver on every count. Two hours later their plane left and our delegation drove back to Kabul before dawn.

As I watched the snow swirling around the windows of the car it reminded me of the circling problems I was having difficulty solving—finding an appropriate office was one of them. There was a building in Kabul that had been previously used by the prime minister before the mujahideen and the Taliban took over. President Karzai had assigned offices in that building to his five vice-chairs; the four men took the biggest offices and left the smallest one for me. However, I decided it didn't suit me—mostly because this was the very building I used to come to when I was searching for information about Ghafoor. And also because I would be one of the only women in the whole building. I decided to find another location from which to launch my dream for the Ministry of Women's Affairs.

I was still working on that plan when President George Bush invited President Karzai and some of us ministers to Washington to be introduced at the State of the Union address in January 2002. That experience was an eye-opener to the corridors of power.

President Karzai, Foreign Affairs Minister Dr. Abdullah Abdullah and I were driven in separate vehicles to Blair House, the official guest house for the president. The next morning, we met with President Bush in the famous Oval Office; he said he was very proud that the Taliban had been defeated and especially proud of me for being in the cabinet as a woman in a difficult environment. He also told us that the Afghan American Zalmay Khalilzad of the National Security Council had his ear, confiding, "After Laura Bush, Khalilzad has the most access to me. Here in this country whoever has access to the president holds power as well." Later, Khalilzad would be appointed US Special Representative and ambassador for Afghanistan. It was a lesson to me about power—one I keenly remembered years later when Khalilzad became the negotiator for Donald Trump and basically declared the Taliban the winner of the war.

We were invited to lunch by Vice President Dick Cheney, had meetings with Colin Powell and Secretary of Defense Donald Rumsfeld, the Congress and the women's caucus, and then I met privately with Paula Dobriansky to discuss the establishment of the US–Afghan Women's Council.

On January 29, the protocol officer took President Karzai and me to the White House ahead of the State of the Union address. While we were there, Laura Bush complimented Karzai on his Afghan traditional coat, and he immediately said, "Dr. Sima fought with me and told me not to wear it." We all shared a laugh at my failure to influence Karzai's style choices.

President Karzai and I were driven together with President Bush and the First Lady in the presidential limousine to Capitol Hill for the State of the Union address and escorted to reserved seats next to a few American soldiers who had been injured in

Afghanistan. When President Bush mentioned our names, we both stood up—which he'd asked us to do earlier—and everyone in the room rose to their feet and applauded us. As I stood there, my scarf slipped off my head and fell onto my shoulders; I didn't even notice it in the moment, but since the State of the Union address was being broadcast live, I realized later that this faux pas could cause trouble for me.

The next morning, we were taken to the airport for a short flight to New York and, sure enough, as soon as the plane took off, my scarf transgression came up. Dr. Abdullah said to President Karzai, "I could not sleep last night because our trip will have the same consequence as Amanullah Khan's trip to the West." I wanted to groan at this dramatic comparison. Amanullah Khan, who was the king of Afghanistan from 1919 to 1929, had traveled with his wife, Queen Soraya, to Europe one time, and the queen was without hijab. After his return from Europe, the mullah announced that Amanullah Khan was an infidel. The conservative agents started a war against Khan and forced him leave the country.

As if the two instances had not happened eighty years apart, Abdullah continued his mournful oration, saying, "This time it was Sima who did not have her scarf on her head." Furious with this sophomoric remark, I threw my scarf on the floor of the plane and told him if everything in Afghanistan depended on my scarf, we were overlooking some very serious problems. Karzai interfered and stopped us from fighting. It was a profoundly discouraging example of the mentality I was dealing with as we embarked on creating a new Afghanistan.

While we were in New York, the Afghan delegation met with Khalilzad. At the end of our meeting, he told me that an Austrian journalist wanted to meet me and asked if I would see her. I said yes, of course. A little later, the journalist approached me and introduced herself as Cheryl Benard, and we talked for a while; then she asked me to come to Austria the next month for the launch of her book about Afghan women, and I ended up attending. Two years later, I discovered Benard was Khalilzad's wife; no one had mentioned that little fact to me. I didn't like her book about the Afghan women and, moreover, I was furious that no one had told me the truth. I'd been used by both of them.

Shady deals and backstabbing were ever-present even as we began to rebuild our shattered country. For example, in early March 2002, just as we began to govern, I was called to an emergency meeting at the palace. The aviation minister, Dr. Abdul Rahman, had been murdered at the airport before his plane took off. His naked body had been thrown out of the plane onto the tarmac.

In the aftermath of the incident, at a cabinet meeting, a totally bizarre collection of explanations and excuses were put forward. One cabinet minister claimed the people at the airport were on their way to Mecca for the hajj and felt the minister was holding up their departure, so while the plane was taxiing down the runway, they killed him. Huh? How did they get inside the plane? How was any of this possible? As each different scenario was proposed, I asked questions that were clearly unwelcome.

And at the end of it all: a whitewash. A man was dead, and there were witnesses, but no one was held accountable. The majority of the cabinet members agreed to look the other way.

This was not the only incident of killing a minister in broad daylight in Kabul. But it was the first high-level execution during the post-Taliban government. As injustice continued on different levels, impunity became the culture.

I tried to concentrate on my goals and projects. Among these was to get a building for the Ministry of Women's Affairs. The building I wanted was where the women's association had been situated before the war began. Now it was occupied by the Ministry of Social Affairs and the minister was Ismail Khan's son, Mirwais Sadiq. It took some lobbying, but by mid-February I got the building back—a bombed-out wreck with broken windows and only a single working office. (The staff of the ministry were so angry with me for getting that place, they even took the electrical outlets with them when they left.) There was a famous cinema called Zainab on the grounds, the only one in the country named for a woman. Even though it was badly burned and filled with debris and dirt, I decided that the cinema would be where we would celebrate International Women's Day on March 8. We had to hurry to clean it up so we could welcome all the women to begin our journey together.

Help came from a variety of sources: the United Nations Development Programme (UNDP) donated a vehicle, and as I was deputy chair of the interim government, they also gave me a computer, desk, chair and satellite phone; we moved in immediately. One of my first visitors at the office was a Swedish woman who was working as a human rights officer at the EU headquarters in Kabul. The meeting went well, but half an hour after it was over, she returned carrying two electric heaters. "Sima," she said, "it's so cold in here you're going to get sick." I had to tell her we didn't have electricity or even the electrical outlets to plug the heaters in. When the American Chargé d'affaires Ryan Crocker arrived to give us

$9,000 to clear and clean the cinema, I didn't even have a second chair for him to sit on. I asked Muslim Hamed to go to the market and find something; he came back with folding plastic beach chairs. Soon after, NGOs and UN agencies turned up with more furnishings.

Just days before the March 8 event, I was at a meeting at the palace and Karzai's advisor Dr. Ashraf Ghani asked me if I was going to write the speech the president would deliver at the event. Put off, I replied that I was not his secretary. Lakhdar Brahimi, the UN special representative of the Secretary-General, who had been walking beside me, asked me what the issue was. He kindly said to me "I am not the secretary for Kofi Annan, but if I want him to say what I feel needs to be said, I write his speech. You should also do it and let the president spread your message." I took this excellent advice to heart, and walked over to Ghani immediately to say that I would write the speech after all.

At last, March 8 dawned. Even though the building didn't yet have a roof, we celebrated International Women's Day at the Zainab Cinema. Mary Robinson, the UN high commissioner for human rights; Noeleen Heyzer, the executive director of the United Nations Development Fund for Women; Chandni Joshi, the regional director of the United Nations Population Fund; a female minister from the federal government of Pakistan; and all of the diplomatic community as well as eight hundred people, mainly women, participated. It was a cold day, but the people who came and the joy they displayed filled the theater with warmth and promise. At the end of the program we released three white pigeons to symbolize freedom. On that peace-affirming day, I could never have imagined that our freedom and rights would be denied again twenty years later.

Although our office was basically funded by donations, we did get a surprise windfall from President Karzai when he came back from a meeting in the Emirates with a suitcase full of cash—US$1.8 million. I asked for $100,000 for the Ministry of Women's Affairs; he said we could have $20,000. He made sure to invite all the local and international media to his office to announce his largesse—it was the only money ever given by the government to the ministry while I was there. The rest came from donors and women's groups around the world.

A friend of mine, Jennifer Jackman from the Feminist Majority Foundation in the United States, came to help me make a strategic plan for the ministry. We started programs for women—English classes and computer training for the staff, a school for married women, a tailoring and handcraft center. Then we launched our strategic plan to establish a ministry presence in every province.

Symbolically, it was a good move for the Bonn Agreement to create a first-ever Ministry for Women in Afghanistan, but I knew women's issues and rights needed to crosscut every ministry. For example, in the discussion about the returning Afghan refugees from Pakistan and Iran, a special commission was called. When I said the commission required a representative from the Ministry of Women's Affairs, another cabinet minister argued and asked why. I explained that it was because 75 percent of the returnees were women and children, and it was our job to know their needs.

The day after our grand celebration of International Women's Day, Lakhdar Brahimi asked me to chair a meeting on human rights that he and Mary Robinson would be attending. As moderator I spoke first, followed by President Karzai. To my astonishment, he mentioned the need for a Truth and Reconciliation Commission to deal with the crimes that had been committed. Unfortunately, that was the first and last time he ever brought up the subject. Mary Robinson and Lakhdar Brahimi also spoke on the importance of human rights for sustainable peace and democracy.

At the end of the event, Robinson and Brahimi announced that I was to be the government leader responsible for establishing a national institution for human rights. Although I said that I was very busy and couldn't make time for this new task, it was a fait accompli in their minds. In fact, this announcement marked the establishment of the National Institution for Human rights, the creation of which had been part of the Bonn Agreement.

It took four more workshops to draft the broad details and the fine print of the Human Rights Commission, which had to be announced before the start of the emergency loya jirga—or grand assembly—being held between the 10th and 19th of June 2002, just three months away. With close consultation, Brahimi and I selected eleven commissioners, four of them women, and presented the blueprint of the commission to the president so he could announce the establishment of the Afghanistan Independent Human Rights Commission. It was written according to the Paris Principles, which had been approved by the UN General Assembly in 1993 and served as a recognized guide for the creation of national institutions such as ours; one of their main conditions was independence from the government.

Later that month, we were invited to travel to Moscow and Germany. I was reluctant to go to Moscow; the Soviet invasion of Afghanistan lingered with me, and I felt it had been the start of all the problems we continued to struggle with. But Karzai insisted I accompany the delegation, and it ended up being an experience that revealed much about the way power is used and abused. In Russia, President Vladimir Putin did not make eye contact with our delegation. He addressed his remarks looking at the table in front of him, hardly raising his head to see us. Moreover, we were never certain whether the translator was telling him what we were saying or, rather, what he wanted to hear. He said he had supported the resistance against the terrorists groups for twelve years, even though the Taliban had not been in existence for twelve years. It is interesting to note that Putin later became a supporter of the Taliban.

I had a private meeting with a senior member of the Putin government. When I told her how important it was for us to support education and then requested scholarships for the Afghan girls, she said, "Afghan girls are so pretty. When they come here they will soon find boyfriends, and how will their conservative families react then?" Her views made me want to shout at her, but instead I replied, "Yes, they are beautiful, and also strong enough to make their own way in life."

Next stop, Germany. On the plane, Dr. Abdullah, who was part of the president's delegation, said, "We are all Kandaharis [a reference to the people who live in Kandahar, mainly Pashtuns] except Sima Jaan." An interesting comment, I thought. I noted the nicety of tacking "Jaan" onto my name, which is used as a common courtesy of respect for friends in our language. I was also the only woman and person of a different ethnicity on this plane—a private jet the German chancellor had sent for us.

We were very well received in Germany, first by the president and then at a luncheon hosted by the chancellor, Gerhard Schröder. In his remarks, President Karzai said, "The people of Afghanistan have a lot of sympathy with Germany, and even during World War II,

Afghans were listening to the news and praying for the victory of Germany." I was surprised by what I was hearing. Chancellor Schröder put his utensils down, paused for a few seconds, and then told our president, "We the German people are not proud of our actions during World War II; in fact, we are ashamed of that part of our history." Afterward, I asked the president why he'd made the statement; he replied that it was the truth. I told him there are certain truths you don't have to mention out loud.

At the end of the visit, when the rest of the delegation went back to Kabul, I traveled to Greece, where I met with the minister of foreign affairs and with a lot of women, including the marvelous Margarita Papandreou, the American-born wife of Prime Minister Andreas Papandreou. She was the famous women's rights activist who once said, "I never dreamed of being the wife of the prime minister of Greece, I dreamed I would be the prime minister of Greece." I was inspired by her dedication to gender equality and promotion of women's rights not only in Greece but worldwide.

Back in Kabul, on top of my other work, I had to monitor the election of the delegation for the emergency loya jirga and to fight for women's participation in it. The commission was traveling to different parts of the country to help local communities elect representatives. I went with the UN team to Bamiyan to observe the election, and also to Qarabagh and Jaghori. A fascinating part of this experience was to discover that the mujahideen leaders were not brave enough to stand for election, which spoke loudly about how they were viewed by the people.

In April 2002 I traveled again to Washington, to receive an award from the International Human Rights Law Group. While there, I had a private meeting with Condoleezza Rice, the national security advisor. Regarding the United States' policies and the establishment of provincial reconstruction teams (PRTs), I suggested that rather than focusing on military security, they put their efforts into labor-intensive projects to provide job opportunities. I also begged her government not to invade Iraq. My theory was this: Building a democratic regime in Afghanistan—promoting women's rights and establishing accountability and justice for war crimes and crimes against humanity—would provide the world with a good example of how to build a people's capacity to promote democracy. Whereas if the United States were to invade Iraq, they would provide more opportunities to fundamentalist groups looking to recruit aimless and unemployed Muslim youth.

Rice's response was that PRTs would be a success story, just as the military intervention in Afghanistan had been. On Iraq, she told me that Saddam Hussein was producing weapons of mass destruction, and she did not think that stopping him would lead to an increase in fundamentalism and terrorist activities.

Next, I traveled to New York to speak at the UN's Security Council. I also met with Secretary-General Kofi Annan, along with the Afghan ambassador, Ravan Farhadi. Again, I raised the issues of accountability, ending the culture of impunity, and the need to fight against the production of opium. Back in Afghanistan, at a cabinet meeting, Foreign Minister Dr. Abdullah made a pointed remark about people who go out and speak against the mujahideen and members of the cabinet. I could tell that Ambassador Farhadi had reported what I'd said to Kofi Annan to Dr. Abdullah, twisting my words in the process. I ignored the remark, but it reinforced my understanding of the fact that there were enemies all around.

———

The emergency loya jirga, which was prescribed by the Bonn Agreement, began a day late, on June 11; the gathering was to run for three to five days, but actually continued until June 19. This was a very important assembly, a test of how people would come together to pave the road ahead. But from the election of delegates to the intimidation tactics of the warlords to the proceedings themselves, it featured all the intrigue of *Game of Thrones*.

The aim of this gathering was to choose a president and a cabinet as a transitional government to serve for two years, until we had a constitution in place and could hold elections. The name of the former king, Zahir Shah, was put forward, but he declared almost immediately that he would not run. Only three candidates were then considered for transitional president: Hamid Karzai; Massouda Jalal, a female medical doctor; and Mahfuz Fedai, a lecturer at Kabul University.

The chair of the loya jirga was Ismail Qasimyar, a legal and constitutional expert. There were to be sixteen hundred people, including two hundred women—the first time in history that women had attended in such numbers. Since we didn't have a hall big enough to hold all the delegates, the German government built an air-conditioned, carpeted tent on the grounds of the Polytechnic University in Kabul.

President Karzai signed the document that formalized the Afghanistan Independent Human Rights Commission on June 6. Later that day there was a meeting to decide whether to invite the mujahideen leaders to the loya jirga. That's when the violations began. In my opinion, since none of the mujahideen leaders had run for election, none should have been invited. But the majority agreed to invite them. This was the first decision taken against the rules and procedures of the emergency loya jirga. Then they broke another rule by inviting thirty-two governors, none of whom had been elected. Matters only got worse.

During the press conference after the AIHRC announcement, one of the journalists asked about accountability, even for members of the current cabinet. I replied that everyone in any position, including cabinet members, should be held responsible for their actions. At the next day's cabinet meeting, a newspaper called *Arman E Mili* had been placed on the table; the headline read, "Sima Samar says everyone in the cabinet should be brought to justice." No one said anything about it. To me, it felt like a warning.

At the final cabinet meeting of the interim government on the morning of June 10, and prior to the 4 p.m. opening of the loya jirga on the same day, the minister of communication, Abdul Rahim, who belonged to Jamiat-e Islami, commented to me, "You had a very dangerous interview." I assumed he meant the one printed by *Arman E Mili*, but he said no, it had been published by *Sadai Mujahid* ("the voice of the mujahid") and came from Shura-e-Nazar, a group within Jamiat-e Islami. I said, "I stand by my comments. " I did not take what he said seriously.

It was close to 4 p.m., time for the official opening of the loya jirga, when we heard there was trouble at the gate. Mohammad Younus Qanooni, the minister of interior, had arrived with more than fifty heavily armed bodyguards and wanted to enter the Polytechnic. He was stopped by ISAF because it was forbidden to enter with arms, but it took so long to diffuse this very tense situation that the loya jirga opening had to be postponed to the next day, June 11.

When I arrived the next morning, I saw that *Sadai Mujahid* had altered an article published in Canada by *Shahrvand* ("Ctizen") six months earlier and distributed the paper among the delegates. The headline read: "Sima Samar Does Not Believe in Sharia Law." *Sadai Mujahid* had edited the story. In fact, what I'd actually said was that I did not believe in the Taliban version of Sharia. Words like that are the kiss of death in my country, but thankfully most people ignored it.

The jirga started and Karzai called the unelected mujahideen leaders to sit in the first row because, he said, they were the ones who'd fought to liberate the country. Of course, after that introduction, each of them insisted on speaking to the gathering. Hamid Karzai won the election as head of the transitional government.

Next, we moved ahead to elect the leadership of the jirga in a secret ballot: the chairperson had already been named; to be elected were two deputy chairs and two secretaries. I had decided to put my name forward for the position of deputy chair just to see where I stood with the delegates.

To my surprise, I won. (What's more, the other people elected were all intellectual and educated; there were no fundamentalists.) When the result was announced, I took my seat on the stage; immediately, a few people started shouting out that I must not be on the leadership team. I thanked those who had voted for me and then told the ten or twelve people protesting that they had used their right to vote, but I'd won fairly, so they didn't have the right to shout at me. I have to admit that I was surprisingly calm in the face of this vocal opposition, which included Afghanistan National Radio and Television, the only national media at that time; it was run, then, by the same person in charge of *Sadai Mujahid*.

On the third morning of the loya jirga, Thomas Ruttig, a German who was working for the United Nations Assistance Mission in Afghanistan (UNAMA), showed me a newspaper with the front-page headline "Sima Samar is the Salman Rushdie of Afghanistan."

Since I'd been named vice-chair of the loya jirga, the fundamentalists had played another menacing card in the power game. They wanted to kill me because I was not a good enough Muslim, or so they said. In fact, they wanted to kill me because I demanded accountability and justice. My other supposed crime was having been photographed without my scarf. These accusations were the basis for their case against me, which was to be taken to the Supreme Court.

These men who saw me as a threat to the status quo in Afghanistan were clearly toiling behind the scenes, seeking ways to discredit and dismiss a woman who was demanding reform. The chief justice at that time, Fazal Hadi Shinwari, an elderly conservative, waited for the chips to fall before deciding whether to send the case to trial. Everyone at the assembly and throughout the diplomatic community in Kabul knew the real issue was the progress I was making for women and girls, including my calls for accountability and justice. But the anti-women warlords made it clear that they would not cooperate with the Karzai government unless he removed me from the cabinet.

Apart from the attacks, there were also moments that spurred me on. At one point I was approached by an elderly Pashtun man who said he had voted for me. "I salute you for what you do and we are going to change our culture in my village," he said. "As you know, we used to fire a gun when a boy was born in the family, but now, watching your behavior, we will fire a gun for girls in my village."

The slander from a small group of naysayers persisted even though there were many other issues to deal with. The interim cabinet ministers from defense, interior and the foreign ministry didn't want to give up their posts to the new transitional appointees; they were adding so much tension to the meetings that the assembly, which had been planned for five days, had to be extended to almost ten. One morning, Nader Nadery, who was working at the loya jirga media center, came to my office at the Ministry of Women's Affairs and said, "Everyone is saying that you have been killed; the news was distributed in a night letter." Half an hour later, a few foreign journalists were interviewing me on the same topic; a day later, the international media had picked up the story. My husband tried to shield my elderly mother from this frightening news. (They were still in Quetta, and everyone was really worried.)

In the meantime, I received a summons from the deputy of the Supreme Court. I went directly to Karzai's office and asked why he was being so quiet while I was under attack. He said he'd talk to the chief judge, but I knew there was more afoot. Lakhdar Brahimi told the ministers that the UN knew about the intimidation and warned them to be very careful of any action they tried to take against me; he reminded them that they had a responsibility to protect me.

The newly established Afghanistan Independent Human Rights Commission was monitoring the loya jirga and, interestingly, the intimidation against me was the first case they documented and shared with the UN. When Canada's foreign minister, Bill Graham, heard about the debacle, he had a visa issued for me and told the UN he would make sure I was welcomed in Canada if they could fly me out of the country. Legions of women from all over the world lined up to support me, and I was offered safe shelter in half a dozen countries. But I knew that leaving during the tumult would be a voyage of no return, so I opted to stay and fight the charges.

The night after the loya jirga, I was awoken by a knock on my door at 1 a.m. It was two people I knew who said, "They are going to kill you tonight. The plan is in place, so please leave the house and go somewhere else." Thirty minutes later, Jean Arnault (Brahimi's deputy) came with an ISAF armored military vehicle and took me into protective custody at the UN guest house. I had been caged not by the Taliban but by the new power brokers, some of whom were members of the government's cabinet.

Karzai summoned me to his office, reminding me to wear my scarf (while in Afghanistan I wore it all the time, although sometimes it fell off my head to my shoulders). Karzai had also asked Chief Justice Shinwari to come and explain the problem his court had with me. Shinwari said, "I don't have a problem, but she should wear her scarf all the time."

I moved immediately with my brother, four bodyguards and two support staff from Shahr-e-Naw to the western part of the city and the neighborhood called Karte Seh where the Hazaras live. A day later, at 8 a.m., the German general from ISAF came to my house and said, "We have credible information that the warlords will kill you, so we want to put our soldiers around your house." I told them that I would not be guarded by foreign forces in my own country. A group of French ISAF soldiers came by and I told them the same thing. By 7:30 p.m., the German general had returned, saying they could not afford the risk of having me killed on their watch. He also mentioned that he'd been to see the three ministers (defense, interior and foreign) to tell them diplomatically that there would be very heavy consequences if they did not use their responsibility to protect me. I realized there was much to fear and I gave in.

For twenty-five days, thirteen to fifteen soldiers and three armored tanks were outside my residence. They installed barbed wire around the perimeter and followed me wherever I went.

On a hot summer day at the end of June, President Karzai called and asked me to come to the palace. Also there were his advisor Ashraf Ghani, the US ambassador, James Dobbins, and Zalmay Khalilzad, all sitting under the shade of the trees in the garden. President Karzai started to talk about people who were very much against me, without mentioning any names. He said I could be the chairperson of the Human Rights Commission, and after a few months he could reinstate me as Minister of Women's Affairs. I could tell he was trying to distance himself from me due to the pressure on him by some members of the government as well as others outside of the government. I told him I would be happy to return to my profession as a medical doctor and that I didn't want to be an obstacle for the new Afghanistan. I wasn't about to beg these men for anything.

There had never been much financial or political support for the Women's Ministry, and the conversation made it clear to me that President Karzai had made a deal and caved into pressure. I was removed from the cabinet; the transitional government took office and the case against me was dropped. When they asked me to chair the Afghanistan Independent Human Rights Commission, I accepted with pleasure, as this was work I wanted to do. At the same meeting, Khalilzad said that I could have the same protocol as a minister, and Karzai agreed with him.

I had seen the threads weaving together that could ultimately destroy the young system we were trying to put in place. Warlords and people accused of war crimes and crimes against humanity were given senior positions. The issue of accountability was not being addressed. When the parliamentary election was held in 2005, some of the previous government and mujahideen commanders who had been accused collectively of killing hundreds of people became members of parliament (including one who was said to be a friend of Osama bin Laden). I wondered if this was the beginning of the end of our brave new world.

I hadn't yet started my new job when President Karzai called me to the palace. When I arrived with my escort of ISAF soldiers, President Karzai told me that he had new intelligence information that I was going to be killed. He said, "I cannot protect you; choose any embassy you want where you can be safe." He said if I worked as an ambassador, I would have direct contact with him and report only to him; I refused the offer immediately. In light of my refusal, he said that he would have to talk with the Hazara leaders to provide protection for me. But I was against the idea; I knew if I were to be killed the Hazaras would be blamed. This proposal was being made to me on July 6, 2002, a day after Haji Abdul Qadir, a minister of public works and one of the mujahideen commanders, had been killed in Kabul. Karzai said my name was on the same kill list.

A few days later, Lakhdar Brahimi raised the security issue with me again. He said, "Sima, you should be an ambassador in one of the EU countries; you can do much more for the future of your country and be safe yourself." He also said Nordic countries were especially good on women's rights, and I would be able to fundraise from those countries for my people. I told him I didn't want to leave the country but was willing to stay out of the government as I didn't want my presence to be a problem in building a democratic Afghanistan. I believed that this idea had been coordinated by President Karzai and Brahimi in order to get rid of me, and this action would be an admission to the people with guns and militias that they had won. I knew this kind of passive response to the extremists was the wrong foundation for Afghanistan.

And so I stayed, beginning my work as the founding chair of the Afghanistan Independent Human Rights Commission. For someone who wanted to change the status quo, this was the perfect posting. I had access to the justice system as well as the jails. I had the ear of NATO, the UN, the diplomats and the Afghan military. I had the mullahs and the politicians on speed dial. But most of all, the most precious jewels in the country—the rural women and girls, their schools and health care centers, their treasured cultural customs that had been buried and, in some cases, obliterated by the Taliban—became my purview. It was among these girls and women that I had begun my adult life as a young doctor. Now I could return to them with support from the government and the international community. I knew they were the future of a successful republic.

Seven

NO PEACE WITHOUT JUSTICE

LIKE A GAME OF TRUTH AND CONSEQUENCES, you can line up countries that respect, enshrine and act on the Universal Declaration of Human Rights alongside those who do not. For those who choose human rights, the truth is a better economy, improved health and productive citizens. For those who don't follow that path, the consequences are the opposite—a poorer economy, a lower score on health measures and unhappy citizens. It is so obvious that I am invariably astounded by the pushback from the handful of power-obsessed, greedy people who disregard the benefits of human rights for all.

I saw my posting to the Afghanistan Independent Human Rights Commission as a way to help end the culture of impunity and the misuse of religion and tradition. I had witnessed these violations in my village and even in my profession as a medical doctor. I also wanted to raise awareness about human rights values in the country and to take steps toward ending patriarchy.

Consider the studies done back in 1985 by the World Bank showing the value of investing in the girl child. If she gets enough to eat, some education and even minimal health care, three things will happen: she will marry later, she will have fewer children and those children will be healthier. Economists claim that these changes alone would eradicate poverty in the village, help the environment and put the country to work. The World Bank has continued to follow the status of girls and its effect on the economy. According to its 2018 report, if girls face limits to their educational opportunities and barriers to finishing twelve full years of education, that deprivation costs their countries between $15 trillion and $30 trillion in earnings and lifetime productivity. I have seen the impact of education in my own life and I have witnessed the hard facts that when girls are not allowed to go to school, child marriages increase and mother and child mortality rates escalate.

Although the president issued the decree that made me chair of the AIHRC, the government didn't show much support, and some high officials were worried we were going to act as investigators and arrest people who had committed crimes. At this time the UN was operating like a shadow government in our country, partly because they were responsible for implementing the Bonn Agreement, but also because they were seen as a mediator who might build trust between the warring factions. So I went to President Karzai and to the UN's Lakhdar Brahimi to try to establish support for the commission.

Once again I had no office, no staff and no budget, but I found a house to rent and bought six meters of cheap Iranian carpet at the market and called the other commissioners to join me. We sat on the floor and started our work.

The first official AIHRC meeting was with donor countries; it was held in the United Nations Assistance Mission in Afghanistan conference room in Kabul on August 19, 2002. We discussed strategy, policy and opening offices in other parts of the country and, of course, funding. Denmark and Switzerland each promised $500,000. But it was a few more months before a trust fund was established by the UNDP and made available to the AIHRC. Since the late 1990s, I had been working with members of the US Congress, especially Senator Barbara Boxer and Congresswoman Carolyn Maloney, on legislation to support women's projects in Afghanistan. As a part of this effort, Maloney would successfully secure earmark funding for the Ministry of Women's Affairs and the AIHRC.

By December 10 we were ready to go public with our plans, and we organized an event to celebrate the anniversary of the Universal Declaration of Human Rights at the Kabul University auditorium. We invited President Karzai, Mr. Brahimi and other members of the cabinet to join us, along with members of civil society and professors and students from the university. My focus was on equality for all people, including gender equality, the rule of law, accountability and justice for victims. After Karzai and Brahimi spoke, we released white pigeons and inaugurated the first monument for human rights, engraved with articles from the Universal Declaration of Human Rights. I also asked that human rights values and principles be added to the school curriculum. It took much effort and quite some time, but human rights principles did become part of the teacher training center and were included in courses at the universities. More importantly, they were added to the curriculum of the Afghan National Police Academy and the

National Military Academy. Eventually, international human rights law was taught at both as well.

The AIHRC set out to conduct workshops in human rights with every sector of society, including prosecutors, judges, journalists, teachers and even the mullahs. Some of the political parties claimed our plan was nothing more than a promotion of immorality among the youth. But slowly we reached people's homes in every corner of the country, and human rights became the discourse in every household.

We opened the first regional office in Herat. Brahimi and Ali Ahmad Jalali, the minister of interior, and some other members of the cabinet traveled there with us for the inauguration on March 18, 2003. A few days before the opening of the office, Human Rights Watch published a report about the human rights situation in Afghanistan. It read in part, "for the first time in over twenty years, Afghans had realistic hopes for stable peace, legitimate governance, increased development assistance, and new respect for human rights norms. At the same time however, ongoing security problems in many parts of the country continued to threaten many Afghans, especially vulnerable populations such as women and girls, orphans, widows, displaced persons, the disabled, and ethnic minorities."

The report named some of the mujahideen leaders—including Ismail Khan, the governor of Herat—as some of the violators of human rights. A journalist called Ahmad Behzad from Radio Free Europe asked Jalali about his reaction to the report and specifically about Ismail Khan; afterward, Behzad was detained and beaten by a National Directorate of Security (NDS) officer. When I was informed, I asked Lakhdar Brahimi to tell Ismail Khan we would not leave Herat until Behzad was released. However, our plans changed suddenly, and we had to leave Herat that day. The US attack on Iraq was about to begin, and the UN plane was required to return to base. As soon we landed in Kabul I learned that the journalist had been released.

The war in Iraq, which began on March 19, 2003, was a turning point for Afghanistan because the world's attention was redirected to that conflict. I had watched the news on February 5, 2003, when Secretary of State Powell spoke at the UN Security Council. Holding up a vial to represent anthrax, Powell tried to convince the members that Saddam Hussein, who was once a friend of the United States, was producing weapons of mass destruction. Powell said, "My colleagues, every statement I make today is backed up by sources, solid sources. These are not assertions. What we're giving you are facts and conclusions based on solid intelligence." As I knew the information they were receiving from my country was flawed, I questioned what was being said about weapons of mass destruction. Two years later, and out of government, Powell described his statement as "a blot" on his career. I was very worried; this accusation was sure to worsen anti-American attitudes in Muslim countries and feed the burgeoning terrorist movements. More importantly, I felt this diversion of attention from Afghanistan to Iraq would mean the job in my country would not be completed. But the United States had already pronounced Afghanistan a success story, and now they were turning their attention elsewhere.

After the inauguration in the Herat office, we opened seven more regional offices. The opening of the AIHRC office in Kandahar was particularly dramatic, partly because, being the birthplace of the Taliban, it was still a difficult place to work. And then my entire team and I were almost killed in the process of getting there.

We had chartered a plane from Bakhtar Afghan Airline, a government-owned company, to fly us to the Kandahar Airport, where the US military was stationed. The night before, the military told us we could not land before 9 a.m. However, the airline told us we would have to land earlier because the vice president, Mohammad Fahim, who was in Badakhshan, wanted the plane to pick him up after dropping us off, to fly him back to Kabul. We tried our best to inform the US military at the airport, but when we arrived at 8:30 a.m. we were refused permission to land and had to circle the airport several times. When finally we were given the signal to land, the plane dove for the end of the runway, hitting the unpaved ground and bouncing up almost a hundred meters in the air. One of the tires burst, and the iron mechanism that holds the tire in place then pierced the ground, which made the plane spin wildly before we came to a stop. Oil was dripping down the side of the plane, but despite the danger we were not allowed to disembark. We sat there terrified for fifteen minutes before US soldiers approached, finally signaling that we could exit; after being made to stand for nearly an hour on the runway in the hot sun, we were finally released by the governor of Kandahar, Gul Agha Sherzai. The soldiers who had done nothing to help us admitted later that they were amazed we had survived.

There are many theories about what happened next in Afghanistan. Somehow, in 2004, like water escaping through a pinhole in a pipe, our future began to leak away. Afghans were being killed by insurgents and also by NATO forces, who bombed wedding parties and other civilian gatherings while conducting their attacks on the insurgents. NATO was getting surprisingly fierce blowback from a reorganized Taliban that had been newly recruiting next door in Pakistan.

Our human rights education pushed further out to try to counter these new concerns. We were certain that once people knew about their rights, they would respect the rights of others and defend their own as well. Women's rights had been suppressed as part of the culture in a patriarchal system before the war, but conflict naturally makes men feel more empowered, and under the name of all the old notions—protection of women, and family honor, and the pride of the tribes—women were increasingly controlled.

It's important to note that discrimination based on gender, which turned into gender apartheid under the Taliban, had already existed, which meant that the AIHRC's task of promoting and protecting women's rights had layers of history to correct. For instance, in 1993 the government said a woman's face had to be covered while reading the news on television. So a woman could read the news, but a photo of a rose would appear on the screen as she did so. A few weeks later they said a woman's voice should not be heard either, and thus women were removed entirely from the visual media. Afghanistan did not participate in important world conferences—such as the International Conference on Population and Development in Cairo in 1994 and the World Conference on Women in Beijing in 1995—because the government said the issues being discussed were un-Islamic.

The AIHRC participation in the drafting of the constitution to be approved at the 2004 loya jirga was incredibly frustrating. It was a tough struggle to bring politicians onside; just adding the word *women* in the constitution was a fight because there were those who said the word *atbah* (follower) would apply both to men and women. The Constitution Drafting Commission had prepared a version but would not share it. So, after consulting with different groups of people all across the country about what they wanted included in a constitution and including their majority views, we at the AIHRC prepared our own draft constitution, translating it into English, Pashtu and Farsi so people could understand the importance of human rights in a people-oriented constitution. The document prepared by the AIHRC was released to the UN, the president's office, the US ambassador and the public. And, in an encouraging development, someone from the office of the Constitution Drafting Commission called and asked for six hundred copies of the draft, promising to put one in the file for every delegate at the loya jirga.

When the assembly began in January 2004 it became clear immediately that the majority of the delegates, including me, favored a parliamentary system over a centralized presidential one. However, Zalmay Khalilzad, the US ambassador, and Ashraf Ghani, the minister of finance and advisor to Karzai, strongly promoted a presidential system. They stacked the meeting with governors who were not official delegates and tried to bribe people to take their side. Once again, the rules and regulations of the loya jirga for approval of the constitution had been broken. On the second day of the assembly, I realized that the AIHRC's draft constitution had not been included in the delegate files. The executive director of the Constitution Drafting Commission, Farooq Wardak, was also in favor of the presidential system, and so he did not share our draft with the participants. He claimed its absence was a mere oversight, but to me it looked like sabotage.

It was also important to the AIHRC that people accused of war crimes and crimes against humanity and those involved in the drug trade should not be allowed to run for office. But the conservatives exerted pressure to soften the language of the draft constitution so that it read that people who were convicted in a competent, trusted and impartial court of war crimes and crimes against humanity could not stand for public office. They knew they were getting their commanders off the hook because the courts during the twenty-five years of war had been neither impartial nor competent.

Despite those maneuvers, in the constitution that was ratified, two chambers were established—the parliament and the senate. The document also contained a Bill of Rights and included a 25 percent quota of women members in each chamber.

And there were other crucial wins. For example, we were able to add equal rights for all citizens—including Shi'ites, who were allowed to exercise their personal status law for the first time. We added the word *women* to the document; we also succeeded in making the Human Rights Commission a permanent institution in the country.

After the constitution was passed, we prepared for the presidential and parliamentary elections; we needed to encourage the people to participate in the election in a transparent way in order to build confidence in the democratic process and promote the legitimacy of the government.

The war had been long. Millions of people were refugees in the neighboring countries and the majority did not have an ID card; they needed help in understanding how to participate in an election.

From the first election in October 2004, and even after, there were confounding roadblocks created by people who were more interested in clinging to personal power than in growing a democracy. For example, in leading the election process, the UN instructed people to register to receive a voting card. Each person was supposed to be photographed for the card, but of course there were some who complained that females must not be photographed. I said if they didn't want to be photographed, fingerprints could be used, but I was ignored. As it turned out, the election process was plagued with fraud. People were coming with fifteen or more female names and obtaining voting cards; young boys put on their fathers' turbans and were given cards.

Elections don't guarantee democracy, but they do allow people to have a voice and role in the political process. I'll never forget one woman in the central highlands, eighty years old, who walked a great distance on a very cold and snowy day to reach the polling station to cast her ballot. It was the first time she had exercised her political right. Although I am sure she voted the way her male family member told her to vote, she still looked so happy and proud to be exercising her franchise.

We have a saying: if you put the foundation wrong the building will go in the wrong direction and be vulnerable to a simple shock. By building our democracy and holding our election on an unstable foundation, we taught our children and our people that democracy is fraudulent and election results could not be trusted.

And there would be repercussions for speaking out against irregularities. When the AIHRC and UNAMA held a press conference, one of the reports documented that Ismail Khan had refused to allow a political party called the Republicans to open an office in

Herat. A few weeks later, when I was in South Korea for a conference, our office in Herat was attacked by his supporters; they set a
fire in the building, looted the electronics and destroyed our vehicles.
When I returned from the conference, I traveled to Herat to see
my staff and Ismail Khan and told him I wanted compensation for
the lost items. After a two-year fight, I got the money from President
Karzai, but the quarrel with Khan did not finish there. He was
removed as governor but came to Kabul as minister of energy and
water. The AIHRC had already started building our office on a piece
of land we had secured, but Khan insisted the land belonged to his
ministry and ordered construction to be stopped. While I eventually
got the land back, he could not resist continuing to interfere with
our work. His actions reminded me of the old expression "a house
divided against itself cannot stand."

Since the AIHRC was new in the country, we needed to focus on
training our staff on different issues, such as documenting all of the
violations of human rights during the prolonged conflict. Because
state institutions and law enforcement were not functional, working
on human rights was complicated.

The toughest file was the investigation of war crimes, dating
back to 1978 and 1979, when the Soviets invaded. We needed
documentation of the crimes committed during those years and
we needed to seek justice for victims, including reparations. We
needed to find a way to achieve proper reconciliation and sustainable peace without revenge. It wouldn't be easy.

From the outset, my mission statement was "no peace without
justice." But bringing war criminals to account in Afghanistan is
complicated. President Karzai himself called for a truth and reconciliation commission "to ensure the people will have justice,"

183

although in the end he didn't keep his word. Still, I leaped at the opportunity to fling open the doors of the PDPA, Soviet, mujahideen and Taliban past and document the crimes that everyone in the country knew about but hardly dared mention publicly for fear of reprisals. Beginning in 2003, I sought the counsel of people who had extensive experience on the issue, including Pakistani jurist Asma Jahangir, the UN's special rapporteur on extrajudicial killing, and Louise Arbour, the Canadian who became the UN high commissioner for human rights.

We wanted to hold a national consultation with the people in Afghanistan to make sure the process was inclusive. I sent my team across the country to consult, interview and conduct focus groups with almost seven thousand Afghans, including refugees in Iran and Pakistan, about the events of the twenty-three years in their lives from 1978 to 2001. It took eight months to gather the evidence—a difficult and dangerous task in the midst of the ongoing conflict— and in January 2005 the report titled *A Call for Justice* was delivered to President Karzai jointly from me and High Commissioner Arbour. It began with an overview of how Afghans arrived at this place: "More than a million people lost their lives and almost the same number became disabled in the course of the war, as a result of antipersonnel landmines, indiscriminate bombing and rocket attacks by the former Soviet Union and the regime backed by them, and attacks by armed militia groups, including the mujahideen and Taliban. Thousands of people were put in jail and tortured for their political beliefs; countless people were disappeared. Thousands of children lost their family members and their fathers. Afghanistan's streets are now full of orphaned children who must beg and work to survive. Almost all the country's major cities were destroyed.

Agriculture was destroyed when the fields were burned. More then [*sic*] seven million people were forced to leave their villages and towns and take refuge in Iran and Pakistan."

The report made international headlines with the shocking claim that 69 percent of the population had suffered human rights abuses, "staggering statistics in comparison to any other conflict in the world," said Arbour.

An action plan based on the recommendations of the people who participated in the national consultation for transitional justice was made at the London Conference on Afghanistan in January 2006 and agreed upon by the AIHRC, the UN, the international community and the Afghan government. The timeline for implementing the action plan was three years. I knew that the concept itself was unheard of in Afghanistan and needed careful explaining lest the enemies of the report use it to sway public opinion. The commission prepared a detailed statement about transitional justice and made it as widely available as possible, sometimes using radio broadcasts to read to the many illiterate people in the country so they would have access to the facts.

In the action plan we explained that the aim of transitional justice was to establish peace and national reconciliation. It was also meant to restore coexistence and cooperation, to heal the wounds of victims and to reintegrate citizens into a peaceful life. Transitional justice goes beyond concepts such as trials, prison and revenge and promotes the culture of forgiveness and affection. It certainly doesn't excuse genocide, war crimes, crimes against humanity and other gross violations of human rights. It was important that our people knew that bold action against these crimes is itself a universally accepted moral principle.

The action plan concluded: "Acknowledging the suffering of the victims, accepting the fact that innocent humans have been oppressed in the country, recording the past events in a historical and comprehensive way, reparations, promoting national reconciliation, removing human rights violators from official positions and restor[ing] the trust of people and victims in state, are the minimums to be addressed."

We knew to achieve these goals we'd need the active and meaningful participation of all national stakeholders, including justice authorities, civil society, professional associations, the mujahideen, traditional and religious groups, victims, ex-combatants and (noncriminal) elements of former regimes, and especially women. And we knew that would be a very tall order.

As UN Secretary-General Kofi Annan noted, justice and peace are not contradictory forces. Rather, properly and simultaneously pursued, each promotes and sustains the other. The question is therefore not whether justice and accountability are to be pursued, but when and how.

The government was reluctant to give the plan the go-ahead, due to concerns and resistance among the mujahideen leaders. Finally, with the cooperation of the special representative of the UN, we managed to get the president's approval. The action plan was publicly announced on December 10, 2006, which was named the National Day for Remembrance of the Victims of War in Afghanistan. When the president spoke that day of the civilian casualties caused by ISAF international forces, it was the first time anyone had seen him cry in public. I also spoke at the event and said, "It has always been the innocent people, particularly the women, children and other vulnerable groups of this land, who have paid the highest price in the conflict. For this reason, we lobbied the government to acknowledge the suffering and the memory of victims of human rights violations."

In support of accountability and justice for major crimes, Louise Arbour directed her office to compile a summary of various national and international human rights reports and release the conclusions. But, to my dismay, the UN in Afghanistan was against the idea, fearing it would destabilize the country and prompt the warlords to take action against the UN or the government. Meanwhile, the national judiciary was lacking political will as well as capacity, while major crimes on all sides continued unabated and without any critical response from the International Criminal Court (ICC).

The treatment of victims of war crimes and crimes against humanity has a shameful history: perhaps if there had been justice for sexual and gender-based violations committed against women during World War II, Boko Haram would not have kidnapped the schoolgirls in Nigeria, and the Yazidi women in Iraq would have not been taken as sex slaves. As long as crimes such as honor killing and violence against women are dismissed as cultural norms, there will never be change. While women around the world have fought to change the law, increase awareness and build shelters where their sisters and daughters can seek refuge, the statistics for gender-based violence have hardly budged. When the brave women of Bosnia who had been gang-raped by enemy soldiers took their stories to the International Criminal Tribunal for the Former Yugoslavia (ICTY) in The Hague in 1998, the tribunal made rape a war crime. But in 2023 women in Ukraine were being raped by soldiers. Impunity for these crimes persists not only in Afghanistan but also throughout the world.

Accordingly, it was no surprise to me when the announcement of the action plan infuriated certain mujahideen leaders, jihadi groups and members of parliament, who began immediately to draft an amnesty law to protect themselves. The law stated that the mujahideen could not be brought to justice or made accountable for anything they did; instead, they referred to themselves as untouchable heroes who had made sacrifices to free the country from the USSR. To me, it was evidence that they were afraid of being caught for actions they knew were criminal. Then, to sow fear and threaten the AIHRC, they organized a protest in the Kabul stadium; they even paid people to attend to make it look as if there was enough support for the proposed amnesty law. In fact, they had never even read the Peace, Reconciliation, and Justice Action Plan.

I waited impatiently for the president to reject this attempt to reverse the action plan, and wondered whether the government's initial welcoming reception of the report was all smoke and mirrors. It seemed so. Somehow, the mujahideen leaders managed to pass the amnesty law in both houses, achieving the necessary two-thirds of the votes from the parliament and the senate. President Karzai did not sign the law.

There were other problems as well. From 1990 to 2003, the UN Human Rights Commission had a special rapporteur on the situation of human rights for Afghanistan, but then they changed that mandate to an independent expert, narrowing the scope of their responsibilities. M. Cherif Bassiouni, an Egyptian judge who was appointed as the independent expert, criticized the handling of prisoners by the international forces. In response, the member states of the Human Rights Commission abolished the mandate;

instead, the high commissioner for human rights was asked to publish a report on Afghanistan.

The report that High Commissioner Arbour filed in January 2008 said: "Human rights and their defenders have come under attack by those who view human rights as a Western-imposed concept, as counter to local religious and cultural traditions, and as a luxury that Afghanistan cannot afford. Yet, insecurity in Afghanistan generally emanates from failure to address ongoing human rights concerns and violations, including effectively addressing past violations. During my visit to Afghanistan, I found Afghans from all walks of life claiming their rights to food, shelter, education, a livelihood, health, justice and physical security. The creation of new institutions to protect human rights is not, and should not be perceived as an attack on traditional systems, but seeks to complement and build upon the latter's strengths."

She went on to add that progress on the action plan had been "extremely limited" due to significant political opposition. She singled out the amnesty law as being a significant factor in undermining transitional justice.

Despite the setback, we made use of the action plan wherever we could. For example, regarding documentation of the truth about what happened, when a mass grave was discovered in Fayzabad, Badakhshan, we decided to build a museum on the site. The remains of the people were properly buried, but we kept clothing, prayer beads, shoes and other artifacts to use in displays.

According to the families of the victims, the massacre had been ordered by Mansoor Haishimi, one of the ministers of the pro-USSR government in 1979, to silence people who weren't supporting the new regime. At one time, Haishimi taught physics with my husband

Ghafoor in the science faculty at Kabul University, and I shudder to remember that I even knew him when he was the minister of energy and water.

When I went to inaugurate the museum, people from all parts of town and the victims' families took part. It was a very moving event; the families were grateful for the closure brought to them by the AIHRC. They saw the museum as a shrine and came to pray for the souls of their loved ones, and they brought photos and mementos to honor the victims. After thirty years of waiting, it was a time to heal.

As for the plan to reform state institutions, we proposed an advisory board made up of people nominated by the president and the AIHRC and UNAMA to check the background of the nominees and disqualify those who were accused of crimes. This way, at least some people were removed from the list to be appointed as governor or district commissioners.

Six months later the president took tentative steps toward the establishment of the advisory board for senior appointments, but it was mostly by way of shuffling provincial governors and friends and relatives of those in power from one post to another rather than sending them to the board, as had been agreed. In one sweeping motion he denied the basic human right of justice to the victims of war.

It is true that the judiciary in place when the government was formed did not have the capacity to manage the trials of war criminals, and letting the guilty go free after a botched trial would have been worse than not charging or at least isolating them. But by now six years had passed. We'd had such high expectations, and they had not been fulfilled. People were tired of waiting.

The travesty in this lack of action is that those accused of gross violations in different parts of the country were never brought to justice. It had taken us two years to interview the victims and collect evidence. There were numerous challenges, including deteriorating security and difficulty in gathering the facts because some witnesses had died; others were displaced and still others were so young their testimony was unreliable. But we pressed on, gathering the evidence we needed. Our documentation showed that the people also suffered from the actions of their own ethnic groups in their villages, in every part of the country.

Although the report of the crimes committed by those on different sides of the conflict was ready by the end of 2009, there was no political will within either the international community or the government to make it public. Since the report included the regimes prior to the interim government—the pro-Soviet and Soviet, the mujahideen and the Taliban—our office and staff would require protection from retaliation if the report were to be released.

Today, the 880-page report is stored in a safe place outside of Afghanistan. I am proud of what my team at the AIHRC was able to document, and I hope the report will eventually be used to teach the history of what happened during the violent conflict from 1978 to 2001.

During the three years in which the work of transitional justice and the action plan was taking place, the AIHRC was also tackling other important reforms, such as a call for a national inquiry about the practice of honor killing.

In many countries in our region, including Afghanistan, if a woman is raped, runs away, or if she's suspected of having a

relationship with a man, she is killed by relatives in order to protect the honor of the family. No one is punished for this act because
it is considered a private matter, not murder. Our national inquiry
examined 130 cases, most of those killings carried out based
on a suspicion of a relationship between the female victim and
an unrelated man, or of a woman escaping a forced marriage. We
succeeded in changing the definitions of rape and consensual sex
in the law that refers to adultery and extramarital sex, and honor
killing was criminalized.

Another issue we tackled was the virginity test. A young woman
running away from a forced marriage, or who wanted to marry
someone she loved but whom the family didn't approve of, would
be picked up by the police and detained, and then sent to a forensic
doctor for a virginity test. We changed that law so that a woman
could not be sent for a virginity test without both her consent and
a court order. Some said this change would promote immoral acts:
in fact, what it did was protect the dignity of women and reduce
corruption in the legal system.

We pushed for the implementation of the UN Convention on
the Rights of the Child, as children's rights were constantly violated: their access to education was denied, for example, and
they were exposed to dangerous work, including the collection
and smuggling of opium and other inappropriate labors such as
brickmaking. The most vulnerable children were those who'd
lost their fathers and whose grandfathers or uncles had sold them
to make money. Children were trafficked in Arab countries; in
one case we examined, a child had been tied to the back of a
camel so that his terrified cries would make the animal run faster
in a camel race.

I remember when we had to deal with a group of children who had been sent to Saudi Arabia by their families to make money. The Saudi police had caught the children without documents and deported them back to Afghanistan, where the AIHRC, UNICEF and Save the Children picked up the file and reunited the children with their families. But we were soon to find out that even more oversight would be necessary with such cases.

Six months later, a colleague from the AIHRC was spending the night in a chai khana in Baghlan Province and noticed that thirteen children and one man were staying in the same place. When the man left the room, my staff member talked to the children and found out they'd recently been deported from Saudi and now were going back because their family could not repay the money given to them by the traffickers; the children had to return to work and pay the family debt. My colleague went to the police, the children were rescued, and after that we made a plan to follow up and monitor any child who'd been deported.

One fact about human trafficking uncovered by the AIHRC was that it wasn't only Afghan women and children being smuggled— our country was on the transit route for neighboring countries as well. We finally criminalized the act and added it to the penal code.

We also managed to increase the age of children in the juvenile justice system from puberty to eighteen years. It wasn't an easy task, as the conservative groups argued that at the age of puberty, girls and boys were adults and therefore criminally responsible for their behavior. The same argument affected the age of marriage: for boys it was eighteen, but for girls, conservative members of parliament wanted it to be fourteen. We managed to push it to sixteen, although in my view that was still legalizing child marriage, another example of a depraved need to use and control a female life and a female body.

One of the worst violations of human rights of children was bacha bazi, which means "boy play"—the sexual abuse of boys by older men. This practice increased during the war in Afghanistan; boys as young as eight or nine would be made to dance for older men who would abuse them sexually and sometimes even "loan" boys to another person for money. The boys were usually dressed as girls and wore bracelets of bells on their ankles, dancing for the pleasure of these men pumped up with money and military arms.

After the AIHRC conducted a national inquiry on bacha bazi, we were able to criminalize this inhumane act. Always at the root of such issues was the impact of war and poverty; the abuse these children suffered earned them food, clothes and money, some of which went to their families. Out of stark need, the families often turned a blind eye.

Another file that we wanted to focus on was monitoring and investigating violence against women and civilian casualties, with the goal of universal accountability for violating international human rights and humanitarian laws. It is true that war is violent and destructive, but still, there are laws for war, as stipulated in the Geneva Conventions of 1949—and those laws were being broken by all sides. What's more, we took on the task of documenting cases of torture, with the goal of eliminating the practice. Once we were able to publicize that torture was a crime, we removed some of the police chiefs from their positions, and we saw a decrease in the cases committed by the government. We also witnessed a reduction in the cases of torture by international forces.

In the meantime, civilian casualties in every corner of the country were increasing, and so were the number of suicide attacks. While the Taliban frequently claimed responsibility, civilian casualties from the international forces had also increased. The AIHRC realized we needed to open more offices where violence was increasing—mostly in the south of the country, such as Helmand, where American and British provincial reconstruction teams were, and later in Uruzgan, where Dutch and Australian soldiers were working.

The AIHRC team had completed its training in the proper documentation of civilian casualties when we took on the first major case in 2007. A US battalion was coming from Iraq to Afghanistan through the Khyber Pass. A man was driving toward them; fearing a suicide attack, the soldiers started shooting at him—and then, for almost twelve kilometers, they shot everyone on both sides of the road. Sixteen people were killed and twenty-four were injured. During our investigation, we asked the US commander for his explanation. He publicly apologized and paid compensation to the families, and the soldiers were called back to the United States. (If there were further consequences for them, we were not informed.) It was actually the first time that an ISAF commander publicly acknowledged a mistake, and it set a precedent for paying compensation to civilian victims. A payment could not replace a father, a worker, a family provider—but it was at least an acknowledgment of the victim's suffering and the mistakes made by the international forces. Other major mistakes had been made by the US forces in different parts of the country, such as bombing a wedding party. Some of the incidents occurred before the establishment of the AIHRC, and we were not in position to document them properly.

When we heard about allegations of torture in the prisons, we requested access to the facilities run by NATO forces. It took more than six years to get that access, mostly because whenever we were close to signing an agreement, our NATO contact would leave (at the end of their six-month to one-year assignment in Afghanistan) and we'd have to start negotiations from scratch again and again. Finally, in 2010, we were able to gain access to the main prison run by the US at Bagram, close to the airport. By now we knew the accusations of torture were true, but what the officials showed us were facilities with cameras in interrogation rooms, created to prevent torture. However, while I was at the prison with AIHRC commissioners Farid Hamidi and Nader Nadery, we were also concerned with the high cost of running this huge air-conditioned building, knowing that the Afghan government would have to run it after the Americans left.

Like a runaway train, the civilian casualties, mostly against Hazaras, were increasing exponentially—brutal attacks on weddings, funerals, sports fields, schools, mosques, protests and any place people gathered. Improvised explosive devices and bombs were taking a dreadful toll of nine thousand to eleven thousand every year, including women and children. We pressed on with reform at the AIHRC, taking on the rights of people with disabilities. A lack of social security meant there was no support for the many who had become disabled during the prolonged war. We had a specific ministry for the martyrs (those who died in the war) and people with disabilities, which provided about ten dollars a month, but even that was misused in a lengthy process by corrupt officials. We lobbied the government to ratify the UN Convention on the Rights of Persons with Disabilities; however, joining the convention was one thing, implementing it another.

Reforming the justice system was another hurdle. In 2005, the United Nations Development Programme Rule of Law department worked with the Ministry of Justice to create a justice-for-all strategy, but they chose to promote the traditional justice system in the country alongside the formal one. To me, that meant reform was being sidelined. For example, there is a traditional law called *bad* that is used in conflicts between families. Although it goes against Sharia law—as well as the Universal Declaration of Human Rights, international norms and standards, and indeed the civil law of Afghanistan—*bad* has persisted. If there is a dispute about a land boundary and someone is killed, the side that loses the dispute gives a girl, or sometimes two or three girls, depending on the size of the harm done, to the offended family. The decision is made by elders in the community, not by the justice system. Although it is applied differently in different parts of the country, *bad* always results in misery, if not death, for the girls.

I felt I had to interfere with the UNDP Rule of Law section that claimed that the majority of people use traditional justice because it is accessible, cheap and quick. I explained that, in the case of *bad* (and there are many other equally unjust traditional laws), it doesn't stop the tension between families. In fact, the angst is perpetuated, and an innocent girl has her life ruined. As well, by not punishing the actual perpetrator, criminal behavior within the tribe goes unchecked and contributes to a culture of impunity.

One of the proudest accomplishments for me was enactment of the Elimination of Violence Against Women (EVAW) law—a combined effort of the AIHRC, the Ministry of Women's Affairs, women's groups, NGOs and female members of the parliament. The criminalization of domestic violence, including *bad,* was a first in our history. While the EVAW law was never approved by the parliament, it was enforced by presidential decree in 2009.

As chair of the Afghanistan Independent Human Rights Commission, I was often asked to meet with foreign delegations. Beyond the usual exchange of information that comes from international diplomacy, they knew very well that I would be frank with my comments, and that I would name the people who continued to commit war crimes or crimes against humanity. And, as a tough-minded broker, I would shame the war criminals. I would steadfastly promote the need for change in Afghanistan. I refused to be cowed—not by religious fanatics, not by warlords, not even by President Karzai. But the cost of that stance is something I felt every day. For six long years, I hadn't been able to go for a walk, go shopping or meet friends in a tea house. I left the sanctity of my home only to go to work, and never without protection.

On January 14, 2008, I was to meet with Jonas Gahr Støre, the Norwegian minister of foreign affairs. The venue was the Serena Hotel, considered one of the most secure places in Kabul (it calls itself an "oasis of luxury in a war-ravaged city"). On that afternoon, my driver checked in with the guards at the gate and then maneuvered the armored Land Cruiser through the anti-terrorist cement blocks ringing the circular driveway to the main entrance.

It was a sunny day but minus twenty degrees, so there was no lingering at the door; my 5:30 p.m. rendezvous with Minister Støre and seven other members of the Norwegian delegation was to take place in a room on the lower level. About forty minutes into our discussion, we heard a sudden dull thud—unmistakably, an explosion. Being somewhat used to such noises after so many years of unrest, I wasn't overly concerned, believing it was far away. But then, thirty seconds later, we heard the rat-tat-tat of automatic machine gunfire—and now I could tell it was close. Then, a second explosion, this time shaking the room we were in. It seemed as if it had happened right on top of us, maybe as close as the floor above.

Later, we would find out that terrorists dressed in police uniforms had stormed the gate of the Serena and shot the guards. As they made their way to the door, a suicide bomber blew himself up in the driveway, acting as a decoy to give the terrorists time to get inside the hotel. That was the first explosion we'd heard. A second suicide bomber detonated his explosives in the lobby of the hotel while the gunmen followed a hallway to the downstairs exercise room, where internationals were known to work out, and began firing as soon as they got the door opened.

Inside our meeting room, two men from the Norwegian embassy barricaded the door; a hotel security agent told everyone to get down on the floor. Then Norwegian bodyguards arrived with their guns drawn and instructed us to get under the round conference table in the middle of the room.

While huddled under the table with the others, I called my driver to find out what he knew. "It's really bad out here," he said. At first, he thought they'd been hit by a rocket. Shrapnel had taken chunks out of the side of the armored vehicle. It took a few minutes before the driver realized that the debris on the windshield was body parts and that this had been a suicide bombing. "Stay in there, keep yourself safe, get close to the wall," he told me. "There's still a lot of shooting. No one knows where the gunmen are now."

Everyone under the table was on a cell phone. We were removed to the bomb shelter, which turned out to be the hotel kitchen. I was impressed by the professional behavior of the security staff in the hotel as they tried to keep people calm, bringing us water and guiding some to the washroom. We were joined by about 130 hotel guests. One man was wrapped in a towel as he'd been in the sauna when the gunmen opened the door; he literally dove out the door still naked and found his way through the hotel garden to a soldier, who took him to the kitchen and gave him a towel. I tried to comfort a man who was crying and lamenting the deteriorating security in the country. "We didn't ask for a palace," he was saying, "just a piece of bread."

At about 8 p.m., American soldiers came into the room with guard dogs and took the Americans out with them, but no one else. A few hours later, President Karzai called Jonas Gahr Støre and said he was sending his bodyguards to bring him to the palace. The minister said, "Sima Samar is here too, and she is more important for Afghanistan than I am and should be rescued." Before being taken out of the room, the minister insisted that I wait for ISAF to come and escort me to my home. Karzai's bodyguards eventually led me out. The lobby of the hotel was a frightful scene—blood and broken glass everywhere. Among the dead were a Norwegian journalist, five other foreigners and six Afghans on the hotel staff; many others were wounded.

I was escorted out of the hotel shortly after 10 p.m. My car was now part of the crime scene; its tires were also punctured, so it couldn't be moved. I had started walking down the street in the direction of my house when the chief of police directed me to a police car and told the officer to take me home. I could tell the assignment made him nervous.

My family was immensely relieved when I walked in the door. As they shared with me their agony of the previous six hours, their angst made me realize once again the price they paid for the work I did. While Tamanna, fifteen, had tried to stay calm, her eyes incessantly blinked and darted at every phone call; my mother, Khursheed, a devout woman who prays most of the day and knew her daughter was the target of the extremists in the country, had been mumbling her prayers, clutching a scarf to her mouth, pacing silently into the room and out again, hoping for news. Rauf had been outside talking to the men who guarded our house and then back inside telephoning contacts, trying to get a handle on the unfolding events. My brother Ahmad Ali, who was my chief of staff, had been on the phone with me and then my bodyguards, as well as office staff and government security, trying to piece together information. My brother Abdul Wahid had fingered his worry beads, sitting cross-legged on the floor with the others. At dinner time everyone gathered around the dastarkhan, and the only sounds breaking the silence were spoons scraping on bowls and cell phones ringing. It was a room full of people who had seen relatives and friends wiped out by the turmoil in the last three decades. The dinner platters were cleared away, but my plate had been kept aside. Pots of tea were refilled again and again.

Reflecting on the attack the next day, I realized that somehow, I hadn't been very afraid, and had remained calm during the whole thing. But then I didn't sleep at all that night, and by morning I suspected I was experiencing post-traumatic stress, because then

I felt scared. But there wasn't time to process the trauma, as I found myself on the receiving end of literally hundreds of callers and well-wishers, most of them performing an Afghan custom called qurbani. While it's normally an offering of food or money to the poor during celebrations such as Eid-ul-Azha (the time when Muslims go to Mecca), qurbani is also performed when someone has been saved from death. All day long people came to my office at the Human Rights Commission and to my house in Karte Seh, leading sheep to the door, carrying dozens of naan bread, bringing packets of money, all of which is meant to ward off the evil eye. We distributed all of what we received to the poor. I was touched by the outpouring of affection and concern. Almost every friend called, and so did Second Vice President Khalili and most of the cabinet ministers, to say they were happy I was safe.

I continued to mull over what had happened. While the attackers were dressed as police officers, one of them actually *was* a policeman, and some of the police who came to rescue us had been drunk. It was a frightening example of how we couldn't trust the legal system; no one was accountable, so there was no justice. I blamed corruption, nepotism, and a lack of commitment from people who benefited from the system the way it was. This wasn't a post-conflict country; we were still *in* conflict. It was no longer clear whom to blame—it wasn't just the Taliban. I imagined how people must have been feeling after seeing what almost happened to me when I was so well-guarded. They probably thought if they just went out to clean the street, they'd end up in pieces.

Like a bad odor, the government's inaction and the international community's lack of support for transitional justice wouldn't go away. Since the action plan had not been implemented effectively and according to its own goals, we felt it needed to be extended for at least another three years in order to implement and promote trustworthy governance. Unfortunately, the political will was not there to support the extension.

Human Rights Watch picked up the case, criticizing President Karzai and the international community for doing little to bring war criminals to justice and instead following a policy of what they called "reliance" on powerful warlords allegedly involved in past crimes.

My life was consumed with the emergencies of insecurity, whether my own or that of the people the commission tries to protect. Just a week after the Serena Hotel attack, I was preparing to leave for Kunduz, a city in the northeast quadrant of the country, to open the newly constructed building for the regional office of the Afghanistan Independent Human Rights Commission. From the view of my security detail, the trip to Kunduz was measured through a sniper's scope, a suicide bomber's vest, an insurgent's preference to wipe the human rights program out.

The night before our planned departure, I was told that heavy snow had forced a change of plans: instead of taking a plane I would have to travel by helicopter, which meant my bodyguards couldn't go with me. The three men who had been my bodyguards ever since I came to Kabul in 2001 to take the post as Minister of Women's Affairs were apoplectic. They knew the risks; with tips from the UN, they had already aborted several attempts on my life. They were adamant; I couldn't go to Kunduz without them. In the end, after some pleading on the phone to the UN, a seat on the helicopter was secured for one bodyguard.

It was still dark, so I needed a flashlight to make my preparations to leave: packing a piece of naan bread and a bit of cheese, swallowing a cup of tea, stopping quickly in my sleeping daughter's room. There was no power in the house—the grid for Kabul was activated only four hours a day, from 6 p.m. to 10 p.m.—so it was cold, so cold you could see your breath in the house. Through the windows thick with frost only the blur of red brake lights and the beam of the headlights were visible as the vehicle waited, guarded by three men toting machine guns. My mother walked like a ghost down the hall whispering prayers for my safety. In fact, we never did make it to Kunduz that day; the weather closed in and we had to return to Kabul after about fifteen minutes of being airborne.

Eight

THEY THOUGHT THEY
COULD BURY US

THERE WAS A SIEGE MENTALITY THROUGHOUT the country in those post-Serena-bombing days. Even the United Nations was in lockdown; staff could not be outside their offices or their homes. Evacuation plans had been reviewed and checkpoints established, just in case the palace collapsed and the international community had to beat a hasty retreat. The strain was evident everywhere, with security even more heightened than usual.

While the government fumbled and the Taliban insurgents did their worst, I relied on a tried-and-true way to fight off despair: making visits to the schools and health clinics I'd started. Invariably, the students and patients I talked to encouraged me to stay the course, and my energy and enthusiasm would be restored.

The race for education began almost as soon as the interim government took office; the official back-to-school date was March 22, 2002. But, like everything else in Afghanistan, the celebration was layered with difficulties. The schools then were in a dismal state of disrepair, and the government didn't have enough money to run them. Nevertheless, a contagious thrill of anticipation had swept across the country.

When the schools for boys and for girls were opened that year, not everyone had the chance to attend. When I heard that some of the schools were terribly damaged and not safe for the students to enter, I'd said, "If the schools aren't ready, let the children sit under the trees. We'll repair the buildings as fast as we can, but the children have to start learning now." Most of them could not afford the uniforms that were mandatory for female students. I used part of the money donated to the Ministry of Women's Affairs to buy sewing machines and fabric and then asked hundreds of volunteers to stitch together more than 500,000 uniforms. I also was grateful for fabric and sewing machines from donor countries. But a bigger issue lurked in the background. The government could not afford to pay all the teachers; they simply didn't have the budget. A lot of the schools, most of them rural, couldn't get off the starting block in this sprint to educate the youngsters who had been denied the right to learn to read and write. But over time the situation did improve, especially in areas that were supported by NGOs and UNICEF.

The problems in running the schools at that time were immense. At the Shuhada girls' school at the center of Jaghori they couldn't dig a well deep enough to provide drinking water, so the kids had to carry water from home. There were five toilets for two thousand students and staff. They didn't have enough books and the buildings were in need of repair, but any time I visited I was witness to more than enough determination to surmount the multiple and confounding problems they faced.

Just up the hill from the school in Jaghori, Shuhada had built an orphanage for the many children who were homeless. Their circumstances were varied: some were there because both parents had died in the civil war; others had been sold to earn money for the rest of the family; and still others had been turned out into the street to beg because there wasn't enough food at home. I wanted shelter for all these kids and housed them in this orphanage they all called "Samar's Nest."

Of course, since it was a Hazara area the problems presented by the government were never-ending. For example, back in 1998 when the Taliban took control and banned girls from attending high school, we'd decided to label our classrooms to create the appearance we were teaching only up to the sixth grade. As a result, our school was the only one where girls had been able to continue a high school education. When the girls who graduated from this school wanted to take the entrance exam for university, I had to explain to the Ministry of Education that we had continued teaching the girls despite the threats, and therefore the girls could participate in the pre-university examination process.

As much as we celebrated the girls being in school, the Taliban was relentless in attacking them. By 2008, the tally of girls' schools burned to the ground in five years was 150, and another 305 schools were closed due to lack of security. But the worst statistic was the 105 students and teachers who were killed, their bodies left with handwritten messages that warned villagers of the consequences of educating girls. As well, the government upheld a regulation written in the midseventies that stipulated that married females, many in their midteens, could not attend the same school as unmarried girls.

It was around that time that another headline about the girls of Afghanistan grabbed international attention. Shamsia Husseini was walking to school with her sister and a classmate in Kandahar when a man on a motorbike stopped beside her and asked where she was going. When she replied, "To school," he threw battery acid in her face. Several teenagers were similarly attacked in the same area that late-fall morning, but Shamsia's injuries were the worst. The acid splashed over her cheeks and eyelids and into her eyes. President Karzai, responding to the worldwide outrage, including sharp condemnation from US First Lady Laura Bush, sent Shamsia to India for treatment and promised her he would arrest the perpetrator and bring him to justice. He didn't. The AIHRC office in Kandahar investigated this case and was told by the police that the man who committed this crime had escaped to a Taliban-controlled area in Uruzgan. But Shamsia said the man and the other hoodlums who acted with him were still walking free right in the neighborhood where she lived with her family.

There was a surprising outcome to this story. After a remarkable recovery, Shamsia returned to school, graduated, and went on to study at the Teacher Training College in Kandahar; she became a language and science teacher for students in grades four to seven. She said then, "President Karzai broke his promise and I'm not very happy about that, but I can say I have given the man who attacked me a bigger punishment than the president ever could. I am teaching the girls. I showed them that they did not win and they will never win. They can't stop girls from going to school even if they threaten their lives." Her powerful words reminded me of a Mexican proverb: "They thought they could bury us; they didn't know we were seeds."

Education is without a doubt the most important tool for achieving peace, prosperity, justice and equality. I recited this formula to everyone who would listen. But old habits die hard. While our primary schools were crowded with students—fifty to sixty to a classroom—the dropout rate for senior students in grades nine to twelve was unacceptably high. There were only about fifteen to twenty girls in the graduating classes because those old shibboleths about the safety—make that purity—of teenage girls hung on like barnacles to a ship. We let primary children walk two hours down mountain tracks to school but forbade the teenagers because they might be kidnapped or raped. The problem was exacerbated by the fact there weren't enough female teachers for the senior students, and many families refused to send their older girls to be taught by men.

Although we Afghans, with the support of the international community, managed to reach the most distant corners of the country with education and with basic health services and trained midwives, we still had not been able to deliver key initiatives such as the reduction of mother and child mortality or access to advanced health care such as radiotherapy. Consider this: In 2004, China began rebuilding a $12 million modern hospital in Kabul. It took several years to complete, but even then the doors were locked for a long time because there weren't enough technicians and medical personnel trained to staff the place. In the meantime, five flights left Kabul every day for India; at least half the passengers on those planes were patients seeking medical treatment. And many more went to Pakistan, Iran and other neighboring countries for the same reason. Why could we not make it a priority to take the necessary measures to get a hospital running? It was utterly exasperating.

This was a critical time, with so many truly astonishing changes in the country: an ever-increasing number of women taking part at every level of society; humanitarian aid services pouring into every province. It felt as if there were endless possibilities out there for all of us. But in fact, there was an undeniable crack in the foundation of the future we were trying to build together. I had for a very long time felt the fault lay with the decision at the loya jirga in 2004 to leave accountability out of the equation. The relationship between the palace where the president works and the warlords with their militias all over the country was not transparent, and nor was it accountable. In fact, the relationship between warlords and the NATO member countries and troops was not transparent either.

And now there was another layer of complexity. The international community, including the military, needed to partner with the Afghan government. But ever since the war in Iraq, I'd wondered if they'd stopped paying attention to the realities in my country. Did they really know what our history meant to us, or the way systems worked here as opposed to the way they worked in the West? It seemed like we were a square peg being jammed into a round hole; were Afghans being shaped by policies that worked in some other country? I am not suggesting that democracy does not work in Afghanistan, but I am insisting that for democracy to be effective, the people need to commit themselves to the promotion of democratic values, and be the owners of the process.

I began to examine much of what we would accomplish in the days ahead through that lens. Policies from the government and international forces needed to be clear and transparent to the Afghan people. We needed to focus on keeping everyone accountable, including the NGOs. A few people had become very rich because of the international troops' presence and the aid money flowing into Afghanistan. Afghans began to resent that fact, which is how the Taliban began to get renewed traction. When the Taliban came calling at night for food or arms or shelter, people knew the government couldn't protect them, so they gave the Talibs what they wanted. The people chose a coping policy to survive, hoping to avoid the backlash from both sides.

Just before the 2009 election I wrote a report card on the eight years that had passed since the world came to our doorstep searching for Osama bin Laden and vowing to get this pariah state back on its feet. Here's what I concluded:

- **SECURITY**: Worse. It improved for a while, but as the promised changes didn't happen and the armed opposition picked up speed, the ranks of thieves, hooligans and terrorists increased.
- **WORK**: Better. Women who could find jobs were back at work, although they were poorly paid. Women were in politics, media, business, sports, music and other jobs, but there still wasn't adequate promotion of gender equality in every corner of the country.
- **SCHOOLS**: Better, notwithstanding the fact that girls' schools had been fire-bombed, teachers murdered and night letters dropped to warn parents against sending their girls to school. While girls made up more than one-third of the students attending classes, the majority of the

four million children still denied education were girls. And there was still work to be done on the training of teachers, the school curriculum and teaching methods.

- **ACCESS TO HEALTH SERVICES**: For women, it was much better, although there was a shortage of female staff in hard-to-reach areas, and less than 10 percent of women had access to contraception. Mother and child mortality had been reduced, but Afghanistan—along with Pakistan and Nigeria—was one of three countries where polio still existed.
- **DOMESTIC VIOLENCE**: Worse. The number of reported cases was very high, although this was perhaps partially attributable to a newly established reporting mechanism as well as institutions such as the AIHRC, the Ministry of Women's Affairs and civil society, including the media.
- **HUMAN RIGHTS**: Much better, but girls and women were still being jailed for running away from their abusive families or wanting to marry someone they loved. And the police still couldn't be fully trusted by women.
- **POVERTY**: A little better. Poverty had decreased a little, but when the international community came to town, prices for everything from food to accommodation rose. Consider that poverty is one of the reasons for fraud during an election, because votes can be bought and sold.

I had tried many avenues to steer my country away from the calamity that was now brewing. I cared nothing about the bounty the political men and religious zealots were seeking. And I knew that a small number of powerful men could get away with dominating many millions of people, and that other countries suffered similar fates and often for similar reasons.

One way I had been gaining perspective on our problems was through a part-time and volunteer role that I had been performing since 2005, when I was chosen by the Human Rights Commission to serve as special rapporteur on the situation of human rights in Sudan. Working with the government and the people of Sudan, also a country in conflict, was an eye-opening experience that gave me another lens through which to better understand international intervention and how the UN functioned in my own country.

Sudan had been embroiled in a civil war for twenty-two years. Like so many civil wars, this one was a battle between religions and ethnicities: North Sudan, with its majority Muslim and Arab population, against South Sudan, with its majority Christian and African people. The result? Two million dead and two million forcibly displaced—a very similar situation to Afghanistan's. When the Comprehensive Peace Agreement (CPA) was signed on January 9, 2005, the UN began its United Nations Assistance Mission in Sudan to facilitate and monitor the agreement's implementation. The CPA included details about sharing power and wealth and holding a referendum so the South Sudanese could decide whether they would be part of one country or separate. The CPA also suggested the government establish a National Human Rights Institution and a border between North Sudan and South Sudan, where the UN had a peacekeeping military presence. My appointment began eight months later.

I knew I was up against some hardline fundamentalists and conservatives. The Sudanese ran a health clinic for women and children in Peshawar, Pakistan, for Afghan refugees, which was extremely conservative; men and women were forbidden to be in the same section of the building. I knew that whenever the male doctor from North Sudan was about to arrive they would ring a bell to make sure all the female staff and patients were out of sight. I also knew that some of the Sudanese had connections with some of our conservative political parties, So I understood the challenge at hand. But still, I hoped that together we could make progress. I traveled to Khartoum in North Sudan and Juba in South Sudan, to El Fasher and El Geneina and Nyala in Darfur, and to many of the provinces, meeting twice a year with government officials, security forces, the armed opposition in Darfur, civil society, the media, women's groups and diplomatic communities.

While I was there, I was able to confirm the connection between the mujahideen in Afghanistan and the Islamists in Sudan. In my first meeting with Hassan al-Turabi, the man who helped Omar al-Bashir with the coup d'état in 1989, he told me that he had traveled often to Pakistan and Afghanistan to meet with the Afghan mujahideen leaders in order to create a strong Sunni Islamic government in Afghanistan. (He didn't realize at that time that I was Shi'ite.) I was astonished to hear him describe the mujahideen as power-hungry men who were fighting amongst themselves and unable to establish the Sunni government he'd hoped for. He told me that eventually he was so disappointed he gave up on them. To my surprise, some Afghans who were related to our mujahideen groups were studying in Omdurman Islamic University right there in Khartoum.

Sudan and Afghanistan had a lot in common: both were complex, poor countries with a sizable conservative population that featured one ethnic group holding power over the others; in the case of Sudan that was the Arabs in Khartoum. Much of the population in both countries was uneducated, and religion and culture were used as an excuse to violate people's human rights, in particular those of women. The judiciary in Sudan was neither independent nor competent, but I found the South Sudanese to be more open to recommendations for positive changes than the government in Khartoum at that time.

My mandate was to make recommendations to improve human rights so people could live with dignity, under the rule of law, and have access to justice. During the four years I was the special rapporteur, I was able to raise the voices of the victims at the international level by bringing their accounts to the UN in Geneva and New York. I advocated for human rights and law reform. But after documenting a range of serious human rights issues facing Sudan, I concluded that there had been little concrete improvement on the situation.

Although my assignment was to examine human rights issues, I could not help but note the differences between the Sudanese women and women in other countries. It reinforced my notion that, in the name of culture and religion, women are often assigned roles that suit a male version of purity or femininity. For example, women in Sudan were not required to cover themselves as much as Afghan women. Their dresses were long but had short sleeves. Of course, I had already noticed legal and wardrobe differences in other Muslim countries as well. In Bangladesh, the arms and sometimes the belly was exposed. In Jordan, women wore tight outfits, and had a choice as to whether they covered their hair or not. In Tunisia, polygamy was not allowed. We Afghans can't claim we are better Muslims than Tunisians or Bangladeshis or Sudanese because women wear burka and girls are denied education.

One of the conclusions I arrived at near the end of my time in Sudan was this: human rights laws are written with the best of intentions, but implementing them depends on the full support and strong political will of the government and all the agencies related to government policy. Despite the critical issues I documented, we had little success in implementing change. And as for the atrocities committed in Darfur, although the government established a special court, only a few nominal cases of petty crimes, such as stealing animals or injuring someone, were listed. The court did not even deign to consider war crimes or crimes against humanity.

Following the Sudanese government's expulsion of international aid organizations on March 16, 2009, its closure of Sudanese organizations, and the increasing repression of human rights activists and journalists, the role of the special rapporteur, as mandated by the Human Rights Council, had become increasingly critical. By now, millions of people had been killed or displaced. Arbitrary arrests and torture were commonplace, and rape had become a weapon of war.

"We are seeing an increasingly dangerous silence on the human rights situation in Sudan," Julie de Rivero of Human Rights Watch said. "Human Rights Council members should focus on supporting the victims in Sudan by extending the mandate of the special rapporteur."

I had been recommending that the International Criminal Court act to end the culture of impunity around international crimes committed in Sudan, particularly in Darfur. But the Sudanese leadership was furious with the international community because the ICC had indicted Omar al-Bashir. Bashir had been a military officer and politician before he overthrew the elected government of Sudan in

1989. He became president in 1993, and he would cling to the post until 2019, when he was ousted in a military coup. In 2008 the ICC accused him of genocide, war crimes and crimes against humanity. He was the first sitting head of state wanted by the ICC, and this was the first charge of genocide ever brought by the court. But since Sudan was not a member of the ICC, al-Bashir was able to avoid the consequences of his murderous actions.

Despite the seriously deteriorating human rights situation in Sudan, the government, the African Union and the Organisation of Islamic Cooperation refused to extend the mandate of the special rapporteur. It came down to this: the authors of the UN documents had very high hopes for their implementation when those documents were written, but they knew that getting leaders to sign and implement them would be a challenge. So, the documents were written without accountability. Look at Afghanistan today—the Taliban has refused girls the right to go to school and women the right to work. Yet Afghanistan joined the Universal Declaration of Human Rights in 1948 and the ICC in 2003, and the right to go to school is embedded in international documents. Time and again, the UN—with no iron fist of accountability— must depend on the politics of embarrassment in its attempts to implement conventions and treaties.

History tells us that justice often comes only when leaders fall from power. Omar al-Bashir, accused of war crimes in Darfur in 2009, was finally charged but not arrested for war crimes and crimes against humanity by the International Criminal Court (ICC) in 2021. Slobodan Milosevic of Serbia was accused of genocide and crimes against humanity in 2001, a decade after the alleged crimes were committed. And in the spring of 2022, the world wondered what it would take to indict and arrest other leaders. For example, although Putin was indicted by the ICC on March 17, 2023, for crimes against humanity in Ukraine, as I write this, I'm still wondering what the outcome will be. No one has been indicted in my country for international crimes.

My term in Sudan had taxed my energy for and commitment to internationalism, and had reminded me of the price one pays in trying to right international wrongs. Then news arrived in September 2009 that brought me full circle: I had been nominated for the Nobel Peace Prize. I was in Kabul and suddenly started getting phone calls from media all over the world asking for my comments. What could I say? I was speechless. I laughed and then I cried. It's hard to describe the feelings I had as an Afghan woman who'd been fighting her whole life for women and girls to have my work noticed in such a way. It was an enormous boost to my confidence in the tough road ahead.

I didn't know who had nominated me, but everyone seemed very excited about it. The media attention kept up for the two weeks before the prize was announced on October 9, 2009. I tried to refuse some of the interviews and promised that I would talk to each one when the decision was announced. It was an almost magical feeling of support; everywhere I went people wanted to talk about what it would do for women and girls and how it would affect Afghanistan. Then the announcement came out: the American president Barack Obama had won. I was enormously pleased for him and felt proud to have been considered.

I have been fortunate to receive many prestigious awards, including the Right Livelihood Award in 2012, which is also known as the "Alternative Nobel Peace Prize." I've been named an honorary member of the Order of Canada, and have also collected a number of honorary doctorate degrees. But I know well that it takes more than awards to move a country in the right direction.

While I was still grappling with my work in Sudan, and before I was aware of the Nobel Prize nomination, I was also engaged with ongoing events in Afghanistan.

The second presidential election in Afghanistan was slated for August 20, 2009. The campaigning began on July 20 amid rising insecurity; the Taliban were threatening harm to anyone who registered to vote. The AIHRC and UNAMA had to carefully monitor the conditions for a free and fair election that the public could trust. The rights of people during an election included four freedoms— of expression, association, assembly and movement throughout the country—as well as three principles: non-intimidation, non-discrimination and the impartiality of the state. One example of the irregularities we investigated was in Logar Province, where more females were registered to vote than men, which we knew wasn't possible. These were what we call "ghost voters." Men had registered thousands of women voters who did not exist—and even if the names belonged to actual women, the women did not vote themselves.

The three main candidates were Hamid Karzai, Dr. Abdullah Abdullah and Ashraf Ghani. During the campaign and on the election day itself, the AIHRC and UNAMA documented violations of political rights and recorded fraud and interference by all candidates, including ghost votes. The Election Complaints Commission did their own investigation and quarantined several boxes of fraudulent ballots.

Because there was no clear majority in the first round, there had to be a second round. Ghani had less than 5 percent of the vote, so he was dropped; then Abdullah declared he would withdraw for the sake of the unity of the country, and Karzai was declared president. However, rumors began almost immediately that Abdullah's supporters were prepared to fight the results—and Abdullah didn't speak up. I quickly arranged a meeting with him and suggested he release a statement to prevent the country from plunging into more trouble. He agreed, the messaging changed, and conflict was averted. Abdullah become the official opposition to President Karzai.

By 2010, with Karzai back in power and the international community planning an exit starting in 2011, we all worried about what would happen to the women in this country when the troops pulled out. Our own military wasn't ready to take over, our government still depended on outside help to function, and terrorism was gaining a foothold. What's more, we were getting mixed messages: one country said it would leave when Afghanistan was stable; another said it would leave soon because the ongoing war was increasingly unpopular with its own citizens; and still another said it would leave when it suited them. Some foreign governments were talking to the Taliban; others equated that with treason.

Now it was time to address the ongoing insurgency and bring everyone in the country together. It began with a loya jirga in June 2010—in the very same tent the German government had built during the emergency loya jirga in 2002. Two thousand delegates gathered to make recommendations for a peace process, including the establishment of a High Peace Council, an independent body that would examine ways to promote negotiations and talks with the Taliban and other insurgent groups. After the idea was adopted that September, sixty-nine council members were appointed—only nine were women.

At the beginning the council gained both national and international attention as it was seen as a real option for achieving peace. But the disagreements came quickly. The truth was that rather than being independent, it was heavily influenced by various members of parliament and government. Furthermore, women were not included in serious discussions, and when the council traveled, women were not usually part of the delegation. Then the chairperson of the High Peace Council, Burhanuddin Rabbani—a former president and founder of Jamiat-e-Islami—died in a suicide attack carried out by the Taliban at his home on September 20, 2011. Seven months later, in April 2012, another member of the High Peace Council, Mohammad Hashim Munib, was also killed in suicide attack, this time in Kunar. After that, the High Peace Council was seen as a weakened body. At the end of the day, the council failed to deliver the promise of holding face-to-face peace talks, and although it continued working, it lost its status and capability both nationally and internationally. The process was so convoluted that a man from Quetta was flown to Kabul by ISAF on November 23, 2010, and paid a bribe to meet with the council because they thought he was Mullah Akhtar Mohammad Mansoor, the Taliban's second-in-command. In fact, he was a shopkeeper who'd been paid off by ISAF as well as the government. He attended three meetings, collected his money and went back to Quetta before anyone realized he was an impostor.

The Taliban did not want to engage with the Afghan government; they only wanted to talk directly with the United States. The US had begun talks with Syed Tayyab Agha, the representative of Mullah Mohammed Omar, at meetings in both Germany and the Gulf States, even before the killing of Osama bin Laden on May 1, 2011, in Abbottabad, Pakistan.

The anxiety throughout the country regarding the exit of the international forces was palpable, and made worse by increasingly brazen attacks on public figures. The plan was that the forty thousand troops would begin to leave in 2011; the process would be gradual, taking place over three years, so that by 2014 there would be only a few thousand foreign soldiers in the country. It's easier to start a war than to set a timeline for ending it.

The drop in security became obvious. An example of this that hit home for me came on June 18, 2013. That day I had broken my routine, having decided to go to Gawharshad University, the school I had founded in 2010, to give a talk to students rather than go to my office. At precisely the time my armored vehicle usually would have pulled up at the gate, a massive explosion ripped through the neighborhood, killing three and injuring thirty. Most of the windows in the Human Rights Commission building shattered.

Some said the target had been the politician Mohammad Mohaqiq, whose car was identical in make and color to my vehicle, but most others assumed it was another attack on me. I had already received a warning from the intelligence service that I might be in danger and needed to be careful. I had asked why they suggested I take care rather than taking action to protect me. Because I call for justice and accountability, I have always been a target. As for who wants me dead, they likely came from both sides—the extremists as well as some people in positions of power.

On that same day the Taliban had opened its office in Doha, Qatar. They called it a political office and raised their flag—with

American consent. That created a lot of anxiety for the Afghan government and for the people, including myself. After strong words of protest from Karzai, the flag was lowered, but events like this kept me wondering about my safety, and that of my staff and the people.

My work with the AIHRC was ever more stressful, partly because we had been warned by the national security office that someone within the commission was working with the Taliban and planning an attack on me. We were never certain that this threat was real, but we increased our security measures at the office, and I made daily changes to the time I would arrive and leave.

Our commissioners were appointed for five-year terms that could be renewed for one additional term. When the terms were completed, the president was to either introduce new commissioners or reappoint the same ones—however, he did neither. We had lost one commissioner to a suicide attack in 2011 when Hamida Barmaki and her husband and four children were killed while shopping in a Kabul supermarket. Then the president had dismissed three capable commissioners and replaced them with four unqualified ones. Not one had the qualifications required by the Paris Principles. However, one of the newly appointed commissioners, Abdul Rahman Hotak, was a former Taliban supporter, and a man who had publicly expressed his opposition to the Elimination of Violence Against Women law, claiming it was un-Islamic.

Because Karzai flouted the rules, the commission risked losing its accreditation from the Global Alliance of National Human Rights Institutions. Everyone from UN High Commissioner for Human Rights Navi Pillay to Human Rights Watch Asia Director Brad Adams wondered what had propelled President Karzai to appoint people such as Hotak to the AIHRC, which been hailed as the biggest success story in the country.

Then Graeme Smith, a senior analyst at the International Crisis Group in Kabul at that time, stated the obvious: "There has been a real reluctance to embrace political pluralism, and there has been nervousness about internationally backed organizations like AIHRC that tell a different story about what's happening in the country than the story the government tells. These appointments seem intended, not to necessarily silence the body, but to change its tune."

The puzzle pieces we had sought, asked for and gathered were here in the country—all the elements it would take to make peace and prosper—but again, the dealings with the government and the strongmen in the country made me come to worrisome conclusions about the way forward.

The concern over the foreign troops leaving now morphed into a feeling, generally expressed across the country, that it was in fact time for them to leave. Their surge into the southern provinces hadn't scored victory; it had sown seeds of defeat. Not only that, but the blame game had also begun, with each group finding fault with the other. The Afghan government criticized the US night raids and the resulting civilian causalities. The United States and NATO member countries accused the government of corruption. During the night raids, which were organized by ISAF, Taliban targets were identified by drones, and those houses were then raided by troops on the ground. ISAF claimed the attacks were held at night because daytime attacks resulted in more civilian casualties, since people in the village would gather to watch.

While it was true that night raids reduced civilian casualties, complaints were made about culturally insensitive searches of houses and female members of the families by men. When I raised this issue with the ISAF commander, General Stanley McChrystal, ISAF invited me and a few members of parliament to Bagram Airport, where they showed us how the night raids were being conducted. As a result of all of the criticism, they began to conduct these operations with Afghan security forces and trained female officers to accompany them. Having seen the control room, with all the high-tech and computerized facilities, I understood how complex the operations were, but I still wondered how so many mistakes kept being made.

In another case, during the early morning hours of March 11, 2012, a US soldier, Sergeant Robert Bales, murdered sixteen Afghan civilians and injured six others in the Panjwai district of Kandahar. Nine of these causalities were children, and eleven of the dead were from the same family. Some of the bodies had been partially burned. Bales was taken into custody, and on August 23, 2013, was sentenced to life imprisonment in the United States. However, the result was not publicized adequately, so most Afghans knew nothing about the conviction and the case further undermined their trust in the judicial process for the international forces.

At the same time, attacks by the Afghan security forces against international forces increased, creating more distrust between the partners. These attacks were called "green-on-blue" (green referring to the Afghan forces, and blue the international forces) and had several causes, chief among them the infiltration of the Afghan security forces by the Taliban. Another reason was anger within the

Afghan forces at some of the behavior of the ISAF troops, such as the Kandahar mass murder by Sergeant Bales.

The withdrawal of the troops was one concern, but there was also the matter of the loss of jobs that would result when they left. At least 200,000 people were employed by the forces with jobs in security, logistics and translating. Being paid by NATO, they were receiving relatively high salaries compared to other Afghans. I estimated that each person employed by the international forces was supporting another ten people. With all those jobs lost, poverty would rise commensurately.

It is also true that we were a country trying to plan its future in twelve-year increments for funding purposes, and yet couldn't plan the next half-hour for fear of attack. Afghanistan became the epitome of "two steps forward, one step back." The obstacles in this fractious place were significant: a stubborn insurgency with an estimated twenty thousand to thirty thousand fighters, a lack of security, and problems with the rule of law, governance and corruption.

Mind you, the confounding security problem didn't keep the people at home, or out of school or away from the markets. The place was teeming with its thirty-eight million citizens. Traffic was notoriously chaotic and the famed Serena Hotel—which was still selling itself as an oasis of calm despite the suicide attack— continued to cater to would-be investors who cautiously saw Afghanistan as a business opportunity. The United States Geological Survey has said there's $1 trillion dollars in mining deposits in Afghanistan. And the Chinese had already won a $3.5 billion contract for the second-largest copper mine in the world—the Mes Aynac mine just forty kilometers southeast of Kabul. (That it sits under a Buddhist monastery is a problem. But today anything goes in a country trying to scratch its way out of its violent past.)

You could be forgiven for thinking the international soldiers bailed out of a losing proposition in Afghanistan, but the facts don't support that story. News of suicide bombers in supermarkets and bombing attacks on guest houses were true, and they did create a sense that the whole place was an armed camp. But consider this: A dozen years after we ousted the Taliban and their misplaced religious rules, you could play golf in the outskirts of Kabul and ski in Bamiyan. There were astronomy clubs, martial art classes, a circus, and youth acrobats. Computers, tablets and mobile phones were being manufactured in Afghanistan. The country had two Afghan-owned airlines and was the most-served destination out of Dubai. You could get Starbucks coffee at a funky bakery in Kabul, buy salmon imported from Norway or taste the highest-quality saffron in the world in Herat, or buy the most delicious and expensive homegrown almonds in the world.

What's more, sports and the arts were flourishing, with women and girls doing amazing things. There were national women's teams for cricket, soccer, running, judo, track, boxing and wheelchair basketball. There was an all-girls orchestra led by a nineteen-year-old conductor—they even played Carnegie Hall. There were rock bands and pop music concerts, technology startups, a coding school for girls, and an all-girls team even won a robotics contest in Europe. There were film festivals, theater groups, reality shows, soap operas and an all-women TV station that was holding its own in the rankings. An Afghan woman won a prestigious innovation award in England for developing a new cancer treatment.

Burkas in Kabul had become a fairly rare sight; but in Kandahar, they were still de rigueur. However, over at the city's Teacher Training College the students doffed their burkas upon arrival and gathered around their computers as though lifting off into the twenty-first century. Gawharshad University was flourishing now, with both boys and girls studying social sciences, math, and human rights, and hotly debating the future of the country. Watching them leave the school at the end of the day, still engaged in discussions, always stirred my soul and reminded me that it was only a dozen years ago that we staggered out of the Dark Ages the Taliban had thrust us into.

You never know when the tide will turn in the work that you do. It may seem unchangeable but then, all of a sudden, an opening leads to a dawning. That's how I felt in September 2013 when the Dutch ambassador came to my office to discuss human rights issues and told me a story that brought closure to a very painful part of my life. His incredible account also gave unequivocal support to the demands I had made for accountability starting in 2001.

The ambassador recounted to me that an Afghan man called Amanullah had arrived in the Netherlands in 1993, claiming he had worked for AKSA, the intelligence service of the pro-USSR regime in Afghanistan that had been responsible for torturing and killing people. Amanullah was seeking asylum because the mujahideen now in control might kill him. He carried with him a secret list of the names of five thousand people who had been killed by the state; there'd been no trial and no documentation of these deaths. The ambassador went on to say that Amanullah had died in 2012, and now the public prosecutor in the Netherlands wanted to release the list.

I could hardly believe what I was hearing. This was the evidence I had been searching for. Was Ghafoor on this list? His brothers, uncle and cousins? I asked the ambassador to send me the list and promised not to make it public before the embargo was lifted. He sent me 154 pages of names that I examined with such a heavy heart that I wondered if I could stay with the task. For two hours I pored over that list, but I didn't find Ghafoor's name. However, those of two of his brothers, his cousins, and a teacher and others I knew were on it.

It was an incredibly painful process for me, but I knew we had to take action. The list would be available to the public on September 23, 2013, so I decided to give it to *Hasht-e Subh* newspaper because I knew they would honor the embargo and be ready to publish at the appointed time. Then I called President Karzai to discuss the action we were obliged to take for the families who had been waiting thirty-five years to learn the fate of their loved ones. I suggested the following:

1. Apologize to the families on behalf of the state and show solidarity with them.
2. Have a collective funeral and a Quran recitation in all the mosques after Friday prayers.
3. Lower the Afghan flag to acknowledge the suffering of the families and show respect for those who were killed.
4. Promise to build a museum in memory of the victims.

My hope was that the president would be prepared to act on the proposals and coordinate his response with the date the list was available to the public. But he did not.

I stressed to President Karzai that the first three actions would require no financial investment and that I would do the fundraising for the construction of the museum. He asked me to send all the information to him in an official letter, but then he discussed the issue with the mujahideen leaders and they decided that building a mosque in Pul-e-Charkhi, where the majority were killed, would be memorial enough. And yet even that promise was never fulfilled. No one from the government stood with the people while they held funerals for their loved ones. I was one of those mourners, and after thirty-five years of seeking closure, I realized the wound would never heal.

The next blow to our entry into democracy came only six months later, in an election held on April 5, 2014. By then, the majority of the troops had left, the insurgency was rising, and corruption had spread like weeds into every department.

I was worried, because when the soldiers who had been with us since 2001 left in 2014, I knew the job was not finished. We had three major transitions to deal with, in the areas of security, politics and the economy.

Until 2014 it was ISAF and NATO who had provided security, with the intention of training an Afghan national army and an Afghan police force to eventually take over. NATO had a force of 130,000, with troops from forty-nine NATO and partner countries. They were deployed in most provinces throughout the country on six-month rotations during that period. Their initial task had been to defeat the Taliban and destroy the Al Qaeda terrorist network sheltering in Afghanistan. Although the Taliban was removed from power and the Al Qaeda network was disrupted, the allies had failed to disable either group or to stabilize the country. I wondered if our

Afghan security force, which was still in training, could handle this task left to them.

On the political front, Ashraf Ghani, a man with fourteen years' experience working as an economic advisor for the World Bank in New York and a former finance minister in the transitional government, seemed to be the perfect candidate for the election. He was adamant about rooting out corruption and claimed to be a reformer. He had run in the last presidential election and failed to get the traction he needed. But since our constitution allows only two terms, Hamid Karzai was no longer a candidate, and Ghani was now the frontrunner.

Ghani said he had a platform for change and that the country was ready for transformation: "The key demand for me from the public across the thirty-four provinces is to transform the state into an instrument of the rule of law, transform the economy into a productive system and improve the education system. We will be able to nurture a democratic culture. For the first time I feel the people understand the political and economic climate." He even evoked historical comparisons: "Our current conditions leading up to these elections are parallel to the US before the Lincoln election, Europe in the 1910s and '20s, Spain after the death of Franco, Chile after the death of Pinochet. These were times when people took elections very seriously. This [interest in the election] gives me the grounds to be able to develop a system that would be responsive to the people, rather than carry out top-down reforms that would alienate constituents."

His promises were music to my ears. He said all the right things: about the difference between stability and security, about inclusion and justice, about job creation for young people, about turning our natural wealth into a productive business. He would sit down with the Taliban to find solutions and extend a hand of friendship to Pakistan. He claimed that women's perspectives on the future of Afghanistan, particularly for peace, were crucial. He also promised that he would do everything he could to promote the principles of human rights and equality among the people in Afghanistan. He said hundreds of times that all Afghans are equal and no one is superior to another.

The election itself, though, was rife with corruption and fraud that was worse than ever. For example, we were expecting six to eight million people to vote but the Independent Election Commission (IEC) printed twenty million ballots. In the end, Ghani won, but the result was so close between him and Abdullah Abdullah that the US secretary of state, John Kerry, had to step in and negotiate an agreement. Eventually Ghani was declared president and Abdullah chief executive, and together they formed what they called the "unity government." That meant 50 percent of the ministers would be proposed by Ghani, and 50 percent by Abdullah.

It was fractious from the start. The two sides couldn't agree on anything and delayed the process of governing. Ghani seemed to want to centralize power and make every decision himself—the opposite of what he had promised. He was dividing people instead of uniting them—the Uzbeks, the Tajiks, the Hazaras; he even tried to create a divide within Pashtuns. I was shocked, surprised and very disappointed. I had backed the wrong horse.

Afghan citizens had been listening during the campaign when Ghani said that, as he had no relatives, there would be no family appointments to his government. Still, once in power, he appointed his retired uncle as the ambassador to Moscow and filled his office with cousins and cronies.

As for his promise to fight corruption, things actually got worse under his watch. The High-Level Commission for Anti-Corruption and Good Governance was a promise that turned into a platform from which he could lecture the members rather than taking action. For all these reasons, the northern province of Kunduz fell to the Taliban during Ghani's first year as president. He'd appointed a young man close to his team for the post rather than a qualified governor. When the province fell, it was a major blow not only to the government but also to the international community. They discovered that, once again, the money provided for defense and especially for local police had been absorbed by commanders rather than paid to the people assigned to defend the area.

I was also concerned about the establishment of tribal militias by the Americans to police the Taliban. This tactic had failed during President Najibullah's government in the late 1980s and early 1990s, as these types of militias were brutal and increased tensions between the various ethnic groups. They also empowered some of the previous commanders to rearm their own people.

It was an all-too-common example of corruption seeping into the donated help for reconstruction. When the Germans brought their provincial reconstruction team to Kunduz, they invested a lot of money in the development of the region, including building the Mazar-e-Sharif Airport. However, the contract went to local commanders, who overcharged for the work they did and enriched themselves at the expense of the donor. This practice was common in other parts of the country as well.

Once in power, Ashraf Ghani became a populist. As long as the people around him were clapping, he thought he was untouchable. For example, soon after he took power, he traveled to Herat and dismissed all thirty department directorates without putting anyone else in place, creating a political vacuum in the province. As a boss he was a micromanager, needing to be in control of every single issue. One time he told me that he worked sixteen hours a day; I told him that if he worked eight hours a day he'd do a better job.

In the meantime, so very much had changed. The young people were experiencing a life of learning and entrepreneurship and reaching for the stars. In the nineties there was one national radio station and one television station. Now there were sixty-four TV outlets and three hundred radio stations. In the 1990s, hardly anyone had a phone, except some of the mujahideen leaders who had satellite phones; now 60 percent of the population had phones, and those who didn't went to the market and used someone else's mobile. More than half a million Afghans were now on Facebook.

While institutions and education and human rights began to take root, the leadership failed to lasso the future. Most of the international troops left in 2014. ISIS turned up in 2015. The consequences ratcheted up the fear of the people. Then Donald Trump became president of the United States in 2016, and I knew we were in trouble.

Nine

TRUMP AND THE TALIBAN

AT FIRST IT WAS RUMORS—WHISPER CAMPAIGNS—and then the gossip took on hard currency: the man who was trying to get elected as the president of the United States was talking about negotiating with the Taliban. His rhetoric gave the impression that the Taliban had won the war. How could Americans and the international community think that a peace process could be conducted with radical fundamentalists and without the government that represented the people of Afghanistan? Since when did the world negotiate with a group that had been called terrorists for twenty years, with men who were on the FBI's most-wanted list, with a network that US intelligence showed had links to Al Qaeda? I knew it was a recipe for disaster.

In 2011, Donald Trump had started tweeting about pulling America out of Afghanistan. He called it "a complete waste" of American money and lives. And in 2013 he said, "We should leave Afghanistan immediately." Such comments were pure bombast, a bully tactic the world would soon see much more of. Another refrain: "Why are we continuing to train these Afghanis who then shoot our soldiers in the back?" (Facts were never his strong suit. Plus, I was amused that he always referred to us as Afghanis, which is, in fact, the term for our currency. We are Afghans.)

To compound the trouble, the international community had been losing interest in Afghanistan ever since the 2003 invasion of Iraq. It was as though there was an unspoken agreement among the allies: we came here to remake a country but we can't tame the insurgents so it's time to take our leave. Afghanistan had made headlines after 9/11, and had gained worldwide support for its efforts to remove its women from bondage. But now silence had fallen.

The end of 2016 was a watershed moment; Donald Trump was elected leader of "the land of the free and the home of the brave" and upheaval around the globe was surging. Whether it was Syria being pummeled by the Russians, or Turkey barely surviving an uprising, or Britain leaving its partnership with the EU, or three African countries turning their backs on the ICC, the old world order had come into question. Despite the disturbing turn of events, I still dared to dream that my landlocked country—a country that had once been best known for its calligraphy and pomegranates and brilliant blue mosques and amazing Bamiyan Buddhas—could somehow latch onto action plans for peace and justice and find its way out of the fractious fighting that had kept us from thriving.

In 2016 one thing was abundantly clear: if the United States withdrew from Afghanistan, the government would fall to the Taliban. After the international community departed there had been a boost in violence. Unemployment jumped from 40 to 50 percent, and economic growth fell from 12 percent in 2012 to 1.6 percent in

2015. The Afghan national army was still in training. Young people were putting their bets on smugglers to get them across the Mediterranean and into Europe. The lack of security and the new trend of insurgents taking hostages added to the sense of helplessness and despair. All of it was a kiss of death to nation-building.

What's more, as in all post-conflict zones, political propaganda was running amok. It was reported that Mullah Omar had died—simply because no one had seen him lately. Or there were claims that President Ghani and Chief Executive Officer Abdullah refused to speak to each other and required a mediator to pass messages between them. I knew that wasn't true—I'd witnessed them at a dinner event chatting civilly if perhaps not amicably. Another story surfaced that President Ghani, rather than stopping rampant corruption, had given a gas contract for the military to his cousin. Major General Gordon Skip Davis of NATO quashed that rumor, calling it an urban myth, and named a Tajik-based company as the actual recipient of the contract. But the innuendo flourished, all the while sowing the seeds of our demise as the governmental disarray fed the egos of the emboldened Taliban. It was clear that Ghani would not support the ministers who had been nominated by Abdullah and blocked whatever actions they took.

There was no denying the Taliban's heightened activity or the serious threat they posed to government forces by placing themselves in rural areas where they could block supply routes and use local taxation sources to set up shadow governments. Their other advantage was an immense opium crop, worth $3 billion dollars in 2016 and constituting about 60 percent of their assets.

It was hard to contemplate the speed of the downward spiral in real time, but in retrospect the American presidential nominee acting as a cheerleader for the Taliban coupled with the departure of the international troops hit us like a double whammy. When NATO ended its combat operation in 2014 after thirteen years of chasing the insurgents, clearing land mines and trying to establish security for the teams rebuilding the country, 130,000 soldiers went home and left a residual army of 13,000 foreign troops whose mission was to train the Afghan National Security Forces (ANSF) and the police, and to conduct counterterrorism operations.

As if to add insult to injury, ISIS (known in the Arab world as Daesh, based on the Arabic acronym) had become a confounding addition to the insurgency. Their incursion began with about fifty to seventy people from the Middle East arriving in Nangarhar Province in December 2014 and taking over a few villages. There, they infected the locals with their barbarous ideas, so in Afghanistan they were referred to as ISKP, Islamic State of Khorosan Province, referring both to Afghanistan and countries beyond Afghanistan's borders.

The original contingency consisted mostly of disaffected Pakistani Taliban and a few Uzbeks, Tajiks and others from Central Asian countries. They had no support from the Afghan people—even the Taliban hated them.

They were about brutality and violence for the sake of brutality and violence, with the goal of breaking the heart and will of the people. Suicide bombs were their modus operandi. Although hyper religious like the Taliban, their goals were different. People already understood that the Taliban's extreme ideology was partially based on the Pashtunwali code, with the goal of ruling over Afghanistan. But ISKP, although smaller and much more violent, had a Salafi ideology and wanted to establish a caliphate across Afghanistan,

Pakistan and parts of Iran and India. In 2016 they were just beginning to cause trouble in my country; it would get worse in time.

Trump wanted to get rid of ISKP. In fact, on April 13, 2017, in the first aggressive foreign action of his presidency, the United States dropped the most powerful and largest bomb in their arsenal on Achin district, the headquarters of ISKP in Nangarhar. They referred to it as the "mother bomb." (I have always been perplexed by the use of the word *mother* to describe something horrific. Mothers give life; they don't take life.) The bombing had a minor impact on reducing violence, but President Trump called it a very successful mission.

By then there were some major insurgencies in action, including the Taliban, the Pakistani Taliban, ISKP, the Haqqani Network, and Al Qaeda, which was back in business but on a much-reduced scale. A year later, in 2018, the Taliban controlled more than 35 percent of the country. Young people were fleeing at the rate of a thousand a month, joining the desperate migration flowing out of Syria and Iraq across the Mediterranean to Europe. Afghanistan had become the second-largest producer of refugees (after Syria) in the world. But it was also the largest recipient of returnees and deportees. Some families sold everything they had so their young sons could risk all to leave the country and reach Europe. Many lost their lives in the jungles and the oceans. And those who went to Australia faced discrimination and even torture in camps and prisons. Some even died by suicide.

What was abundantly clear was that we needed the United States and NATO to stay the course. Back in 2014, the government had signed a bilateral security agreement with the United States, which suggested they would stand with us until we could stand on our own. To me, this legal milestone was a key to our future.

Another key priority was finding a leader who would stop the corruption. Transparency International—a global organization leading the fight against corruption—declared Afghanistan the third most corrupt country in the world (after Somalia and North Korea). Whether it was police officers demanding bribes for safe passage along a highway or shopkeepers selling extorted goods or the proliferation of schemes such as smuggling and kidnapping, corruption was rife, and the funds pouring in from the international community turned it into an art form. The money that was supposed to build our institutions and bring health care and education to our people was an irresistible source of quick cash to those in positions of power and influence. Some of those people brought their ill-gained wealth to the West—to Canada, the United States and various European countries—but none were ever charged for corruption.

One outsized instance of corruption came to light between 2010 to 2013, as details of the Kabul Bank scandal slowly emerged. The scheme involved a small collection of powerful insiders including the vice president's brother, Hassin Fahim; the president's brother Mahmood Karzai; and others. Together, they took US$912 million of the bank's funds to support their own lavish living style, and also loaned money under the table to family, friends and associates. The government was able to recover less than half of the money taken. Many people wanted to see the revelations as a turning point, but in fact, since there were very few repercussions—most admitted taking the money but only two went to jail—there was no accountability.

President Ghani could talk the talk of unity and development, but he could not walk the walk. He wanted a peace agreement, but only on his own terms: he thought the Taliban and the warlords should come into the fold of the government, although such an outcome was never possible. He said he wanted a national consensus on peace-building but failed to reach one, and he couldn't even keep his supporters on his side.

We at the AIHRC and all Afghans kept waiting, hoping Ghani would change course, select new people, and deliver on his promises to build peace and stop the war. I tried to convince him both publicly and privately to unite the people by building their confidence in a good government. I told him this was the way to isolate the Taliban. But he didn't want advice. He surrounded himself with people who would agree with him and fired those who questioned him. He also played the ethnicity card very badly, favoring certain Pashtun warlords over others. Instead of creating peace and unity he was constantly creating new divisions.

By the time our 2019 presidential election campaign had begun, the US government had already started official talks with the Taliban, which seriously undermined the legitimacy of our election process. Most people were focused on diminishing security, increasing poverty and the worrisome thought that we were about to be abandoned by the world again. More business owners lost confidence and took their money out of the country.

Afghans needed to take responsibility for and manage the peace process. I also felt we had to put the emphasis on democracy and human rights. With this in mind, we launched a National Inquiry on Women, Peace and Security. We went to fourteen provinces to hold public hearings and focus groups and do interviews. More than thirty-five hundred participated; the majority supported the inclusion of women and victims in the peace process. But by the time we published the results everyone's attention was focused on a new development with the election.

The IEC said the parliamentary election should be postponed for two reasons: the vote counts for the recent presidential election had been delayed, and the American talks with the Taliban were creating confusion about who would be leading the country. The international community was also divided about postponing the election.

Ghani insisted that the election go forward. It became obvious that Donald Trump wanted the peace deal with the Taliban in Afghanistan to help secure his own re-election in the United States. It also became abundantly clear that the fate of Afghans was not even being considered. Just before the 9/11 anniversary, President Trump invited the Taliban to the presidential retreat at Camp David, but the Taliban claimed they wanted a signed agreement first. The meeting was held by telephone instead.

The 2019 election went ahead on September 28. It then took five months for the IEC to declare Ghani the winner, and only a few hours for Abdullah to dispute the result and claim he had won. Less than one-fifth of the registered electorate had bothered to vote—although to be fair, some stayed away due to threats of violence. In the end, according to IEC, Ghani received 9.6 percent of the registered votes and Abdullah received 7.5 percent. The numbers alone tell a story about a country in fear, a people in hiding, a loss of trust and belief.

The telling fact was that the IEC failed to confirm the number of people who had turned out to vote or even the number of invalid votes that were cast. This lack of transparency by the people appointed to guard the accuracy of the result was another blow to a population beginning to question the democratic system. Not surprisingly, doubts had been cast about the impartiality of the IEC, and all of it led to suspicions of fraud.

But in a quintessentially Afghan way, this election also featured at least one miraculous success that showcased the ability of the Ministry of Women's Affairs, the AIHRC and the women-run NGOs to mobilize quickly to address a problem. Just two months before the presidential election, it had become obvious that women wouldn't be able to vote because there were not enough women "searchers" (security checkers) posted at voting booths. The UN team and the rest of the international community contacted the Ministry of Women's Affairs and women's groups across the country and hired and trained five thousand women searchers in time for the election. Despite all the disappointment and failure associated with the election, this endeavor at least was a step in the right direction.

Regardless of the election result, the Taliban were taking control of one territory after another. And they were operating outside of our borders too, via the ubiquitous "Talks with the Taliban"—Taliban meetings with officials in Pakistan, in Qatar, in the United Arab Emirates, in Saudi Arabia, Russia, Iran, China and the United States. But there were no serious Taliban talks with the Afghan government. What's more, the UAE and Saudi Arabia started their own grab for power, telling the Taliban not to have talks in Qatar and to set up an office in UAE. Russia brought Karzai, some jihadi leaders and some non-jihadi politicians from Afghanistan together with Taliban representatives and neighboring countries at two days of meetings in Moscow, with no Afghan government officials and only a few women delegates. These were ominous warnings to a people who had been promised reform and democracy.

The most significant piece of the puzzle for me was that the warlords and corrupt intellectuals had never left center stage. After 9/11 they'd been tamed with appointments such as vice president, cabinet minister, governor or a dozen other powerful posts. They profited immensely in real estate, drug-running and government appointments. They had become the power brokers, arranging meetings with the Taliban without consulting the people and the government.

Another puzzle piece that perplexed me was that somehow, despite our now robust civil society, the Taliban were able to carry out deadly attacks that required support from the people—even though the majority of Afghan people were against them. The government had tried to reach out with a plan notifying the Taliban that formal peace talks could begin if they agreed to three conditions: reject violence, cut their ties with terrorist organizations and respect the Afghan constitution. But the Taliban knew they could bypass the government because the American president had offered them an olive branch. Why should they talk to the government when the shots were being called by a man in Washington, and Khalilzad as his representative?

I spoke publicly about the consequences of leaving the government out, but I could not counter the influence of all the talks with the Taliban in so many other countries. While Donald Trump was launching a political gambit to get himself re-elected as president of the United States, he was encouraging other countries such as North Korea to flout protocol and also giving nodding approval to

Islamic countries with connections to Al Qaeda that were looking for training grounds for radical Islamists.

The atmosphere in Afghanistan remained tense, with the country situated as it is in a critical geopolitical location, with neighbors and near neighbors that include three nuclear states (China, Pakistan and India) with a combined population of several billion people. Instability in the region could have profoundly negative consequences. Regional and economic cooperation could unlock tremendous opportunities for the world economy, but that path was dependent on a trio of tenuous factors: the involvement of the international community, the confidence of Afghans, and the unity of the people in the country.

Corruption and nepotism had become such a cancer on our population—metastasizing from one bureau and district to another—that we were increasingly losing trust in our leaders and in each other. The attacks increased in Kabul, and a siege mentality began to take hold. Even as the UN was declaring steady progress, and NATO was insisting the Taliban gains were not what people said they were, I noticed something telling in the announcements from both about wins and losses. The Taliban were taking a lot of ground, but it was in largely unpopulated areas. So their wins were being measured by geography rather than head count and were described as "areas not in government control." It was obvious we were losing ground.

I also began to notice other subtle but significant changes. The Belgian embassy had closed right after the international forces left the country in 2014. But now Australia and most of the EU countries had also reduced their staff and operations. As well, the language being used by the international community to refer to the Taliban and their activities had altered. The terms had become nuanced: "terrorist acts" were being replaced with "violence," and "terrorists" with "insurgents" or "groups spreading terror." These were words of capitulation, and they took some of the sting out of murderous attacks and replaced it with the salve of soft language.

No wonder the Taliban had no interest in power-sharing; it was quite clear to me they had already decided to take Afghanistan and establish an Islamic emirate as soon as the Americans left. They were at war with the Afghan army, but I knew they would eventually be at war with anyone who opposed them. They made a show of attending meetings, but they never wanted to negotiate, only to buy time. I wondered where the UN and the international community thought this would go. Wouldn't a Taliban victory ensure that terrorist-fueled fundamentalism would increase in intensity and spread to Europe, Africa and throughout the world?

I raised these concerns when I met with students at Gawharshad University. Seeing the negative effects of the peace talks, they were losing faith in the international community. One said, "I think they are only here for our mines. Why else would they be building an airport in Helmand Province, just a few kilometers away from the rare earth deposits?" Another asked, "If they wanted to end the opium trade, why is it still active in Helmand?" I told them they were the future owners of this country and needed to participate in the democratic process and promote values that were based on rights and freedom. But I was concerned about the impact of the propaganda on the mentality of the citizens and particularly on the youth.

Supporting the international community had become a tough sell. Sixty-five percent of the population was under the age of twenty-five, and 35 percent was under fifteen—young people like these students who had defied the naysayers and believed in the future of the country; they were grabbing all the brass rings the international community had tossed to them. But the consequences of increasingly entrenched corruption and deteriorating security were blocking their progress. When I think of those days, I can see that the gains were really extraordinary. Women as well as men were doctors and lawyers and CEOs. Women had become politicians and governors, Olympians and artists. We could be forgiven for thinking the epicenter of our world had now twisted on its axis and was in danger of spinning out of control.

Meanwhile, I tried to lobby and carry on with the reforms I felt could get my country back on track. My team and I were trying to fundraise enough money to compile reports of civilian casualties and violations of human rights between 2002 and 2020. We wanted to hold another national consultation about transitional justice. We needed to know what people were thinking and how to heal the wounds of the victims. We interviewed women, men, state institutions, civil society and, most important, the victims themselves. The peace process had to be victim-centered, to avoid revenge. What was clear in the final report was that people wanted peace with dignity, and peace with human security. As I participated personally in some of the public hearings, I realized that people were also very concerned about the reduction of the presence of international forces. I was also concerned, although I never thought the government would collapse quickly or that the president would run away with his team. When I reflect on this, I wonder why I didn't see that the collapse was coming so fast.

My term as chair of the AIHRC had been set to expire in July 2018, but Ghani kept delaying the appointment of new commissioners, so I stayed in the role for nearly a year longer. Finally, in July 2019, he made the decision about the new team, although he ignored all the established regulations for appointing commissioners. Since he wanted me to be on his side for the upcoming election, he established a position for me as state minister for human rights and special envoy on international affairs. He then abolished this new ministry before it was even established and without any consultation with me. I did not support any candidate, and when people asked for my advice I told them to vote for the person they trusted. The AIHRC did not do the political rights monitoring for the election that had been used in the past.

Needless to say, I did not support President Ghani during his re-election campaign. Of course, he was very unhappy about my decision, but he had not fulfilled his promises for human rights and good governance. He had stopped serving the people and clearly saw my work as expendable.

In December 2019, as the tide was turning perilously in my country, the secretary-general of the UN, António Guterres, appointed me as a member of the UN Secretary-General's High-Level Panel on Internal Displacement. Before this appointment I had also been named to the UN Secretary-General's High-Level Advisory Board on Mediation. Both appointments honored the work I had been doing in Afghanistan and Sudan, and obviously there was tremendous need the world over to deal with internal displacement and mediation. But a new enemy appeared on the scene just weeks later: COVID-19.

Of course, the pandemic had serious negative impacts on every country, but in underdeveloped countries such as mine, the situation was even worse. The Afghan economy was already under stress, and so was every institution in the country. Relief money was misused by corrupt officials, and, as a result, the suffering was off the scale. The impacts on women were especially severe. They lost their jobs. Domestic violence increased because women were quarantined with their abusers. Women's shelters and all the protection mechanisms were closed. Poverty increased, particularly where women were head of the household. To be fair, everyone was in quarantine, and the conditions were difficult for the men as well, since they also lost their jobs. Overcrowded hospitals didn't have enough beds or oxygen. The number of the COVID-19 casualties was high, although grossly underreported by an overwhelmed Ministry of Public Health.

Like everyone else, we on the panel found ways to work online during the pandemic, but by the time our final report with recommendations to improve the situation of internally displaced persons was delivered in September 2021, there were many more people in my country and around the world displaced by conflict, violence and climate change.

In my life I have seen colossal changes in the country where I was born in 1957. The tribal history is better understood now, if not tamed into national cohesion, and the abhorrent treatment of women has been exposed, if not corrected. But the level of violence in Afghanistan, which has risen and fallen over the years, catapulted to calamitous levels after President Donald Trump began his ill-conceived Talks with the Taliban.

Back in 2018 when the peace talks began in earnest—not just with the United States but also with countries such as China, India, Pakistan and Russia, who also had an eye on these proceedings—Trump had played another shocking card: pitching the exit of the United States as part of the peace negotiation. However, it was simply a disgraceful ploy to deflect his failings at home.

The so-called peace agreement was officially called the Agreement for Bringing Peace to Afghanistan, though it was also referred to as the US-Taliban Deal and the Doha Agreement. Signed on February 29, 2020, it was nothing short of a calamity in the making. It came after more than eighteen months and nine rounds of peace talks. A joint statement was issued, covering four elements:

1. Intra-Afghan negotiations: The Taliban agreed to start talks with the Afghan negotiation team.
2. Ceasefire: Negotiators agreed that a lasting ceasefire among US, Taliban and Afghan forces would be part of Afghan negotiations.
3. Withdrawal of foreign forces: All NATO forces would withdraw from Afghanistan when the agreement was signed in return for the Taliban's counterterrorism commitments. The United States agreed to reduce the number of its troops from roughly twelve thousand to eighty-six hundred within 135 days of the agreement being signed. If the Taliban followed through on its commitments, all US and other foreign troops would leave Afghanistan within fourteen months.

4. The Taliban guaranteed that Afghanistan would not be used by any of its members, or other individuals or terrorist groups, to threaten the security of the United States and its allies.

The information coming out of Washington, NATO countries, and also from the Talks with the Taliban was mostly contradictory. For example, all comments by the international community—including those made by Zalmay Khalilzad (the US negotiator) himself—indicated that the gains of the last twenty years were to be safeguarded, and yet this was not mentioned in the joint statement. As well, if the negotiators had been honestly committed to success, they would have involved the people in the discussions and not limited them to the Taliban and the United States. The Afghan government, regardless of all the mistakes it had made, was still the representative of the Afghan people. But it was not one of the signatories. And the document the signatories issued did not include a single word reflecting women and human rights. It was impossible to see peace coming from this agreement.

On the day the peace agreement was signed, President Ghani, US Defense Secretary Mark Esper, and NATO Secretary-General Jens Stoltenberg issued a statement in Kabul. Stoltenberg stated, "We went in together in 2001 and we are going to adjust [troop levels] together and when the time is right, we are going to leave together, but we are only going to leave when conditions are right."

The United States also committed to closing five military bases within 135 days and expressed its intent to end economic sanctions on the Taliban by August 27, 2020. The Doha Agreement was supported by Pakistan, China and Russia and unanimously endorsed by the UN Security Council. India also welcomed the pact.

Washington hailed the agreement as a pathway to an intra-Afghan dialogue involving the Taliban and an Afghan government delegation that would lead to a lasting political settlement of the long-running conflict. Within the limits of the English language, it's hard to imagine a statement that is more flawed or incomprehensible. While the agreement in the short-term was designed to reduce the number of US troops, it didn't commit the Taliban to a ceasefire or curtail their operations against Afghan forces. Nor did it oblige anyone to engage in dialogue. As Afghans, we felt we'd been sucker punched.

It's incredibly hard for an Afghan to believe that the United States had our best interests at heart when they engaged in a discussion with the Taliban. While this extraordinary pretense of a dialogue was going on, the Taliban were escalating their attacks on the ground, inflicting incredible casualties and expanding their territorial control by taking back many more districts in the country. (Not to mention the fact that Al Qaeda and ISKP and a collection of criminal gangs across the country also remained active.) Although I was in favor of dialogue and had always made that clear, I also called for accountability, justice and reconciliation to promote sustainable peace in the country.

The leaders on both sides, including Khalilzad for the United States, had been dodging the truth and using self-serving statements to assist with a power grab. They promised the troop withdrawal would follow a ceasefire—there was no ceasefire. They claimed they negotiated in good faith—they did not.

In the aftermath of the deal, insurgent attacks against the Afghan security forces surged, and thousands were killed. Then the Americans successfully pushed Ghani to agree to the release of five thousand Taliban prisoners from Afghan jails in exchange for one thousand Afghan soldiers held captive by the Taliban. The United States dramatically reduced the amount of air support they provided, leaving the Afghan National Security Forces at a huge disadvantage; the result was a sense of abandonment within the ANSF and the Afghan population.

Taliban violence increased exponentially. There was a shocking rise in the number of journalists being killed; not only were the Taliban against freedom of expression, but it was also known that Trump referred to journalists as the enemy of the people. And so journalists became an immediate target for lunatics. Judges and female human rights defenders were being murdered. Civilians were being slaughtered because of their ethnicity and religion. In fact, during the fifteen months after the Americans signed the Doha Agreement there were more civilians killed than in any other year since the war on terror began. At the same time, the attacks on American soldiers stopped, except for one American killed in a suicide attack in Kabul; President Trump vowed he would take revenge.

As David French wrote in *Time* magazine three days after the deal was signed, "The war in Afghanistan was no 'war of choice.' On 9/11 our nation suffered its worst attack since Pearl Harbor. It suffered its worst attack on an American city since the British burned Washington DC on August 24th, 1814, and the Taliban were intimately involved. That attack came from an enemy operating with the permission and under the protection of the same Taliban the Trump administration deals with today. . . . But there is no hope for peace when your opponent intends to continue the fight, and the hope for peace diminishes further still when the proposed peace agreement diminishes allies and strengthens your enemies."

The negotiations were by any measure a gift to the Taliban: a lack of management by Ghani and his team, alongside the withdrawal of troops, the release of Taliban prisoners and the removal of sanctions including travel bans, asset freezes and the arms embargo. As French said, this was an exchange "for unenforceable promises from an untrustworthy enemy."

In January 2021, I had a meeting with some members of the negotiation team from the Afghan government who were in Doha, trying to negotiate with the Taliban. Though the team was initially energetic and optimistic about the potential of the negotiations, they admitted their immense frustration with the intransigence of the Taliban as well as the distressing lack of unity and guidance from the Afghan leadership.

The conclusions of our discussion were distressing. First, there was the Taliban: they would not end the violence; they were silent on and disapproved of the progress of the past two decades; and they were against human rights and certainly the rights of women. What's more, the immense increase in violence from the Taliban proved it was a tactic for them—a means to gain points at the negotiation table. Now, predictably, they were claiming that the peace negotiations wouldn't work until the current president of Afghanistan stepped down.

Second, there was the government: The negotiating team described President Ghani as a man who had started acting like a dictator and was not respecting the rule of law, the constitution, or human rights and women's rights. They claimed there was a lack of political will to stop rampant government corruption and political bickering, which were seriously undermining the position of the negotiation team. I witnessed some of the meetings held between Ghani, Khalilzad, the American ambassador and his staff at the palace, and other government officials; instead of listening, managing and directing the meeting, Ghani was shouting and cutting meetings short without a final result. Dr. Abdullah had been given the chairmanship of the peace process after the disputed election in 2019, but Ghani was reluctant to give him the authority and financial support to do the job.

Afghans were watching this peace process initiated by the United States that now included talks between the Afghan government and the Taliban. Despite evidence to the contrary, I saw this as an opportunity. In the past forty-three years of war, Afghans had never been closer to the possibility of having peace than they were now, and many of us were ready to contribute. However, in order to protect the peace process and not endanger the investments made on all sides, I decided I had to draw the world's attention to a few crucial points, and through media interviews I spoke out to the many international partners who had worked with us to build a democratic country:

- The agreement between the United States and the Taliban did not address the voices and demands of the Afghan people, who were now being targeted and killed at higher rates than ever before. For instance, during the same week the agreement was signed, two female Supreme Court judges were assassinated in Kabul; the gunmen remained unidentified.

- The peace process requires more time and more determination by both sides in order to achieve sustainable results.
- The May 20 withdrawal deadline should be revisited; the end of war and conflict cannot be defined by a deadline, but must reflect the realities and conditions on the ground.
- The Taliban must be specific in stating a change in their policy, especially regarding women's rights, freedom of expression and other basic rights. Currently their policies are as harsh as they were between 1996 and 2001.
- Although Afghanistan is not a stable country and relies heavily on foreign aid, it has begun to form institutions for democracy. It has taken steps, in its constitution, to provide equal rights for men and women, and it has begun to support a flourishing free media.
- Afghanistan's fledgling democracy is at stake, and the country needs its international partners to intervene. An insecure Afghanistan is not only a threat to Afghans but also to the whole world; an unstable Afghanistan could become a breeding ground for terrorism sponsored by different states, including our neighboring countries.
- To avoid another 9/11, the United States must not prematurely withdraw from Afghanistan. Afghanistan's security must be considered an essential element of US national security.
- The Afghan president must respect the constitution of Afghanistan and the rule of law, and must work for Afghan unity and peace, which must include the protection of women, journalists, human rights defenders, civil-society

activists, and the rights of minorities and victims of human rights violations.

- Afghanistan's politicians must stop political bickering and work to unite the country.
- Peace negotiations must have the support of the people of Afghanistan. An immediate ceasefire is required to turn cynicism into optimism and to create a culture for peace that includes closure, acknowledgment, reparation, restitution and protection from victimization. Peace must also include accountability and justice to stop the culture of impunity.
- Space must be created for more consultation among the people and to build confidence in the process to guarantee the sustainability of the peace. Afghans have witnessed too many deals that did not end violence or bring peace.

I tried to state as clearly as possible that the country was in turmoil, that people had lost faith, had suffered enough. My plea to the international community was to ask those who supported us from the beginning to now turn their attention to the government of Afghanistan and the Taliban, to demand they both come to the table with the common good of the Afghan people on their minds. If that happened, I felt we could move forward; in fact, I felt we could flourish. This was a time for the international community to own the work they had done here, to be proud of the enormous accomplishments in Afghanistan.

But my words fell on deaf ears. The very people who had come with funds and plans and high hopes looked the other way while the so-called peace process followed a dishonest script that was doomed to fail.

People ask me who was at fault in this debacle. The answer is obvious: everyone was. It was the fault of the Americans and the international community for allowing a peace process to be conducted with the Taliban and without the government that represented the people of Afghanistan. How could a process like that succeed? It was the fault of the Afghan government that watched corruption rise and practiced exclusivity rather than inclusivity. And it was our fault as Afghans because the lack of unity in our country made us unable to take the lead and manage the peace process.

I can't fault the Americans for wanting to get out of the longest war they have ever fought, but I can fault them for the way they executed their end game. Under President Trump, they formalized an agreement that would declare peace—but they didn't care who that so-called peace was with and subsequently gave the Taliban the erroneous impression that they were the victors of the war. But the whole world knew what the Taliban had done.

It's fair to suggest that President Ghani's office should have been able to save the day. Unfortunately, the endless political bickering in the president's office seriously undermined the work the negotiating team was doing in Doha. Ghani began acting like a lone wolf—all the decisions were being made by him and were not shared with his cabinet. He began to fire anyone who brought him bad news. When generals told him the police and the soldiers were not being paid, he dismissed them. Ultimately, Ghani did not have the political will, skills or ability to govern. And the negotiation team was not able to make their points because the Taliban would not talk with them, and Ghani wouldn't allow Abdullah or Karzai to get involved either.

Interestingly, we hardly ever examine the fine details of failed leadership. Here was Ashraf Ghani—a man who completed a PhD at Columbia University in the United States, who worked at the World Bank in New York City for fourteen years as a respected economist, who returned to his country as advisor to President Karzai and minister of finance, who became the chancellor of Kabul University and even the president of the country. But then he exchanged his reputation for pariah status. How do these things happen? What propels intelligent, experienced people like Ghani to turn their backs on justice?

Of course, negotiating with the double-dealing Taliban, who kept saying in their pseudo-piously religious way that they wanted an Islamic Emirate, was an Achilles' heel for everyone on the other side of the table. No one dared to counter their religious arguments, even though our constitution already stated that no law can contradict Sharia law and Islamic principles. The Taliban insisted on what they referred to as *their* version of Sharia law, which is what we'd seen when they held power from 1996 to 2001. There is no place in the Quran that says girls cannot go to school and women cannot go to work. There is no other Islamic country that interprets Sharia this way. Even in the strictest countries, girls can go to school. At the peace table the Taliban were never precise about how they would interpret Sharia. They simply said, "All will be according to Sharia."

Another huge flaw in this entire peace process was that it was conducted without the meaningful participation of the people. In many cases, civil society and women's groups tried to consult with Afghans, but getting their ideas to the negotiating table never happened. The people want what they have always wanted: a chance to live and raise their families in peace without terrorist threats. Part of the Taliban strategy was to keep up the violence—the murders and bombings—to put pressure on the government. It's hard for people to come together, to show solidarity, when terrorists are on the street targeting women and ordinary civilians while the leaders of those groups are negotiating with the Americans.

Americans bring human rights and minority rights and women's rights to the table, which is a positive, but in our case, and when the chips were down, they looked the other way in the face of horrendous violence, claiming a ceasefire was coming. Who ever heard of a peace deal before a ceasefire?

History is replete with stories about Afghanistan—that the British couldn't defeat the Afghans, that the Russians couldn't either, and now the Americans and NATO member countries had also failed to find a peaceful resolution. So the world wonders why we can't find peace. The answer is complicated.

Afghanistan's geopolitical situation includes tension between many powers. The Pakistan leadership harbors the Taliban openly in Quetta, Peshawar and Karachi. The Taliban flew to Doha from Pakistan with Pakistani passports for the meetings with the Americans. Pakistan gathers insurgents to fight in India's Kashmir region and has them trained in Afghanistan. (That's why India supported an "Afghan-led and Afghan-owned" peace process.) Iran rejected the peace talks because the Afghan government was excluded. Then Qatar got mad at Turkey for hosting the peace talks in Istanbul when the Americans decided the talks should be in Turkey rather than Qatar.

Everyone in this shifting and unstable region is related—from Syria and Iraq and Yemen to Turkey and Iran to Pakistan, India and the "stans" (Turkmenistan, Uzbekistan, Tajikistan, Kazakhstan). They all have toxic oppositions to their governments, and they are almost all Islamic countries that have some connection to Al Qaeda. History has shown us that they are looking for training grounds for radical Islamists who oppose their own governments.

Insecurity in this region means a surge of refugees, burgeoning drug trafficking and flourishing global terrorism. The countries in this region share common marks of instability: economic hardship, organized crime, environmental degradation leading to poor crops and poverty. It's a formula for trouble.

War has always been a destructive force in my country. But even in the peace process, we were very divided, and this current problem goes back to 2004 and the loya jirga during which we were drafting the constitution. Political parties, the mujahideen, and the tribal leaders were all in the same tent, vying for power. The mistake made then was that the people who had destroyed the country during the Soviet occupation and the civil war that erupted after the Soviets left in 1989 were never held accountable for their crimes. Our rights and freedoms were simply ornaments to dress up the position of the power brokers.

Impunity is an ugly truth that festers and feeds revenge. We can trace it precisely if we choose to—the criminal acts committed; the citizens killed, maimed, disabled, wounded; all of the commanders and militiamen responsible. It may not be easy to make every single commander accountable but reconciliation and healing is possible if there is political will. However impunity is worn like a protective skin—*If you tell what you know about me, I will share my secrets about you.* It is the poisoned chalice of a nation.

———

Like every Afghan, I was living in a state of fear during this unsettled time. And like most Afghans, I can say I had begun to distrust the foundation on which the progress of the last two decades had been built. Just consider my own ethnic group, the Hazara minority, targeted by the Taliban, and ISKP as inferior; they called us "Islam unbelievers." Hard facts about atrocities were still being ignored as the attention had switched to peace talks and troop withdrawal. The attacks by opponents of the government increased and became more complicated and coordinated. For example, in Jalalabad, located in southeastern Afghanistan, there were violent incidents every week, including attacks on offices, the mosque, and sports stadiums. However, the attacks on the Hazaras were much more violent and inhumane everywhere. In western Dasht-e-Barchi, a Hazara area in the west of Kabul, they launched suicide attacks at the maternity hospital, educational centers, sports clubs, wedding halls and mosques. Attacks occurred during voter registration and at anti-government demonstrations. The casualties were very high.

We'd known throughout our lives that Hazaras were targeted, but even in the presence of NATO forces the atrocities against us continued. For example, in 2015, the Taliban took as hostages seven Hazara—men, women and a young child—who were traveling from Quetta through Zabul Province back home to Jaghori. They were held hostage for several months, and then the Taliban beheaded all seven and put their bodies on display. In protest, once the Hazaras had gathered the remains of these murdered people, they carried their coffins through the streets and held demonstrations first in Ghazni and then in Kabul.

The protestors arrived in Kabul on the evening of November 10 with the bodies. I called the president around 8 p.m. to urge him to take action to prevent violence. I asked him to make a short statement on television, showing solidarity with the people and promising that he would do everything in his power to bring the perpetrators to justice, to guarantee the government would provide more security for the Hazaras, and to assure them that development projects would begin in the area and that their demands would be considered. He listened to me, but said he was not going to give in to pressure. I ended the call by telling him that this was his responsibility. Then I went to see the bodies and tried to convince the people to take the coffins to the morgue at the hospital, but they were too agitated to do so. The next morning the demonstrations continued, with almost a hundred thousand protestors carrying the bodies to the Presidential Palace. As they approached the palace, a few tried to climb the cement protection wall. The police shot and injured the protestors. I then received calls from both the palace and the organizers of the demonstration asking for my intervention. When I went to the president's office, I saw how terrified he was. Later, in a meeting with Hazara representatives, Ghani was defensive, but ultimately he agreed to some of the conditions. However, he never acted on punishing the perpetrators or providing enough protection for Hazaras, despite my advice to him. We have a proverb that says: Why would a wise person commit a deed that bears regret? Surely Ghani realized later that this cost him support among the people.

Indeed, the attacks on the Hazaras continued unabated. And yet, I was expected to focus on making peace with the Taliban. Is this not what duplicity looks like?

———

The Taliban played the international community like a fiddle. They managed to divert international opinion, present themselves as credible and impose their views on the international community and Afghans.

When Joe Biden defeated Donald Trump in the 2020 US presidential election, most of the world breathed a sigh of relief. While I was happy Biden had won, we were worried that his election would not change US policy in Afghanistan. Biden said he'd review the peace process—which he did—and then he declared that he'd withdraw the troops. This is what I had feared: everyone would leave, as they'd done before, and we would be left with our fledgling democracy and a very questionable future.

The US Congress had established the Afghanistan Study Group in 2020 to make recommendations for American policy in Afghanistan. They concluded that the May 2021 withdrawal date should be extended and emphasized that a key objective of US military presence was to create conditions conducive to an acceptable peace agreement. They recommended that the US should not leave Afghanistan without an evaluation of the situation on the ground, finding that: "The United States is in a position where effective diplomacy, modest continuing aid levels, and strong coordination across civilian and military lines of efforts against a clear and unified objective can create the conditions for a responsible exit from Afghanistan that does not endanger our national security." Even these recommendations were not taken seriously.

Afghanistan is surrounded geographically by neighbors who all want something. India wants development projects; Iran wants water; Pakistan wants water as well as a stake in our politics to ensure Afghanistan doesn't end up with a pro-India government.

China wants a strict monitoring of the border with northern Afghanistan due to the proximity of the Uyghurs, and they also want access to our mineral resources. The warlords want assurances for their assets and incomes and positions in the government. It all created a powerful sense of déjà vu.

These factors mean that human rights defenders and activists have many enemies in Afghanistan—from militants, warlords and tribal chiefs to those who stifle criticism. As spring turned to summer in 2021, the unimaginable began to unfold.

Ten

THE IDES OF AUGUST

THE UNIMAGINABLE ALWAYS TAKES US BY SURPRISE. The inside story about what happened on August 15, 2021, is about the United States, NATO, the United Nations, the mujahideen leaders, the tribal elders and President Ashraf Ghani, along with his handpicked associates. It also involves the Taliban and those who funded them. Collectively, they made a deal that would come back to haunt us.

The ancient Roman calendar referred to the middle of a month as "the ides"—the expression lives on thanks to Shakespeare. In his play *Julius Caesar*, Caesar is warned by a soothsayer to "beware the ides of March"—the date in 44 BCE on which he was assassinated. Today, the quote invariably refers to a bad omen, and such an omen came to pass in Afghanistan on the ides of August 2021.

The confounding thing about conflict is that the ending is never scripted in the playbook. There was a time when the end of a conflict was about winners and losers. Not anymore. These days, it's about deals being struck and gains being made—political deals, business deals, land grabs, resource grabs. And none of it achieves results that benefit the vast majority of the people. Somalia, Iraq, South Sudan . . . even Bosnia did not end with measures in place to secure the democratic governing of the country.

It has to be said that the collapse in Afghanistan was spectacular. It looked to the watching world as though the Taliban had fought hard to capture provinces such as Kandahar, Helmand and Herat, but when they took Kabul they hardly had to fire a shot. While there's more to the story, the truth is it took less than nine months for the Taliban to reverse twenty years of change. More than 100,000 Afghan civilians and another 176,206 Afghan soldiers died or were wounded during the last two decades. The toll for soldiers from the international community was 3,579 deaths and 23,536 wounded. The financial cost was a staggering $2.3 trillion.

The ides had been years in the making. The US negotiations with the Taliban had started behind the scenes in November 2010, when Richard Holbrooke, the special representative of President Obama on Afghanistan and Pakistan, tried to convince them to end the war, and again in 2013, when the United States agreed that the Taliban could open their official office in Qatar. The deal made was that there would be a prisoner exchange—an American soldier, Bowe Bergdahl, being held by the Taliban for five Taliban prisoners in the Guantanamo Bay detention camp. It was agreed that the Taliban prisoners would stay in Qatar. Although that news was released to the media in 2014, the talks continued in secret until late 2018. Collectively, the talks achieved nothing. When they were finally made public, it was only a matter of time before the

collapse was complete. The only reason we were all caught by surprise was because we were so desperate to make our date with
democracy work; we were too afraid to acknowledge the signs that
we'd been jilted.

Betrayals were a sign of the times. According to witnesses in
Herat, on August 13, 2021, the newly appointed commander of
the army telephoned former mujahideen leader Ismail Khan, who
was leading an armed group of young people to fight against the
Taliban and defend the government, and told him to come to the
military post for discussions; when Khan arrived, the National
Directorate of Security kept him under observation and denied
him an exit to Kabul.

Khan had fallen prey to the Taliban, who had insiders working
as spies at the NDS. The infiltration had actually begun in 2008,
when the Taliban managed to have their own people posted as
civilians within the ministries. The attacks the Taliban took credit
for were mainly in Kandahar and Helmand Provinces and occurred
because they had learned battle plans from insiders. In fact, every
ministry had a back channel with the Taliban, as well as with the
Americans. Our foes were braided together with our own leaders.

The year had dawned with perilous signs of trouble. With the
NATO troops gone, the military losses were climbing fast and demor-
alizing soldiers. The tensions between the mujahideen factions, as
well as the tribal chiefs and village elders, were at a boiling point.
For many, the Taliban became an escape hatch: joining them was a
way to take revenge on one faction or another. And remember,
these were mostly uneducated young men who could not read and
write and were promised they would go to heaven and have seventy-
two virgins waiting for them if they joined the jihad.

By the summer of 2021, most of the generals had been removed and replaced with unqualified people who were close to Ghani. Army officers were told not to fight the Taliban. The soldiers, who hadn't been paid in months, lacked food and medical care and weren't being resupplied.

And meanwhile, Ghani had his finger in every pie, interfering with the decisions made by his ministers and his generals. Corruption and nepotism were rife. The signs of defeat were all there. Embassies were closing, and by the time the middle of August rolled around, the US staff had been burning documents for several weeks. The television news kept announcing a delay in the government delegation's departure for Doha, where they were to sign an agreement with the Taliban.

At the end of June I traveled to the United States to visit my family. Both of my children, now grown with families of their own, live in the US, and so do my sister and four of my brothers. Since Ghani was obviously steering clear of me, and the job he'd appointed me to do was abolished in December 2020 without ever having materialized, I felt it was a good time to get away to catch up with the family and clear my head about what lay ahead. My plan had been to return to Kabul on August 10, but as that date drew near I faced a dilemma, caught between my need to get back to my country and my family's concerns for my safety. In the end I made the very difficult decision to stay in the United States, hoping my country could survive.

We all knew that deals were being made for power, for land, and for resources—everyone wondered if the United States had secretly negotiated a surrender. When we considered all the blood that had been shed in Afghanistan, it was too hard for us to contemplate that we'd be back where we started in 1996. And our wishful thinking about the future was reinforced by constant messages from the United States and the NATO countries reassuring us that they would not leave Afghanistan in the lurch.

The truth about what was going on behind the scenes would eventually be revealed in a 2022 report by the US government's Special Inspector General for Afghanistan Reconstruction (SIGAR). The report noted that the most important factors in the collapse of the Afghan National Defense and Security Forces (ANDSF) were the decisions made by two US presidents to withdraw US military and contractors from the country. According to one former US commander, "We built that army to run on contractor support. Without it, it can't function. Game over . . . when the contractors pulled out, it was like we pulled all the sticks out of the Jenga pile and expected it to stay up." After having invested $89 billion in the defense project, the United States walked away. As a result, Afghan soldiers in isolated bases ran out of ammunition or died for lack of medical evacuation capabilities.

According to a senior Afghan official, it was not until April 14, 2021—when President Biden announced the final troop and contractor withdrawal date—that President Ghani's inner circle said they realized that the ANDSF had no supply and logistics capability. But they had been supplied by outside contractors for twenty years—how could the president's office not have been aware of that?

As it turned out, the step-down of the ANDSF had been carefully calculated. The Taliban had brokered a series of surrenders along the way by assassinating military leaders, threatening their families and offering them money to lay down their arms, and more money if they would join forces with them. It's easy to suggest—as President Biden did when he made his announcement—that the military should have fought back. But the SIGAR report puts the blame squarely on the Doha Agreement, which "was a catalyst for the collapse." What's more, the report acknowledges that after the signing of the Trump administration's US–Taliban Agreement, the US military abruptly changed its level of support. A former commander of Afghanistan's Joint Special Operations Command told SIGAR that "overnight. . . 98 percent of US airstrikes had ceased."

We knew about the many factors affecting the ANDSF—low salaries; poor logistics that led to food, water and ammunition shortages; and corrupt commanders who colluded with contractors to skim off food and fuel contracts. But SIGAR said the root cause of the morale crisis may have been the lack of ANDSF buy-in with the Afghan central government.

The government had certainly gone rogue. Ghani feared that the international community was turning against him, and he no longer trusted the Americans. But it was the outrageous secrecy around the US-Taliban negotiations and the Doha Agreement that I feel bore the greatest responsibility. They had even talked about rewriting the constitution, creating a transitional government with an expanded parliament to accommodate many Taliban members, and reconstituting the courts. I wasn't the only one suggesting that the secrecy created collusion between the Taliban and the Americans—the SIGAR report later put the truth to it when it said, "Taliban propaganda weaponized that vacuum against local commanders and elders by claiming the Taliban had a secret deal with the United States for certain districts or provinces to be surrendered to it. One former senior Afghan official told SIGAR that the Taliban used this tactic quite effectively, telling forces, 'They're going to give us this territory, why would you want to fight? We will forgive you . . . we will even give you 5,000 Afghanis for your travel expenses.' Having not been paid for months, the police would abandon their posts. Then, 'the army panicked; they thought the police made a deal, and they're going to be butchered. So, the army made a run for it too. That started a cascading effect.'"

Insiders knew the Afghan army was heavily dependent on the American soldiers and suppliers. But the conclusion of the SIGAR report stung us to our core: "The February 2020 decision to commit to a rapid US military withdrawal sealed the ANDSF 's fate."

What the SIGAR report did not mention was the role being played by neighboring countries, particularly Pakistan, in supporting the Taliban.

Soon enough, various Afghan provinces began falling to the Taliban. In Faryab Province in early August, the Taliban promised the special forces they would be safe if they surrendered. When they did, all twenty-two of them were executed. And the governor of Nangarhar—Ghani's man—was seen on social media welcoming the Taliban in his office on the morning of August 15.

The Taliban declared to the world that they had turned more moderate. They managed to fool many with that pretense, but Afghans knew the truth. The vengeance was terrifying; members of the Afghan security and defense forces, women lawyers and judges, journalists, Hazaras and Afghan Hindus and Sikhs were hunted down. As well, anyone who had helped the West over the previous twenty years—the fixers who worked for journalists, the translators, the drivers—had to gather their families and hide. In the chaos during the takeover of Kabul, the airport was overwhelmed with desperate people trying to get away. The world watched aghast as a military cargo plane moved down the runway with desperate people clinging to its fuselage—two young men fell to their deaths as the plane rose into the sky.

As the Taliban made their way to Kabul, these men who had promised moderation announced that girls over the age of fourteen and widows under forty were to be taken as brides for their soldiers. Videos flashed around the world of people being tormented and then drowned—being pulled from the river and plunged back in again and again in a show of such brutality and hatred that the coverage was too graphic for most news outlets to air. Men were beheaded, their heads paraded on sticks around the village like something out of the Dark Ages. Women were flogged for being on a cell phone, pleading for mercy while old, bearded men passed the whip one to the other.

It was evident that as much as the government had failed the people of Afghanistan, the United States and NATO had failed in their planning and decision-making about departing. The proof was evident not only in the rapid retreat but also in the fact that the United States left Bagram Airport in the middle of the night without telling a single Afghan member of its team. When the Afghans arrived for work in the morning there were more than a thousand armored vehicles on the base without any keys. What followed were rampant rumors that the United States had been defeated and the Taliban were taking over.

The Taliban and the Americans had agreed that there would be a political agreement between the Islamic Republic of Afghanistan delegation and the Taliban, with the creation of a transitional government to safeguard the achievements of the last twenty years. Initially, Ghani said he would step down only when he could hand the presidency to an elected person, a demand that was not practical or possible. After much convincing from Karzai, Abdullah and others, Ghani said he would be willing to leave power after a loya jirga. US Secretary of State Antony Blinken pushed Ghani to send a delegation to Doha to secure the deal with the Taliban, claiming it would get them the ceasefire they had been asking for. But Ghani backed out and did not allow his delegation to fly to Doha.

On August 15, the world woke up to the news that the president of Afghanistan had run away and the Taliban were walking down the streets of Kabul toward the Presidential Palace. Soon enough, we heard that Ghani had taken about fifty people with him in three helicopters to Tajikistan. In a turn of events that must have surprised Ghani, the Tajik government did not give them permission to land; they went instead to Termiz, a border city of Uzbekistan, and spent a night there. The next morning the United Arab Emirates sent a plane to take them to Abu Dhabi and granted the president asylum. His aides claimed afterward that this flight had been arranged the day before; they knew Ghani was preparing to escape.

When it was known that Ghani had fled, someone at the palace called former president Karzai and asked him to come to the palace and take command of the country. Karzai called Abdullah and gave him the details he had, and at about 4 p.m., Abdullah posted a video on social media about Ghani running away. He asked the citizens to stay calm and avoid disturbances.

By 6 p.m., the Taliban were in Kabul and entering the palace. Everyone was in shock, including the UN, but the reaction was powerful and the message was clear: after the American retreat, our leaders ran away. We Afghans were now on our own.

My niece, who was working at the Ministry of Finance, went to work that day as usual. At around 10:30 a.m., someone from the ministry came by her desk and said, "Everyone has gone, the Taliban are in Kabul—what are you doing here?" She ran outside and saw terrified people running in all directions; after forty-five minutes she found a taxi and went home. A female police officer told me she was starting her workday in Karte Char, as usual, when suddenly her colleague found out that the Taliban were in the city. The women were terrified and started to strip off their uniforms, knowing they would be in great danger if the Taliban entered the office. They raced around the room looking for scarves and burkas to cover themselves. The male officers were also in shock and attempted to hide the insignia on their uniforms.

As the Taliban arrived in each village and town, they opened the doors of the jails and detention centers and let the criminals go free. The smugglers, the suicide bombers, the drug dealers and criminals, including the ISKP members, who had murdered thousands of Afghans, were released. The Hazaras were hit again with multiple bomb blasts outside a high school and an education center in Kabul's Dasht-e Barchi neighborhood. Then a mosque in Mazar-e-Sharif was attacked, and another in Kunduz. Two minibuses full of Hazaras were hit with explosives in Kabul and Mazar-e-Sharif. Altogether, more than one hundred Hazaras were killed and as many injured in six to eight weeks.

As news spread of Taliban takeovers in Herat and then Mazar-e-Sharif, my family in Kabul as well as the United States insisted I postpone my return. You can only imagine the size of my heart-ache when I turned on my phone on August 15 and saw that the Taliban were in Kabul, posing for selfies in the president's office at the palace, and that Ghani had run away. I called my husband, who confirmed the terrible truth. He said the streets were full of people trying to reach their homes, on their phones calling family members to make sure they were safe, telling them to come home immediately. It was as though all of Kabul had been hit by a stun gun. An eerie quiet eventually filled the streets; the shops were closing, the usually chaotic traffic was stilled, and the crowded sidewalks emptied.

At this point, the cabinet ministers, including the second vice president, were on their way to the airport. The scene captured by the media and shown to the world was a country running away from itself. The Afghan special forces, trained by the CIA, were supposed to be providing security at the airport and managing the crowds, but in fact they were hustling their own families onto the few departing planes.

Families began to be displaced—some running for the borders, which were closed, and others finding relatives in rural areas. It didn't take long for the Taliban to come pounding on the door at my own house. Less than twenty-four hours after arriving in Kabul, Commander Juma Khan Fateh from Badakhshan was at my gate. "Is this Sima Samar's home?" he demanded. "Where is she?" He and his associates pushed past the guard, entered my home and demanded my bodyguards hand over their Kalashnikovs and pistols. Some men were left outside the house to watch who came and went.

I needed to evacuate my family, several of whom were living with me at my house, including my brother Ahmad Ali and his wife. Given my work as a defender of human rights, I feared for their safety. I called previous ambassadors and the US embassy and the NATO civilian ambassador and the current Canadian and German ambassadors. Ahmad Ali was my chief of staff and everyone knew him, so he was in immediate danger. Fortunately, the Canadian embassy staff reacted quickly, got them on a list, and evacuated them with their own staff the next day. My husband and the rest of the family, including my mother, were not ready to leave at that point.

I also had to consider the consequences for the staff at the AIHRC and people related to me. They were all terrified and knew they were at risk because of their association with me. When some people suggested they take down photos of me in the offices for fear of retaliation from Taliban soldiers, I supported the decision. Although the leaders were telling people there was a general amnesty, in truth they were ransacking houses, and arresting, torturing and killing people.

What followed was like the script of a horror movie—the Taliban were at my home, taking first one car provided for me by the UN (we had actually been in the process of handing the vehicle over to the government) and later my personal car, and threatening my brother Abdul Wahid, who'd stayed behind with our mother. The United States promised to get my husband and brother as well as a colleague from the Human Rights Commission and his pregnant wife out. But the chaos at the airport prevented them from leaving, and in fact, they were only a few meters from the suicide bomb that killed fourteen American soldiers and more than two hundred Afghans.

Another of my brothers, Abdul Aziz, and his son and daughters were promised that if they could get to Tajikistan they'd be evacuated to Sweden. They were beaten up by the Talibs at the border and returned home. So many times they packed up a few belongings and made the dangerous drive to the airport; so many times they narrowly escaped capture and returned to the house wondering what the next day would bring.

Imagine being on the other side of the world watching your life's work collapse and your family dodging catastrophe. I could not sleep. I couldn't stop crying. My thoughts were such a jumble of agony, I could hardly manage. I was being contacted by media from all over the world asking me to comment, to speak out. But at the same time my colleagues, friends and family back home were asking me to remain silent, telling me that they would be punished for anything I said. I'd been speaking out for my whole life but now I was muzzled.

Rauf knew he was being watched, so he decided to go into hiding. He left the house in the dead of night and found shelter with friends. He changed lodging every few days, traveling to Jaghori and Bamiyan so they wouldn't find him. He tried to cross the border to Quetta but could not pass. The looting and shooting were everywhere, with Hazaras getting the worst of it. At last Rauf made it to Islamabad, but by then the stress had sent his blood pressure through the roof. When he tried to obtain a US visa, he was beaten and robbed by the Pakistani police. Eventually the German government arranged his evacuation and he left Pakistan in mid-November, twelve weeks after the nightmare began.

On the day Rauf had gone into hiding, the Taliban had come back to our house in Kabul. The first time they had a letter from the minister of justice, and the next time, one from Mawlawi Abdul Salam Hanafi —even though they had announced publicly that no one has the right to enter anyone's home and push people out or take people's possessions. In reality, they came whenever they chose to and took whatever they wanted, and if you dared to argue, you could be beaten, even killed. To add to the fear, these men had a photo of me taken when my scarf had fallen to my shoulders; they thrust the photo at my brother Abdul Wahid's face and shouted their insults: "Shame on you as an Afghan and Muslim man to have such a sister and you are still saying that you are the brother." They demanded to see his ID card, to see if we had the same name as our father, and made him go from one office to another explaining himself and providing the documents of our house, all the while extorting money from him.

On August 17, Zabihullah Mujahid, the spokesperson for the Taliban, held a press conference in the government media center and announced an amnesty for everyone who had worked with the previous administration; as long as they apologized to the Taliban, they would be given immunity. I thought about that piece of nonsense for a while and wondered what I was supposed to apologize for. Was it for working as a medical doctor or for helping the Afghan refugees in Pakistan, or should I apologize for establishing hospitals for Afghans? Or maybe I should apologize for trying to save the lives of people who are vulnerable and poor. Perhaps my crime was taking care of the children suffering from malnutrition or providing an education for the girls and the boys. Or did they think I should be sorry for building all those schools and hospitals or training the midwives, nurses and teachers? Or was it opening the first-ever Ministry for Women's Affairs? When I think of the time I spent, the delicate conversations I had to make Afghan women visible again, I shudder because history is repeating itself.

Perhaps they were asking me to apologize for my crime of promoting and protecting human rights for all, including the Taliban. Perhaps they'd forgotten that I fought for the elimination of torture and for a moratorium on the death penalty for everyone, including the thousands of Taliban in detention. I remember the day I visited an American-run prison in Bagram; a group of prisoners was outside at the time, and when they saw me arrive, some ran to the fence shouting "Sima Samar is here." Then they called out that they were not being treated fairly. Later, I sent my staff to get the details. They knew I insisted on the rule of law and the doctrines of human rights for prisoners. They knew it then and they know it now. But still the Taliban entered my home and threatened my family.

On November 4, the Taliban came again and searched every corner of the house. Two of them stayed in our home until the next day, when others arrived and declared the house to be government property. An Uzbek Taliban commander had moved in next door and insisted he wanted my house too. The harassment continued until finally they pushed my brother and our ninety-three-year-old mother from the house into the cold. I sent copies of the documents proving our ownership of the house to Fatima Gailani, who was the former director of the Red Crescent Society, and to Hamid Karzai, asking for their help. They responded immediately, and the Taliban mob finally left my home.

When the Taliban took over, the backlash began, like a blueprint of betrayal. The first thing they did was to abolish the Ministry of

Women's Affairs and replace it with the Ministry of the Promotion of Virtue and Prevention of Vice. It was a difficult day for me, as I had devoted my energy and enthusiasm and commitment to the Afghan people in opening that ministry and repairing and refurbishing the building itself; now the Taliban was using it to eliminate women from public and social life all together.

The Taliban possessed very few strategies for governing, but the measures to restrict women's rights were rolled out one by one as though they were recreating the old regime:

Dress Codes

Posters appear with photos of two acceptable dresses for women, the burka and the black niqab. Dress code violations such as females with hair showing or wearing a colorful hijab are crossed out with an X.

- Female mannequins in store windows must have the heads cut off.
- Police from the Ministry of the Promotion of Virtue and Prevention of Vice monitor women's dress styles in a shopping mall and claim, "The real cause of moral corruption is the face." An official from the ministry adds: "For all dignified Afghan women, wearing hijab is necessary and the best hijab is chadori [the head-to-toe burka] which is part of our tradition and is respectful. Those women who are not too old or young must cover their face, except the eyes. . . . Islamic principles and Islamic ideology are more important to us than anything else."

- The clothing edict is revised: all women must cover their faces and wear head-to-toe clothing that covers the entire body with loose fabric, making sure faces are not seen in public. If women don't cover their faces, their male relatives will face punishments that begin with a summons and escalate up to court hearings and jail time. From past experience, everyone knows that punishments can include lashing, beating, drowning and murder.

Women in Public

- Women should leave home only when necessary and only if accompanied by a close male relative.
- Women are told to stay at home. When women and girls gather on the streets in protest, the Taliban spray them with fire hoses and beat them. Some are jailed, others are disappeared; and some women, such as former member of parliament Mursal Nabizada, are murdered. But the women keep protesting, hoping to let the world know of their plight.
- Women cannot travel by air or road and are only permitted to go 70 kilometers from home unless accompanied by a close male relative.
- Taxi drivers and any other public transportation vehicles must refuse female passengers who are not covered properly.

Female Education

- Schools are closed, with the promise they will reopen soon. Women and girls are beaten on the street for daring to protest and calling for access to education.

- The schools almost open, but just as the girls gather in their classrooms, a new edict is declared by Supreme Leader Hibatullah Akhundzada—no education after grade six.
- Classes for females and males at the university must be separated, and the students must enter through separate doors so as not to see each other.
- Later, universities are closed to women. Many male students walk out with the women in protest.

Women Working
- Women can work only in the health sector.
- Women are banned from government jobs.
- Women presenters on television must cover their faces. Soon after, the edict changes—women are banned from most of the positions.
- In July of 2023, women's beauty parlors were banned, taking away a source of income. (Women came out to protest against this ban, but faced violence.)

Civil Society
- The Taliban close 153 media centers. The Ministry of Women's Affairs is closed. The Afghanistan Independent Human Rights Commission is shuttered. They announce that it is not necessary for women to play sports.
- Driving lessons for women in Herat are canceled.
- Public parks are now segregated: certain days are for women, others for men. Then women are banned from being in parks at any time.

All of this is about duplicity as well as ignorance. They obsess about women covering their faces, but the holiest place for Muslims is Mecca, where people come from all over the world for the pilgrimage and men and women don't cover their faces. Only Afghanistan forbids education for girls and transfers the punishment for a so-called crime to another person. What's more, we have proof that some of the Taliban members' daughters are studying in Pakistan and Qatar, even attending universities and private schools. Some are even playing soccer for their school teams.

The Supreme Ruler, Mullah Hibatullah Akhundzada, who lives in Kandahar and is never seen in public, ordered that every Talib must implement the rules of the Ministry of the Promotion of Virtue and the Prevention of Vice. But now, as in 1996, there are divisions within the ranks of the all-male cabinet. I don't believe we should hold any false hope for a so-called moderate Taliban. The Taliban are all the same. But their divisions are what might ultimately bring them down.

The United Nations Assistance Mission in Afghanistan responded to Mullah Hibatullah's order by saying, "This decision contradicts numerous assurances regarding respect for and protection of all Afghans' human rights, including those of women and girls, that had been provided to the international community by Taliban representatives during discussions and negotiations over the past decade."

Khalid Hanafi, acting minister at the Ministry of the Promotion of Virtue and Prevention of Vice said, "We want our sisters to live with dignity and safety." There's not much dignity or safety in a burka, since you lose your identity and become invisible. And since you are fully covered, you are deprived of the vitamin D that comes from the sun. I remember in the 1980s, when I was living in

Pakistan as a refugee, some of the fundamentalist Pakistani members of parliament were saying that women should not participate in sports because their skin color would become darker and they would not find a husband as a result. At that time, I was thinking that Afghanistan was lucky not to have people with this kind of mentality. I did not know then that Pakistanis were training our people to be even more extremist than they themselves were.

In a stunning turn of events, the supreme leader announced that Talibs should not marry a second, third or fourth wife. Two days later he added a caveat—if the couple does not have children, or does not have male children, or if there is "another legitimate reason," the man can marry more wives.

It didn't take long for the Taliban to throw women back into the Dark Ages, and to make a mockery of the deal they had cut with the United States. The fallout was just as swift. Poverty increased so much that people were willing to sell their organs to get money to feed their families. Daughters were sold because families could no longer feed them or because the money from the sale was needed to feed the rest of the family. Child marriages increased dramatically as a source of income. The age of marriage according to the law is sixteen, but the Taliban do not respect the law, and some girls are being married as soon as they reach puberty. Forced marriages became acceptable again. The mechanism to protect victims of domestic violations of human rights was abolished. As soon as they took power, the Taliban announced that girls and widows who were not married should marry a Talib, and their job would be to serve the husband and take care of the children and family matters.

———

When spring came to Kabul in 2022, the collapse of all the work I had done to improve the health and education and human rights of our people was almost complete. The current government is composed mostly of one ethnic group, with a few token people from other groups who think the same way as they do. And they don't know how to govern: they have no strategy for their own soldiers, their security forces or the disarmament program they talk about. They have no idea how to respond to the needs of the people and they are obsessed with controlling women, seeming to forget that they were born and brought up by women. It makes me wonder how they treat their mothers and why they see women as their enemy.

Our neighboring countries who didn't want a NATO presence in Afghanistan are happy that the international community has gone. Pakistan was the first to place the Taliban flag on the Afghan embassy, in Islamabad; Russia, China and Iran followed a few weeks later. The Taliban is being funded in a variety of ways: by taxes, by extortion, by opium production and by jihadi networks from countries that support them. Some report they are also funded by wealthy Arab sheiks who had connections to bin Laden; the Taliban has already promised mining contracts to some of these countries. Meanwhile, the donor countries we had counted on pledged only $2.44 billion—half the funds required to avoid a humanitarian catastrophe.

The Taliban is not a united group, and although I believe they have not changed and cannot be trusted, there are a few who don't accept the orders from the supreme leader. For example, schools for girls were open in Mazar-e-Sharif and other provinces in the north while they were closed in most of the country. (Although they were all closed in less than a year.) It felt like the jury was out regarding which Taliban faction would win this argument. Within months of the Taliban takeover, a rumor began that Mullah Hibatullah, who had rarely been seen or heard by the people, was being controlled by Pakistan's Inter-Services Intelligence and used to veto the decisions of those Taliban leaders in Afghanistan who promised moderation to Afghans and to the international community.

I remember telling US Secretary of State Colin Powell that his country's intelligence had failed them when it came to the Taliban in the early days, and I also felt that their information had failed them on Iraq. Now I realize their intelligence had failed them again. In the twenty years they were here, the international community never really understood how to build a democratic Afghanistan, how a tribal country works, how loyalties are managed and what it takes to pull a country like this together. We were so grateful for the help we were getting, and were able to see the enormous changes to health, to education, to governance—but all the while I worried that the international community thought that what we wanted was a version of what they had. And of course we wanted peace, good governance and human rights for everyone. But we didn't want a Western life—rather, we wanted an Afghan life with dignity, fairness and safety.

On August 3, 2021, I wrote in my diary that history was repeating itself. The people in Kabul were on the street shouting "Allahu Akbar" in support of the Afghan security and defense forces who were fighting to stop the Taliban. I remembered the same situation in 1979. In protest of the Soviet invasion and the puppet regime, people across Kabul had shouted "Allahu Akbar" from their houses at night. The majority of the people in the city participated.

Those of us who lived in Kabul at the time remember the impact of that historic collective protest. Four decades later, young people were using social media to mobilize in Kabul. But this time the protest lasted only one night. I felt there were six million people who could have attended and swung public opinion, but they didn't turn up in numbers that mattered, and those who might have supported the protest looked the other way. It wasn't a good sign.

Corruption, nepotism and mismanagement caused the collapse of our country. Knowing the history of the Taliban, I wondered what would happen to the women who had risked joining the police and the army. In late August I called the ones I knew. They were trying to hide, but even their relatives were afraid to give them shelter. One said, "I have studied so hard and was hoping to be a useful citizen for the country to help protect my fellow sisters in Afghanistan. But now I cannot take care of myself, and no one is here to help me." I felt her pain and heartbreak.

Zaki Anwari, a football player for Afghanistan's youth team, was one of the victims who died falling from the evacuation plane. His mother had been praying for her son and for his safety. We have a tradition that when anyone from a family wants to leave the house to travel, the mothers usually hold up a Quran and ask the person to walk underneath it as a blessing. When families watched the horrific scene on TV, how many mothers' hearts were beating fast? How many were running to hold the Quran and pray for the safety of their sons and loved ones? I would like to ask everyone in the world to imagine the level of pain felt by those mothers who were hoping their sons would be safe, and how it must have felt for a mother to watch her son fall from the plane like a piece of fabric.

Some people stayed at the airport for days, some even for more than a week, hoping to board a military plane. On August 28, 2021, one woman even delivered a baby girl on a Turkish Airlines flight to England; another woman barely made it to the hospital in Germany. These women had to labor on the floor of cargo planes, squeezed in beside strange men. They even had to stifle their cries of pain so as not to upset the other passengers. Such were the risks they took to avoid being killed by the Taliban.

I have always said that Afghan women are brave. They witnessed the killing of their husbands, brothers, sons and daughters. They watched the destruction of their properties and were forced to leave their homes. They became internally displaced or refugees in neighboring countries, where most of the time they were not welcomed by the authorities or local people. They have had to build a new nest over and over again.

In February 2022, another bombshell hit. American president Joe Biden signed an executive order concerning $7.1 billion in Afghan Central Bank assets that had been deposited in the United States for safekeeping. Biden declared that the money would be split evenly between humanitarian assistance to Afghanistan and a fund to cover the lawsuit that the 9/11 families had brought against the Taliban. The idea that $3.5 billion worth of funds from Afghan people would be kept by the United States is contrary to every law in their land and in mine. Fortunately, a us judge decided that the 9/11 victims could not receive compensation from that reserve money since the Taliban was not recognized by the United States as a legitimate government.

John Sifton, the Asia advocacy director of Human Rights Watch, spoke on the issue. "The Biden administration's decision creates a highly problematic precedent for a policy of essentially commandeering a country's sovereign wealth and utilizing it for things that are not what the people of Afghanistan necessarily wanted it to be used for," he said. The Afghan-American Foundation added: "The funds at issue belong to the people of Afghanistan, not any government or entity, past or present—that is not a policy position, it is a fact."

On February 13, the following open letter was addressed to President Biden:

Dear Mr. President,

We are profoundly saddened by the news that the Afghan funds deposited by the Central Bank of Afghanistan with the Federal Reserve Bank will be taken by the US Government to be split between humanitarian assistance and payments to the families of the victims of September 11th. While we share the sorrow of 9/11 and the lives lost as a result, both in the US and Afghanistan, this decision by the world's most powerful country over the resources of the world's poorest country is extremely unfair. It will drive Afghanistan's economy further into the ground.

Our people stood side by side with your nation for years, sacrificing more than any other nation in the war on terror. Moreover, the funds that the US seeks to redistribute belong to the Afghan people, who were not responsible for the acts of Al Qaeda terrorists or the Taliban. The 9/11 terrorists were not Afghans. Evidence shows that the mastermind and co-conspirator, Osama Bin Laden, who lived in Pakistan military custody for ten years, and Khalid Sheikh Mohammed, a Pakistani radical Islamist, were killed and captured in Pakistan.

Today, Afghans are going through some of the darkest days of our history, partly because of over-confidence in our friends and allies during the "cold war" and "war on terror". The support of the US for the most radical elements of the mujahideen during the Cold War, and the abandonment of Afghanistan by the international community after the Soviet withdrawal, gave rise to the terrorists that have victimized both of our countries. Thousands of Afghans have died every year in what was called the "war on terror" by the US and allies.

We are now dealing with the pain of a hasty withdrawal of troops, and a "peace deal" which allowed for the safe withdrawal of your troops and return of the Taliban to power yet brought nothing but pain for Afghanistan and its people. Many of us are now in exile, uprooted from our country and having left everything behind, trying to save what little dignity we can. Although we lost everything personally, it is this most recent decision by you which has been even more painful. As women, we do understand the hurt and sorrow experienced by each family member of the victims of September 11. However, we are sure they will not be healed or appreciate one penny of Afghan money when the men and women of Afghanistan feel they are being forced to sell one child to feed another because of life-threatening poverty.

We are also the victims of the shortsighted policies of big nations and the corrupt leaders that our international allies chose for us. The people of Afghanistan should not be victimized again by this collective failure. The assets of Afghanistan belong to its people. The Central Bank and the economy must be supported if the people are to survive.

Taking funds from the Afghan people is the unkindest and most inappropriate response for a country that is going through the worst humanitarian crisis in its history. It is the squeezing of a wounded hand. We ask you to reconsider this decision as we are still trying to heal what is left of us as a nation.

Thank you for your consideration.

The letter was signed by me and others on behalf of the Afghan people.

There are those who say the United Nations, NATO and the United States could never have saved Afghanistan. They claim that as long as we were so dependent on foreign aid, we could never have been true to our own structures, our own history. I don't agree. We do have problems to address. For example, analysts have pointed out that the Pashtuns are the largest ethnic group in our country; the majority of the Taliban are Pashtun as well, and, in fact, former President Ghani is Pashtun, as is former President Karzai. And yet we are a country of many ethnic groups and tribes. I believe our problems will persist until a leader figures out how to bring all of us together at the same table for the good of the whole country. However, I also believe we know how to correct our problems. In this post-COVID world, we see nations both reconsidering the common good—as with the world's reaction to the Russian invasion of Ukraine—and, at the same time, succumbing to a disturbing level of me-first thinking and populism.

The lessons Afghans have learned is that *we* must direct the future of our country. We are the ones who must find a way to unite the country, to bring the ethnic groups together. If international organizations such as the United Nations and NATO support our work toward unity, the extremists will know they have no future without us, and Pakistan will know that cutting deals with insurgents is the same as having pariah status. Countries that want to invest in Afghanistan would know that this is a country that respected the rule of law and the human rights of every citizen. It may sound like a pipe dream, but it's one I believe in. If the Talibs went to school and learned to think for themselves, they could use their religious fervor for the greater good. As Afghans we're sick of fighting, sick of duplicity, sick of waiting for the other shoe to drop on our lives.

Two thoughts linger with me: First, the lament that the international troops left after fourteen years because their leaders claimed it was long enough—while after the ceasefire was signed between North and South Korea in 1953, the troops stayed for thirty-five years. And second, not a single country has recognized the Taliban.

Eleven

GETTING TO NEXT

THERE ARE NO WINNERS IN WAR. Everyone loses in one way or another.

Starting over requires a scrupulous examination of the past, a critical analysis of the population, and an invitation to nation builders to come to the table. We are a country of many ethnic groups. Our population is mostly uneducated. We have used and abused religion and culture to elect and expel people in power throughout history but in particular for the last four decades. All of this has contributed to the fissure in our land—we are not united, so we cannot stand as one, but we are passionately and proudly Afghan, so no one has been able to defeat us.

Peace talks never could have worked. What we need first is unity among Afghans and a regional consensus in support of the process. The international community needs to guarantee that our neighboring countries will stop this game they play with Afghanistan. Pakistan must be reined in. Everyone knows these things, but no one acts.

Now is the time to right the wrongs we have lived with since the late 1970s. There are three keys to the future: human rights and equality for all, universal education, and unity among the ethnic groups and the provinces. Not one Afghan can be left behind in that formula. We need an approach that is people-centered rather than one that is ethnic-centered or seeks short-term political gain. I am a product of this tribal society; I was brought up in an oppressed and persecuted ethnic group that faces horrendous discrimination. As a young girl, I was taught to believe that men were superior to women and that I did not deserve the same opportunities as they had. None of those barriers stopped me, nor did they deter my work and projects. I am proof that we can move forward, that we can be the changemakers this country needs.

Internationally, the UN needs to use the tools they have to guide this country to democracy and ensure we have free and fair elections. You can't build a democracy with military intervention; the people need to own the process. It cannot be a quick-fix project, but rather requires a long-term, multidimensional strategy. The Responsibility to Protect program, known as R2P, would work here because of its three-step approach: Pillar 1 says every state has the responsibility to protect its populations from mass atrocity crimes: genocide, war crimes, crimes against humanity and ethnic cleansing. Pillar 2 says the wider international community has the responsibility to encourage and assist individual states in meeting that responsibility. Pillar 3 says that if a state is manifestly failing to protect its populations, the international community must be prepared to take appropriate collective action in a timely and decisive manner and in accordance with the UN charter.

To the Afghan people I say:

We are a country of minorities; none of the ethnic groups is in the majority. We have ignored that fact for centuries. If we address it and find unity, we will have sustainable peace. As citizens we must take the responsibility to bring peace. It cannot be done by force or by killing. We should learn from history; it was our own people who invited the USSR to come to our land in 1979; it was our own people who brought the other nationalities into the country, like the British who came in 1839 and the jihadis who came during the last four decades from all over the world. It is easy to blame others for invasion and aggression, but it is the lack of unity and our own insiders who facilitated the failures in Afghanistan. We also need to acknowledge our mistakes, overcome our denial and be proud of our courage. As our proverb says: You can make a golden frame for the mirror, but the mirror will not lie.

Religion must be hailed for what it is—a spiritual and holy relationship with Allah. It must not be used as a political tool that promotes aggression, terrorism and misogyny. Access to quality education and health services, including reproductive health services, are key for healthy populations and for responsible and productive citizens. Without human rights, peace and development will not be sustainable, and the lack of peace will impact everyone, regardless of geographical distance. Peace-building requires an honest, practical and inclusive approach that becomes a reality on the ground and includes accountability and justice. Justice is not only criminal justice; it is also an acknowledgment of the suffering of the victims and their need for reparation.

We must acknowledge that Afghanistan belongs to all Afghans, and they have equal rights and equal responsibilities. No one is superior to anyone else; the majority and minority votes must be counted through the equal participation of the people in a free and fair democratic process. Don't use excuses such as lack of education and lack of awareness to exclude citizens. They fully understand justice and injustice and must be included at every level.

A presidential system of government does not work in Afghanistan; the majority want a decentralized, parliamentary system. The government must be accountable and responsive to the needs of the people, including by providing basic social services and justice and enforcing the rule of law. A system should be people-centered, responsive to the needs of the people. We've witnessed the problems with a centralized system throughout the last five decades.

Human rights and dignity for all must be the way we approach every single issue in our country. Inclusion is the way to build trust and confidence between the people and the government. The foundation for democracy is trust among the people and in the process.

Corruption and nepotism are an enemy that kills from the inside more efficiently than any enemy from the outside. We must fight corruption at every level relentlessly.

Quality education is the strongest tool to fight ignorance and poverty. Universal education makes peace-building and development possible. The plan must be long-term and never seen as a quick fix.

Access to health care, and reproductive health care, including access to contraception, is a basic human right. It is also the key to a healthy society and to the reduction of poverty, which is invariably a root cause of conflict. Rather than ten hungry children who cannot go to school and wind up contributing to the problems of aggression and criminal gangs, Afghanistan needs many fewer children, healthy children—per family so they can have enough food and good-quality education. Reproductive health care also means empowering the women in Afghanistan, who are vital in their contribution to development and peace.

Access to justice must be people-centered and based on principles of human rights. When you keep power in the hands of one ethnic group, as we have always done, you favor their view of justice. The law must be fair and equal for all.

Every citizen must be accountable for their actions, whether a failure to stop corruption or a crime against humanity. I am not in favor of revenge, but the need to respect the right to justice for victims overrules amnesty announcements made by those seeking to hide the past in order to keep the status quo.

The role of women in all these processes must be promoted. Their participation in every program will contribute to a more equal and peaceful society.

Militarization and budgets for advanced weapons will not protect us—respect for human rights and healthy, educated citizens will be our front line for safety and prosperity. Making ever more advanced weapons generally gets priority over feeding poor people; the danger in that decision is those hungry and jobless youth will be more dangerous than our neighbor's nuclear bombs.

The blame game must stop, not only with our neighbors but also with the international community. We Afghans must negotiate honestly with our neighboring countries and reduce their intervention in our nation. We need to acknowledge our own problems; in the past, denying them has only led to more distrust, more conspiracy theories, more national damage. It's like the old adage: When you try to make a fire in your neighbor's house it will come back to you—if not with flames, then with crippling smoke.

Now is the time to address injustice toward women, first and foremost. And until men decide to walk with us, we will never get to the finish line. I'm not talking about the perpetrators alone; I'm talking about every single man—every single father, husband, brother and son. This is their problem, and I think they ought to fix it. I call on the female family members to stand up to their sons, husbands, brothers and fathers, and any other family member who treats women with disrespect. They must be told that it is wrong, it is shameful and it is also illegal. And despite what the fundamentalists say, it's against Islam.

To my Afghan sisters, let us channel our fears into tangible solutions that ensure our rights and freedoms are protected. Given the culture of isolation that has historically framed our participation, we must focus on inclusion, which means that Afghan women and men are fairly represented regardless of their sexual orientation, ethnicity, religion or economic background.

My beloved country and the wonderful men and women who live here are everything to me. I have dedicated my life to them and I will continue to do so. I seek for them a prosperous, peaceful country where people can live in dignity, free from fear and want, with their rights and freedoms respected and protected. Success for me would be helping people to see the world from a different perspective so they can value each other, enjoy their rights and freedoms, be part of the goodness that helps each person to rise and defeat the menace of poverty, conflict and oppression.

I am not afraid of the Taliban; I know they will not survive. Radicalism does not have a place in Afghanistan. Afghanistan will once again be a country of peace and tolerance, and home to the moderate Islam it was more than forty-five years ago. But I am afraid of the vicious cycle of conflict imposed by the geopolitical/geostrategic rivalries that surrounds us. I am afraid of the rubber stamp system of the loya jirga, and I am afraid of the international community abandoning Afghanistan.

I leave you with hope—hope that my own story helps Afghans to invest in the female members of their families, to respect freedom of choice for their daughters and sisters, to create a future with values that see women as partners.

I hope our government responds to the emerging needs of individuals. I hope it is a government that is representative, not autocratic, that is egalitarian and democratic, and that does not concentrate power in the hands of a few in a central government but delegates power as well to the provinces and districts.

I hope for citizens who live with honesty and honor their commitments, stand true to their values, and keep their promises should they hold a government office. We need leaders who are available to the people they serve, and who refuse to lower their standards despite the pressure brought to bear and the challenges of governing. These are the leaders who refrain from corrupt practices, build a transparent system and celebrate the goodness and resilience of the Afghan people and the history of this land.

The calamities the whole world has experienced—from COVID-19 to climate change—must be the undercurrent of the changes we make. We depend on a healthy environment, on the foliage of our mountains, the water of our rivers and springs, the wildlife of our country, the food of our traditional farms, the wood of our forests, the people in our villages and communities. We've been so busy fighting insurgents and opportunists, but we now need to take stock of what we love about our homeland, the beauty that surrounds us, the ancient traditions that we still honor, the ones that honor all of us.

I write this book from a distance. My husband, Rauf, is in Germany, and I am in the United States, where I worked as a scholar at risk at Harvard University in the Carr Center for Human Rights until December 2022, and am now working as a scholar at risk at Tufts University's Fletcher School. I hope my story tells you about the life of a physician who took an oath—*first do no harm*. I fought child mortality, smallpox and measles, and I fought those who refused justice and equality for women. Getting to next—the next stage of being a changemaker—means we understand that the world no longer operates as isolated landmasses but rather as humans interconnected with shared values and dreams of the future. In the midst of the brutal reality of the conflict ravaging my homeland, I found purpose in advocating for the human rights of the people, particularly those of women and girls. The fight for human rights and equality requires long-term commitment for generations to come—we need to walk the path of nonviolence, and choose the leadership and system of government through democratic processes and peoples' participation.

I'm ready for next.

ACKNOWLEDGMENTS

This book is a small part of my life and struggle in Afghanistan, particularly during the forty-five-year-long conflict. It is also a testament to the support I have received over the years.

I am grateful to the donors who have supported my work at Shuhada Organization. Foremost among these are the late Frederick Ines from Inter Church Aid and the late Thorvald Stoltenberg of Norway, who were instrumental in funding my first hospital in 1988, and the late Vreni Frauenfelder of Help Committee Schaffhausen, the organization in Switzerland that she created to support Afghanistan, which has been providing aid for more than three decades. I am also thankful to the international institutions that recognized my work and gave me the courage to continue despite difficult circumstances.

The talented and committed staff of Shuhada Organization, the Afghan Ministry of Women's Affairs, and the Afghanistan Independent Human Rights Commission have helped to make these institutions vibrant forces to improve and bring dignity to the lives of Afghans and their communities.

My profound thanks also go to the Feminist Majority Foundation, which along with Congresswomen Carolyn Maloney, Senators Barbara Boxer and Dianne Feinstein, and so many other women in the 1990s, raised awareness of the atrocities faced by women under the Talban regime and helped stop the United States and the UN from recognizing the Taliban, and advocated for support for Afghan women and girls. My fortuitous meeting of Eleanor Smeal and Jennifer Jackman of the Feminist Majority Foundation in Brussels in 1998 began not only a decades-long collaboration on behalf of Afghan women and girls but also resulted in long-lasting friendships. I also owe thanks to Mavis Leno, who led the Campaign to Stop Gender Apartheid in Afghanistan from 1997 to 2001.

When the Afghan government fell to the Taliban, I could not return to my country. I am indebted to Susan Cohen and her colleagues at Mintz, Levin, Cohn, Ferris, Glovsky and Popeo, PC, who secured my legal status in the United States; to Evelyn Murphy and Jacque Friedman, who introduced me to Susan Cohen and have continued to provide their friendship; to Deborah Stone, whose friendship and support have been enduring; and to Jane Unrue, who helped make possible my positions as scholar at risk at Harvard University and Tufts University. I have appreciated the support and insights of my colleagues at the Carr Center for Human Rights at Harvard University's John F. Kennedy School of Government and at the Fletcher School of Tufts University, who facilitated work on this book.

Over more than twenty-five years, Jennifer Jackman has been my close friend and supported my work. Jennifer's friendship has helped me survive since I became a displaced person with the Taliban takeover in August 2021. Jennifer shared with me her house, her cats and the ocean, and has provided all manner of assistance in adjusting to my new life in the United States as well as with this book.

Sally Armstrong has been critical to every stage of the book's evolution. As a journalist and longtime friend, Sally has devoted herself to bringing global attention to the plight of Afghan women and girls for more than two decades. Our collaboration over the years laid the foundation for this book and brought it to life.

Finally, I am grateful to members of my family who supported me and faced dangers because of my work, including beatings, imprisonment, torture and threats. Their support was crucial to my work, where I could facilitate access to education and basic health services to the people who were in need, and in making the topic of human rights a discourse in every household in my country. I know we have a long way to go to achieve equality, women's rights and human rights in Afghanistan—it is a difficult road but not an impossible one.

INDEX

9/11 attacks on the United States of America, 6–7, 48, 136–141, 236, 242, 244, 253, 256, 289–291

A

Abdullah, Abdullah, 154, 155, 161, 163, 219–220, 232, 237, 242, 255, 258, 274

Adams, Brad, 223

Afghan government, 196
  commissioner of, 96
  criticizing US, 224
  election of, 232
  international community and, 185, 210
  Iran and, 260
  Taliban and, 221–223, 243, 251–252, 254–255, 258, 304

Afghan National Military Academy, 176

Afghan National Police Academy, 175

Afghan-American Foundation, 290

Afghani (currency), 13, 32, 33, 61, 65, 105–106, 236, 272

Afghanistan. *see also* Afghan government; women and girls in Afghanistan
  about, 2–3, 6–13, 19–20, 25–27, 197, 202, 227–228, 260
  American soldiers injured in, 154–155
  child abuse in, 194 (*see also* women and girls in Afghanistan)
  democracy and, 210, 297
  election in, 219, 242–243
  Geneva Accords and, 94
  hippies in, 56, 88
  illiteracy in, 16, 117, 123, 185
  insecurity in, 22, 118, 129, 140, 189, 205–206, 226, 240, 245, 267–268
  international community and, 24, 143, 177, 196, 211, 220, 226, 227, 235, 265, 293, 294, 300
  making improvements in, 97, 100, 143, 163, 198, 256–257
  mujahideen in, 15, 100, 214 (*see also* mujahideen)
  new vision for, 151, 170–172
  the People's Democratic Republic of, 60, 69
  pipeline through, 132
  refugees from, 109, 239
  report on, 176, 184, 191

Samar and, 71, 115, 123, 144–145,
    155, 200, 248, 296–301
security forces of (*see* ANSF (Afghan
    National Security Forces))
Taliban in, 102, 104, 111, 115,
    125, 230, 287
transitional justice in, 185–186,
    189, 191, 197, 202, 247
US and, 14, 142, 148, 195, 236, 264
violence in, 178–179, 184–185,
    249–250, 262, 269
women and girls in, 51, 87, 89, 98,
    112, 120, 130, 133–134, 175,
    217, 284, 288 (*see also* women
    and girls in Afghanistan)
Afghanistan National Radio and
    Television, 166
Afghanistan Study Group, 264
Africa, 42, 50, 118, 213, 246
African Union, 217
Aga Khan University Hospital, 128
Agha, Syed Tayyab, 221
Agreement for Bringing Peace to
    Afghanistan. *see* Doha
    Agreement
AIHRC (Afghanistan Independent
    Human Rights Commission),
    241, 277
  chair of, 30–31, 170, 172–174,
    198, 248
  closing of, 283
  creation of, 160, 164–165
  explosion at, 222
  office(s) of, 177–178, 183, 195,
    202, 203, 208
  threats against, 188, 277
  work of, 168, 175–176, 179–182,
    185, 190–198, 212, 219,
    223–224, 243

Akhundzada, Hibatullah, 283, 284,
    287
Akram, Fatima, 61, 62
Al Qaeda, 7, 131, 140, 230, 235,
    239, 245, 252, 261, 291
al-Bashir, Omar, 214, 216–217
al-Turabi, Hassan, 214
Albright, Madeline, 136
Ali Asghar (uncle), 25, 37
  Fatima, wife of, 37
Amin, Hafizullah, 62, 68
  assassination of, 69
Amnesty International USA, 124
Annan, Kofi, 158, 163, 186
ANSF (Afghan National Security
    Forces), 238, 253, 270–272
Anwari, Zaki, 288
Arab, 14, 88, 123, 192, 213, 286
Arabic, 37, 117, 238
Arbour, Louise, 184–185, 187, 189
Arman E Mili, 165
Armstrong, Sally, 125
Arnault, Jean, 169
Aryana Girls' School, 98
Ashrar, 62. *see also* mujahideen
Atrafi (sports teacher), 48
Australia, 54, 141, 195, 239, 245
Axworthy, Lloyd, 124–125
Aziza (sister), 28, 31, 39–40, 43–45, 51

B

Badakhshan, 178, 189, 276
Bagram, 280
  airport in, 152, 196, 225, 273
Bakhtawar (cousin), 33
Bales, Robert, 225–226
Balochistan, 87, 102
Bamiyan, 4, 7, 9–11, 102, 104, 107–108,
    110, 137, 162, 227, 236, 278

Bangladesh, 50, 215
Barmaki, Hamida, 223
Bassiouni, M. Cherif, 188
Battle of Maiwand, 91
BBC, 73, 141, 144
Behzad, Ahmad, 176, 177
Beijing, 179
Bellamy, Carol, 124
Benard, Cheryl, 156
Bergdahl, Bowe, 267
Biden, Joe, 264, 270–271, 289, 290
bin Laden, Osama, 118, 131,
    139–140, 144, 171, 211, 222,
    286, 291
Blair, Cherie, 142–143, 153
Blair, Tony, 153
Blinken, Antony, 274
Boko Haram, 187
Bonino, Emma, 133–134
Bonn, 143, 144, 145, 147
Bonn Agreement, 150, 159, 160,
    164, 174
Bosnia, 187, 267
Boxer, Barbara, 175
Brahimi, Lakhdar, 158–160, 168,
    171–172, 174–176
British. see UK (United Kingdom)
Brunet, Ariane, 148
Brussels, 96, 133
Brzezinski, Zbigniew, 14
Buddha statues, 9–11, 104, 106, 236
Bush, George W., 140, 142, 153–155
Bush, Laura, 142, 154, 208

C

Canada, 124, 125, 141, 144, 146,
    165, 168, 240. see also individual
    places names in
    ambassador of, 277

House of Commons, 146
    Order of, 219
    Royal Canadian Mounted Police,
        146
    welcome delegation from, 145
Canadian Women for Women in
    Afghanistan, 124
Carr Center for Human Rights
    (Harvard University), 301
Carter, Jimmy, 14
Central Bank of Afghanistan,
    289–292
Cheney, Dick, 154
China, 11, 14, 49, 108, 209, 226,
    243, 245, 250–251, 265, 286
Chrétien, Jean, 146
CIA (Central Intelligence Agency),
    14, 276
Clinton, Hillary Rodham, 130
CNN, 144
Cold War, 15, 49, 88, 89, 95, 101,
    127, 147, 291
Columbia University, 259
Constitution Drafting Commission,
    180
COVID-19, 249, 293, 300
CPA (Comprehensive Peace
    Agreement), 213
Crocker, Ryan, 157
Current Medical Diagnosis and Treatment,
    75

D

Daesh. see ISIS (Islamic State of Iraq
    and Syria)
Darfur, 214, 216–217
Dari (language), 8, 49, 117
Dasht-e-Barchi, 2, 17, 21, 262, 275
Davis, Gordon Skip, 237

Davos, 109
de Rivero, Julie, 216
Dobbins, James, 170
Dobriansky, Paula, 147, 154
Doctors Without Borders. *see* MSF
  (Médecins Sans Frontières)
Doha, 23, 222, 254, 258, 260, 269,
  274
Doha Agreement, 250–251, 253, 271
Dutch. *see* Netherlands

E
Edmonton, Alberta, 144, 145
Eid, 1, 202
Election Complaints Commission,
  219
Emirates. *see* UAE (United Arab
  Emirates)
England, 227, 289
Esper, Mark, 251
EU (European Union), 96, 97, 134,
  157, 171, 236, 245
Europe, 155, 227, 231, 237, 239,
  240, 246
EVAW (Elimination of Violence
  Against Women), 197–198,
  223

F
Fahim, Hassin, 240
Fahim, Mohammad, 178
Farhadi, Ravan, 163
Farsi, 50, 180
Fateh, Juma Khan, 276
Fayzabad, Badakhshan, 189
FBI, 235
Fedai, Mahfuz, 164
Federal Reserve Bank, 290
Feminist Majority Foundation, 124,

  130, 132, 134, 136, 148, 159
Ferdowsi, 36
Fletcher School (Tuft's University), 301
Flower for the Women of Kabul, 134
France, 83, 141, 169
Franco, Francisco, 231
Frauenfelder, Vreni, 88, 109, 110,
  118–119
French, David, 253, 254

G
Gailani, Fatima, 134, 280
Gailani, Pir Sayed Ahmed, 134
Gates, Bill, 109
Gawharshad University, 2, 222, 228,
  246
Geneva Accords, 94
Geneva Conventions, 19, 194
Gerhard, Mr., 96
Germany, 73, 141, 289
  colleagues from, 82, 166, 169, 277
  meetings in, 133, 142, 160–162,
    222
  support from, 164, 220, 233, 278
Ghafoori, Ali, 57–58, 63, 70, 74–78,
  81, 84–86, 89, 101, 108, 144, 148
Ghani, Ashraf
  about, 259
  as advisor to President Karzai,
    158, 170, 180
  conflict with Abdullah, 237
  election of, 219–220, 231–233, 242
  fleeing of, 274–276
  interference of, 269
  as Pashtun, 8, 292
  presidency of, 234, 241, 254–255,
    258–259, 270–271
  Samar and, 248, 263
  Taliban and, 240, 251–254, 266

Ghazni, 25, 30, 74–75, 81, 137, 262
Ghor, 137
Global Alliance of National Human
    Rights Institutions, 223
Global Leader for Tomorrow Award,
    109
Gorky, Maxim, 47
Graham, Bill, 168
Guantanamo Bay, 267
Guterres, António, 248

H
Habibula, Shakiba, 110
Haishimi, Mansoor, 189–190
Halima (father's second wife),
    27–29, 51, 102
Hamed, Muslim, 148, 158
Hamidi, Farid, 196
Hanafi, Khalid, 284
Hanafi, Mawlawi Abdul Salam,
    278–279
Haqqani Network, 239
Harakat-e-Inqilab-e Islami
    Afghanistan, 82
Harvard University, 301, 304
Hasht-e Subh, 229
Hazara(s), 232
    about, 2, 4, 8–10, 104, 169, 207
    attacks on, 15–16, 18, 105, 108,
        136–137, 196, 263, 272,
        275, 278
    discrimination against, 41, 49,
        106, 118, 128, 262
    girls' education and, 48
    leaders of, 171
    misconceptions about, 12, 127
    mujahideen group of, 92
    Pashtuns and, 80
    as refugees, 87

Hazarajat, 8
Helal, Isabelle Solon, 144
Helmand Province, 12, 47, 100
    about, 38, 52, 75
    airport in, 246
    family in, 27, 39, 70
    Hazara community in, 48
    reconstruction in, 195
    Taliban in, 267, 268
    Helmand Valley Development in,
        27, 40
Help Committee Schaffhausen, 88
Hephthalites, 9
Herat
    about, 7–8, 227
    AIHRC in, 176–177, 182–183
    Ghani in, 234
    Red Crescent in, 125
    Taliban in, 104, 267, 268, 276
    women in, 283
Herodotus, 11
Heyzer, Noleen, 158
Hezb-e Islami, 93, 107, 111
Hezb-e Wahdat Islami, 107, 111
High Peace Council, 220–221
High-Level Commission for
        Anti-Corruption and Good
        Governance, 233
Hills of the Martyrs, 21
Hindu Kush, 86, 105
Hindus, 272
Hitchcock, Mrs (teacher), 48
Holbrooke, Richard, 267
Homemaker's, 125
Hotak, Abdul Rahman, 223–224
Hotel Bost, 55
Human Rights Watch, 176, 203,
    216, 223, 290
Hushek, Tom, 129

Hussein, Saddam, 163, 177
Husseini, Professor, 66
Husseini, Shamsia, 208

I

ICC (International Criminal Court), 187, 216–218, 236
ICCO (Inter-Church Organisation for Development Cooperation), 96–97
ICTY (International Criminal Tribunal for the Former Yugoslavia), 187
IEC (Independent Election Commission), 232, 242–243
India, 108, 208–209, 239, 245, 250, 252, 260, 264
Ines, Frederick, 86, 88, 90, 97
Inter Church Aid, 86, 87, 90, 92, 100
International Conference on Population and Development, 179
International Crisis Group, 224
International Human Rights Law Group, 162
International Security Assistance Force. *see* ISAF (International Security Assistance Force)
International Women's Day, 157–159
Iran, 8, 13, 107, 109, 260, 264
  family in, 85
  ISKP in, 239
  Islamization in, 89
  medical treatment in, 209
  mujahideen in, 15
  refugees in, 84, 110, 159, 184, 185
  surgeon from, 96
  Taliban in, 243, 286
Iraq, 187, 195, 239, 260, 267, 287
  invasion of, 163, 177, 210, 236

Irish Times, 141
ISAF (International Security Assistance Force), 48, 141, 144, 165, 169, 171, 186, 195, 200, 221, 224–226, 230
ISI (Inter-Services Intelligence), 94, 287
ISIS (Islamic State of Iraq and Syria), 12, 234, 238. *see also* ISKP (Islamic State of Khorasan Province)
ISKP (Islamic State of Khorasan Province), 12, 22, 238–239, 252, 262, 275. *see also* ISIS (Islamic State of Iraq and Syria)
Islam, 14, 126, 262, 299–300
  fundamentalism in, 20
  fundamentals of, 135–136
  mujahideen and, 13, 15
  separate arms of, 11
  Taliban's interpretation of, 12, 16, 134, 281
  women in, 46, 114
Islamabad, 143, 278, 286
Islamic Emirate, 246, 259
Islamic Republic of Afghanistan, 273
Israel, 136

J

Jackman, Jennifer, 136, 159
Jaghori, 25, 82, 93, 262, 278
  about, 36, 52
  girls' school in, 100, 206–207
  home in, 28–30, 36–38, 40, 43, 45, 74–75, 77–78, 81, 85, 97, 106
  hospital for women in, 92
  MSF in, 82
  mujahideen in, 84
  visiting, 118–119, 162
Jahangir, Asma, 184
Jalal, Massouda, 164

Jalalabad, 104, 144, 262
Jalali, Ali Ahmad, 176
Jamiat-e Islami, 111, 165, 221
Japan, 109, 152
John Humphrey Freedom Award, 144
Joint Special Operations Command, 271
Joshi, Chandni, 158
Julius Caesar, 266

K
Kabul
  about, 8–9, 49, 78, 151, 227–228
  colleagues in, 109, 133–134, 178, 183, 221, 224
  family in, 75, 84, 276
  hospital in, 71, 128, 209
  living in, 54–55, 57–58, 76, 148, 153, 177, 203–204, 218, 269, 278
  locations in, 2, 6, 55, 143, 149, 152, 226 (*see also* Serena Hotel)
  peace agreement signed in, 251
  protests/resistance in, 70, 188, 262–263, 287–288
  Taliban in, 111, 118, 150, 267, 273–275
  UN in, 104
  US in, 147
  USAID in, 47
  violence in, 1–6, 16, 21–22, 69, 73–74, 102, 105–106, 156–157, 171, 223, 245, 253, 255, 262, 272–273
  working in, 81, 167, 175
Kabul Bank, 240
Kabul Polytechnic University, 64, 65, 164, 165

Kabul University, 53, 164, 175, 190, 259
  Faculty of Medicine at, 13, 54, 63
  Faculty of Science at, 52
Kalashnikovs, 276
Kandahar
  about, 7
  AIHRC in, 177–178, 208
  airport in, 178
  Pashtuns of, 161
  security in, 53
  Supreme Leader in, 284
  Taliban in, 16, 102–104, 128, 267, 268
  traveling through, 39, 119
  violence in, 5, 225–226
  women in, 5, 228
Karachi, 82, 125, 128, 260
Karmal, Babrak, 60, 69
Karte Seh, 105, 106, 169, 202
Karzai, Hamid, 167, 243
  candidacy of, 219–220, 231
  Ghani and, 180, 258–259, 274
  as Pashtun, 8, 292
  problems with, 161–162, 198, 203, 208, 223–224
  support from, 159, 183, 200, 280
  transitional presidency of, 164, 166
  working with, 144, 149–155, 160, 168–172, 174–175, 184, 188, 229–230
Karzai, Mahmood, 240
Karzai, Qayum, 150
Kerry, John, 232
Khakash, Musa, 61
Khalili, Karim, 202
Khalilo, Haji, 80–81
Khalilzad, Zalmay, 154–156, 170, 180, 244, 251–252, 255

Khalq party, 50, 59–60, 62, 73
Khan, Amanullah, 12, 155
Khan, Genghis, 108
Khan, Ismail, 8, 104, 157, 176, 182, 183, 268
Khan, Mohammad Daoud, 13, 50, 51, 59, 67
Khartoum, 214–215
Khursheed (mother), 43–45, 102, 144, 168, 201, 204, 277, 280
about, 25–33, 37–38
as grandmother, 57–58, 70, 75, 77–78, 84–85
Khwaharan Musalman (Sisters of Muslims), 99
King, Angela, 125
Kunduz, 104, 203–204, 233, 275

L
Lafferty, Elaine, 141, 149
Lashkar Gah
activism in, 49
classmate from, 56
family in, 27–30, 37, 38, 43–45, 51–52, 57–58, 63, 75, 102
Lavrov, Sergey, 151
Leno, Jay, 133
Leno, Mavis, 132–133, 136
Logar Province, 219
London Conference on Afghanistan, 185
Lutter, Dr., 86–88

M
Mahaz-e-Milli, 80
Malalai Hospital, 90–91, 97
Maloney, Carolyn, 175
Mandela, Nelson, 109

Mansoor, Mullah Akhtar Mohammad, 221
Martin Luther King Jr. Memorial Library, 97
Massoud, Ahmad Shah, 8, 9, 111, 139
Mazar-e-Sharif, 7, 102, 104, 105, 107, 116, 233, 275, 286
Mazari, Abdul Ali, 8
McChrystal, Stanley, 225
Mecca, 38, 83, 156, 202, 284
Mediterranean Sea, 237, 239
Mes Aynac (copper mine), 226
Mestiri, Mahmoud, 99
Milosevic, Slobodan, 217
Ministry of Education, 207
Ministry of Finance, 275
Ministry of Justice, 197
Ministry of Mining, 61
Ministry of Public Health, 249
Ministry of Social Affairs, 157
Ministry of the Promotion of Virtue and Prevention of Vice, 113, 281, 284
Ministry of Women's Affairs, 157, 168, 198, 206, 212, 243, 279, 280–281
closing of, 283
funding for, 159, 175
Samar as minister of, 153, 170, 203
Mission Hospital (Quetta), 86, 89, 96
Mohammad Khail (refugee camp), 87
Mohammad, The Prophet, 41
Mohammed, Khalid Sheikh, 291
Mohaqiq, Mohammad, 222
Moore, Tristana, 141
Moscow, 151, 160, 233, 243
MSF (Médecins Sans Frontières), 17–18, 79, 82–83, 86
Muhammad Akram (brother-in-law), 61, 62

Husnia, sister of, 61
Muhammad Amin (brother-in-law), 78–79, 81
Mujahid, Zabihullah, 279
mujahideen, 261
  about, 8, 13–16, 62
  factions of, 83, 89, 101, 105
  fighting against, 123
  Geneva Accords and, 84
  leaders in, 107, 139, 145, 162, 164, 166, 176, 188, 230, 234, 266, 268
  Samar and, 80, 82, 97, 100, 186
  Sharia law and, 146
  speaking against, 163
  Sudan and, 186
  Taliban and, 16, 104, 111, 116, 153
  US and, 291
  violence of, 92–93, 99, 106, 171, 184, 228
  warring with Soviets of, 81
  women and, 13, 102–103, 143
Munib, Mohammad Hashim, 221
Muqur, 38–39
Muslim Brotherhood, 49, 73
  ideals of, 13
Muslim(s), 11, 38, 127, 202, 213, 279, 284
  countries, 134, 177, 215
  law, 135
  Samar as, 167
  youth, 163

N

Nabizada, Mursal, 282
Nadery, Nader, 168, 196
Najibullah, Mohammad, 94, 233
  murder of, 111
Nangarhar Province, 238, 239, 272

Nasiri, Dr., 127
Nasiri, Humaira, 127
National Day for Remembrance of the Victims of War in Afghanistan, 186
National Human Rights Institution, 213
National Inquiry on Women, Peace and Security, 241
NATO (North Atlantic Treaty Organization), 24, 141, 196, 230, 237, 266. *see also* ISAF (International Security Assistance Force); Stoltenberg, Jens
  ambassador of, 277
  Article 5 of, 7, 140
  attacks by, 178–179
  failure of, 273
  member countries of, 210, 224, 251, 260
  presence of, 262, 270, 286
  responsibilities of, 292, 293
  Samar and, 172
  Taliban and, 245
  withdrawal of, 238, 239, 250, 268
Naveed, Abdul Rauf, 56, 66, 69–70, 81, 101–102, 127, 145, 201, 278, 301
NDS (National Directorate of Security), 176, 268
Netherlands, 96, 195, 228. *see also* individual place names in
New York, 124, 126, 139, 142, 155, 163, 215, 231, 259
New Zealand Human Rights Commission, 48
Nigeria, 187, 212
night letters, 16–17, 60, 74, 120, 168, 211

Nobel Peace Prize, 218–219
Noorzad, Maryam, 18
North Korea, 240, 244, 293
Northern Alliance, 9, 131, 139
Norway, 92, 96, 116, 141, 198–200, 227
Norwegian Refugee Council, 100

O

Obama, Barack, 218, 267
Ogata, Sadako, 109, 152
Omar, Mullah Mohammed, 104, 113, 222, 237
Omdurman Islamic University, 214
Operation Enduring Freedom, 7, 141
opium, 122, 129, 163, 192, 237, 246, 286
Organisation of Islamic Cooperation, 217
Oxfam, 98, 110, 116

P

Pakistan, 264, 293
  about, 8, 51
  bin Laden in, 144, 222, 291
  family in, 78, 85, 101
  Inter-Services Intelligence of (*see* ISI (Inter-Services Intelligence))
  Islamization in, 13–14, 89
  madrassa schools in, 16, 103
  mujahideen and, 15, 62, 94
  nuclear arms of, 245
  peace talks with, 250–251
  police from, 91, 141, 278
  refugees in, 109, 115, 159, 184–185, 214, 279, 285
  representative from, 158

Taliban and, 125, 136, 179, 239, 243, 260, 272, 284, 286
  US and, 131, 267
  women's rights in, 87, 89, 120
  working in, 82, 151
Palestine, 136
Panjshir Valley, 7, 8
Papandreou, Andreas, 162
Papandreou, Margarita, 162
Parcham party, 50–51, 60, 69, 74
Paris Principles, 160, 223
Pashtu (language), 8, 117, 180
Pashtun (area), 103
Pashtun(s), 7–9, 50–51, 80, 87, 95, 136–137, 161, 167, 232, 238, 241, 292
Pashtunwali, 8, 238
PDPA (People's Democratic Party of Afghanistan), 13, 50–51, 59–60, 71, 84, 85, 184
Peace, Reconciliation, and Justice Action Plan, 188
Persian, 6, 11, 36, 90
Peshawar, 86, 99, 119, 214, 260
Pfau, Ruth, 82, 86
Pillay, Navi, 223
Pinochet, Augusto, 231
Powell, Colin, 147, 148, 151, 154, 177, 287
Presidential Palace, 151, 263, 274
Pul-e-Charkhi, 66, 69, 75, 230
Pul-e-Khumri, 102
Putin, Vladimir, 161, 218

Q

Qadir, Haji Abdul, 171
Qamber, Haji, 84–85
Qanooni, Mohammad Younus, 165
Qasimyar, Ismail, 164

INDEX

Qatar, 23, 222, 243, 260, 267, 284
Qudsia (friend), 42, 53
Quetta, 87–88, 137, 221, 278
 family in, 102, 144–145, 168
 home in, 85, 127, 139–142,
  148–149
 medical work in, 93, 95–96, 98,
  115–116, 123
 refugees in, 99, 101
 Taliban in, 103, 119, 138, 260,
  262
 work in, 100
Quran, 31, 37, 83, 115, 116–117,
 134–135, 229, 259, 288

R
R2P (Responsibility to Protect), 295
Rabbani, Burhanuddin, 108, 111,
 150, 221
Rahim, Abdul, 165
Rahman, Abdul, 156
Ramadan, 1, 22
Ramon Magsaysay Award, 108
RAWA (Revolutionary Association of
 the Women of Afghanistan),
 74, 97
Reagan, Ronald, 14
Red Crescent Society, 110, 125, 280
Refugee Women in Development,
 124
Republicans (Afghan political party),
 182–183
Revolutionary Council, 69
Rice, Condoleezza, 162–163
Right Livelihood Award, 218
Rights & Democracy, 144
Robinson, Mary, 158–160
Rose, Karel, 96
Rostam, 36–37

Rumsfeld, Donald, 154
Russia, 161, 243, 250, 251, 286, 293.
 see also USSR (Union of Soviet
  Socialist Republics)
Ruttig, Thomas, 166

S
Saberi, Toorpikai, 72–73
Sadai Mujahid, 165–166
Sadiq, Mirwais, 157
Safar (bodyguard), 105–106
Safi, Mahbooba, 40–41
Salafi, 238
Samar, Sima, 137, 145
 about, 28–29, 279–280
 awards won by, 54, 108, 109, 162,
  218–219
 as chair of the AIHRC, 30–31, 248
  (see also AIHRC (Afghanistan
   Independent Human Rights
   Commission))
 childhood of, 25–27, 35–36
 early activism of, 119–120
 education and, 31–32, 40–42, 48,
  53–56, 62–63, 70, 71, 98
 family of (see Akram, Fatima; Ali
  Asghar (uncle); Bakhtawar
  (cousin); Ghafoori, Ali;
  Halima (father's second wife);
  Khursheed (mother);
  Muhammad Akram (brother-
  in-law); Muhammad Amin
  (brother-in-law); Naveed,
  Abdul Rauf; Sultani, Abdul
  Ghafoor; Tamanna (step-
  daughter); Yaqubi, Abdul
  Aziz; Yaqubi, Abdul Kayum;
  Yaqubi, Abdul Samad;
  Yaqubi, Abdul Wahid;

Yaqubi, Ahmad Ali; Yaqubi,
     Aqila; Yaqubi, Qadim Ali)
   headscarf and, 78, 125–126, 155,
     167, 169, 279
   Marzia (childhood name of), 40, 75
   medical practice of, 71–73, 74,
     78–80, 90–94, 97–98,
     110–111, 115–116, 117–118,
     120–122
   message to the Afghan people
     by, 295–301
   as Minister of Women's Affairs,
     144, 151, 157, 170, 203
     (see also Ministry of Women's
     Affairs)
   Nobel Peace Prize and, 218
   plan for Afghanistan by, 255–257
   political achievements of, 160,
     166–167, 181, 197–198
   RAWA and, 74
   report on Afghanistan by, 211–212
   security concerns for, 148,
     165–170, 178, 199–202, 203,
     222–223, 276–278, 280
   as Sima Jaan, 161
   as special rapporteur for Sudan,
     213–216
   UN appointments (other) of, 248
Sangi Masha, 77, 92, 100
Saudi Arabia, 193, 243
   aid from, 123
   madrassa funded by, 88
   mujahideen and, 14, 62
   Taliban support from, 125, 136
   women and, 13
Saur Revolution, 60
Save the Children, 193
Sayed Al-Shuhada school, 15, 21, 24
   attack on, 2–6, 18–19

Schröder, Gerhard, 161–162
Second Anglo-Afghan War, 91
See Paya, 25
Serena Hotel, 140, 141, 198–199,
     203, 205, 226
Shah, Mohammad Zahir (King), 12,
     50, 74, 104, 164, 203
Shaheed, Farida, 135–136
Shahnameh, 36
Shahr-e Gholghola (City of Woe),
     107–108
Shahrvand, 165
Shakespeare, William, 266
Sharia law, 120, 146, 166, 197, 259
Sherzai, Gul Agha, 178
Shi'ite(s), 9, 11, 12, 42
   rights for, 181
   Samar as, 214
   traditions of, 40–41
Shinwari, Fazal Hadi, 167, 169
Shuhada, 97–102, 105, 108, 136, 206
   bombing hospital of, 137
   orphanage of (Samar's Nest), 207
   as Shuhada Organization, 116,
     151
Shuhada Girls High School, 100
Shura-e-Nazar, 165
Sifton, John, 290
SIGAR (Special Inspector General for
     Afghanistan Reconstruction),
     270–272
Silk Road, 7, 11
Smeal, Eleanor, 132, 134, 136
Smith, Graeme, 224
Sohrab, 36
Somalia, 240, 267
Soraya, Queen, 155
South Korea, 183, 293
South Sudan, 213–215, 267

Soviet(s). *see* USSR (Union of Soviet Socialist Republics)
Stoltenberg, Jens, 251
Stoltenberg, Thorvald, 92, 96
Støre, Jonas Gahr, 198, 200
Sudan, 123, 213–219, 248
Sultani, Abdul Ghafoor, 92, 97, 101, 149, 190
  about, 51–53
  arrest of, 65–66
  arrest of family of, 61–62
  disappearance of, 75
  engagement and marriage to, 54–55
  family of, 64, 74, 77 (*see also* Muhammad Amin (brother-in-law))
  news of, 84–85
  search for, 67–69, 153, 229
  sharing chores with, 56
  son and, 58
  support from, 60–61, 79
Sunni Islam, 12, 214
Sunni(s), 9, 11, 12, 41–42, 134, 214
Supreme Court, 167, 168, 255
Sweden, 96, 116, 157, 278
Switzerland, 88, 109, 175
Syria, 236, 239, 260

T
Tajikistan, 150, 261, 274, 278
Tajiks, 8, 9, 87, 95, 232, 237, 238
Taliban, 104, 127, 169, 202, 205, 220–224, 232, 237, 239, 241, 256, 290, 293, 299. *see also* Talks with the Taliban
  about, 12, 16–17, 102–103, 178
  in Afghan security forces, 225
  amnesty offer from, 279
  bin Laden and, 139
  defeat of, 23, 128, 141, 144, 152, 154, 227, 228, 230
  edicts of, 112–114, 121
  emboldening of, 237
  harassment by, 120, 133, 262, 280
  international community and, 161, 246, 264, 266
  negotiations with, 250–251, 254, 257–259, 263, 269–270
  Pashtuns in, 8, 292
  poor governance of, 128–129
  renewal of, 179, 211, 233
  report on, 191
  Sharia law and, 146, 166
  takeover by, 21, 118, 135, 150, 153, 207, 236, 267, 272–275, 280–281, 287
  terrorism and, 6, 7, 10
  Trump and, 154, 235, 237–238, 253
  US talks with, 241, 244, 252, 267
  violence of, 22, 124, 137, 140, 142, 172, 184, 195, 219, 260, 277, 278, 280, 289
  women and, 15, 95, 112, 114–115, 116, 119, 217, 281, 285
  (*see also* women and girls in Afghanistan)
Talibs. *see* Taliban
Talks with the Taliban, 243, 250–251
Tamanna (step-daughter), 101, 201
Taraki, Nur Mohammad, 59, 68
Teacher Training College, 208, 228
Temor, Mohammed, 64
Time, 253
Transparency International, 240
Trump, Donald, 154, 234, 236, 253, 258

Al Qaeda and, 244–245
defeat of, 264
ISKP and, 239
Taliban and, 235, 237–238, 242, 250, 271
Truth and Reconciliation, 109, 159
Tufts University, 301, 304
Turkey, 236, 260
Turkish Airlines, 289
Turkmen, 8–9
Turkmenistan, 104, 131, 132, 261

U
UAE (United Arab Emirates), 125, 136, 159, 243, 274
UK (United Kingdom), 14, 141, 236, 260
invasion by, 6, 8, 296
prime minister of, 152–153
Ukraine, 187, 218, 293
UN (United Nations)
Convention on the Rights of Persons with Disabilities, 196–197
Convention on the Rights of the Child, 192
General Assembly of, 125, 160
High Commission for Human Rights, 184–185, 223
High-Level Panel on Internal Displacement, 248
Human Rights Commission, 188, 213, 216
intervention by, 133, 213
local offices/compounds of, 104, 105, 111, 205
meetings of, 99, 119, 131
problems with, 95, 98, 107–108, 124, 182, 187, 217, 292

responsibilities of, 292, 293, 295
Secretary-General, 131, 158, 186, 248
Secretary-General's High-Level Advisory Board on Mediation, 248
Secretary-General's High-Level Panel on Internal Displacement, 248
Security Council of, 163, 177, 252
Special Adviser on Gender Issues and Advancement of Women, 125
support from, 145, 158, 169, 177, 203, 277
Taliban and, 132, 245–246
UNAMA (United Nations Assistance Mission in Afghanistan), 166–167, 182, 190, 219, 284
UNDP (United Nations Development Programme), 157, 175, 197
UNESCO, 10–11, 98
UNHCR (United Nations High Commissioner for Refugees), 109
UNICEF (United Nations International Children's Emergency Fund), 107, 124, 193, 206
United Nations Assistance Mission in Sudan, 213
United Nations Development Fund for Women, 158
United Nations Development Programme Rule of Law, 197
United Nations Population Fund, 158

Universal Declaration of Human
 Rights, 125, 130, 144, 173,
 175, 197, 217
working with, 107, 110, 142, 162,
 168, 172, 180, 185
United States Geological Survey, 226
University of Maryland, 127
University of Toronto, 146
Unocal Corporation, 132–133
Urgent Action Fund, 148
Uruzgan Province, 117, 195, 208
US (United States of America)
 Afghanistan and, 24, 129, 224,
  236, 260
 ambassador from, 180, 277
 attacks by, 141, 177, 239
 attacks on, 118, 131 (see also 9/11
  attacks on the United States
  of America)
 Central Bank of Afghanistan
  and, 289–291
 congress of, 175
 election in, 242, 264
 family in, 269, 276
 House of Representatives, 130
 Islam and, 14
 madrassa funded by, 88
 military forces of, 178, 195, 200,
  225
 mujahideen and, 13, 62, 101
 prison run by, 196
 Secretary of State, 274
 Special Representative for
  Afghanistan, 154
 Taliban and, 132, 221, 223, 233,
  235, 242–243, 253, 255–256,
  266–267, 271, 285
 visiting, 97, 125, 127, 136, 147,
  301

 withdrawal of, 250, 251, 252, 256,
  270
US-Afghan Women's Council, 154
US-Taliban Deal. see Doha Agreement
USAID, 27, 46, 47
USS Cole, 131
USSR (Union of Soviet Socialist
  Republics). see also Cold War
 fighting against, 123, 143
 invasion and occupation by, 6, 8,
  13–15, 69, 88, 118, 160,
  183–184, 188, 260–261,
  287, 296
 oversight of doctors from, 72–73
 peace talks with, 250
 resistance against, 70–71, 74
 support for Doha Agreement of,
  251
 Syria and, 236
 Taliban and, 243, 286
 war with, 69, 112, 129
 withdrawal of, 94–95, 99, 102
Uyghurs, 265
Uzbekistan, 69, 261, 274
Uzbeks, 8–9, 106, 232, 238, 280

V

Vendrell, Francesc, 131
Voice of Germany (Deutsche Welle),
 52

W

Wahhabism, 12, 14, 123
Wardak, Farooq, 180–181
Washington DC, 119, 126, 129, 148,
 153, 162, 244, 251, 252, 253
Wazir Akbar Khan (district), 149
Wazir Akbar Khan Hospital, 63, 71
WEF (World Economic Forum), 109

WLUML (Women Living Under
Muslim Laws), 134–135
women and girls in Afghanistan.
 see also under Afghanistan
 bride price of, 32–33
 celebrating, 158, 218
 child marriage of, 108, 117, 193,
  273, 285
 education and, 22–23, 98, 161,
  174, 207–209, 212, 282–283
 forced marriage of, 43, 49, 51, 99,
  108, 117, 192, 273, 285
 health of, 123, 128, 174, 209, 212
 hospital for, 90, 98
 HRW report on, 176
 international support for, 142–143
 misogyny toward, 13, 120–122
 rights of, 7, 44, 91, 121, 133,
  143, 179, 212, 281
 so-called protection of, 13–14,
  89, 209
 status of, 13, 15, 46, 48, 89, 110,
  134, 174
 under Taliban, 104, 112–115,
  117, 136, 281–284
 trafficking of, 50, 89, 117,
  192–193, 207, 285
 violence against, 108, 117,
  135, 143, 191–192, 212,
  272–273, 275

Women's Alliance for Peace and
 Human Rights in Afghanistan,
 124
World Bank, 127, 143, 174, 231, 259
World Conference on Women
 (Beijing), 179
World Food Programme, 107
World War II, 161–162, 187

Y
Yakawlang, 110, 137
Yaqubi, Abdul Aziz, 61, 69, 278
Yaqubi, Abdul Kayum, 52–53, 56,
 59, 61, 64
Yaqubi, Abdul Samad, 85
Yaqubi, Abdul Wahid, 28, 31, 39, 56,
 70, 102, 201, 277–279
 Nasreen, wife of, 70
Yaqubi, Ahmad Ali, 148, 201, 277
Yaqubi, Aqila, 48, 64
Yaqubi, Qadim Ali, 26–30, 34,
 37–40, 42–46, 48, 51–52,
 54–55, 75, 96, 102
Yazidi, 187
Yemen, 131, 260

Z
Zainab Cinema, 157–158
Zia-ul-Haq, Mohammad, 14

SIMA SAMAR is a doctor for the poor, an educator of the marginalized and a human rights defender. She established and nurtured the Shuhada Organization that operated more than one hundred schools and dozens of hospitals and clinics. Samar served in the Interim Administration of Afghanistan and established the first-ever Ministry of Women's Affairs. From 2002 to 2019, she chaired the Afghanistan Independent Human Rights Commission, a commitment that has put her own life at great risk. Having served as the UN special rapporteur on the situation of human rights in Sudan from 2005 to 2009, she was appointed in 2019 as a member of both the UN Secretary-General's High-Level Panel on Internal Displacement and the UN Secretary-General's High-Level Advisory Board on Mediation. She is currently a visiting scholar at Tufts University's Fletcher School.

SALLY ARMSTRONG is an award-winning author, journalist and human rights activist. She is the author of four bestselling books: *Ascent of Women*; *The Nine Lives of Charlotte Taylor*; *Veiled Threat*; and *Bitter Roots, Tender Shoots*. Armstrong was the first journalist to bring the story of the women of Afghanistan to the world. She has also covered stories in conflict zones from Bosnia and Somalia to Rwanda, Afghanistan, Iraq, South Sudan, Jordan and Israel. She is a four-time winner of the Amnesty International Canada media award, the recipient of eleven honorary doctorate degrees, and an Officer of the Order of Canada. In 2019, she delivered the CBC Massey Lectures, *Power Shift: The Longest Revolution*.